Two Pioneers

Other Titles from Potomac Books

The Most Famous Woman in Baseball: Effa Manley and the Negro Leagues, by Bob Luke

Pull Up a Chair: The Vin Scully Story, by Curt Smith

Jewish Sports Legends: The International Jewish Sports Hall of Fame, fourth edition, by Joseph M. Siegman

Two Pioneers

HOW HANK GREENBERG AND
JACKIE ROBINSON
TRANSFORMED BASEBALL—AND AMERICA

ROBERT C. COTTRELL

Potomac Books
Washington, D.C.

Library of Congress Cataloging-in-Publication Data
Cottrell, Robert C., 1950–
    Two pioneers : how Hank Greenberg and Jackie Robinson transformed baseball—and America / Robert C. Cottrell.
        p. cm.
    Includes bibliographical references and index.
    ISBN 978-1-59797-842-2 (hardcover: alk. paper)
    ISBN 978-1-59797-843-9 (electronic edition)
    1. Baseball players—United States—Biography. 2. Greenberg, Hank. 3. Jewish baseball players—United States—Biography. 4. Robinson, Jackie, 1919–1972. 5. African American baseball players—Biography. I. Title.
    GV865.A1C67 2012
    796.3570922—dc23
    [B]
                                                                    2012000672

Potomac Books
22841 Quicksilver Drive
Dulles, Virginia 20166

First Edition

10 9 8 7 6 5 4 3 2 1

For Sue and Jordan,
and in memory of Sylvia Light Cottrell,
a lifelong St. Louis Cardinals fan

CONTENTS

ACKNOWLEDGMENTS

Once again, I owe a debt of gratitude to my literary agent Robbie Hare of Goldfarb & Associates. She provided entrée to Potomac Books, where I have had the pleasure of working with senior editor Elizabeth Demers and production editor Aryana Hendrawan.

This book acquired its gestation many years ago, receiving impetus from an extended stay in Cooperstown, New York, where I conducted research at the Baseball Hall of Fame Library. Helping me rifle through files and examine photographs were my wife, Sue, and my then nine-year-old daughter, Jordan, who photocopied a large number of materials on both Hank Greenberg and Jackie Robinson. Tim Wiles, director of research at the Baseball Hall of Fame, proved friendly, helpful, and supportive. I returned to Cooperstown on other occasions, and also carried out research at the Sporting News Archives in St. Louis, where Steven P. Gietschier, director of historical records, also assisted in my research endeavors. Visits to the Library of Congress provided additional useful information, enabling me to acquire primary documents on Robinson's military service and to pore over a large number of microfilm reels, particularly those associated with newspapers in Brooklyn, New York City, and Detroit; black-run newspapers; and sports publications such as *Baseball Magazine*, *Sporting Life*, and *The Sporting News*. More recently, John Horne of the Photo Archives at the National Baseball Hall of Fame has been very kind in fielding queries, providing information, and delivering pristine images of my two subjects.

As always, Sue and Jordan were supportive throughout the entire writing process, serving as sounding boards and fans of two of baseball's—and America's—most important sports figures.

INTRODUCTION

Hank Greenberg and Jackie Robinson are forever linked because of the barriers they encountered, the discrimination they endured, and the athletic gifts they exhibited. Greenberg was the first great Jewish major leaguer and Robinson the first African American player in organized baseball during the twentieth century. Both suffered ridicule and abuse. Each nevertheless excelled. Greenberg became one of the preeminent sluggers of the 1930s and 1940s. Robinson, from the mid-1940s into the following decade, helped bring back speed and a thinking man's approach to the game, both of which had largely been discarded for a generation.

Greenberg's numbers, compiled in a sport where statistics are more important than in any other, are arguably more impressive. He garnered four home-run and runs-batted-in (RBI) titles, came within two round-trippers of tying Babe Ruth's single season mark, and fell one RBI short of Lou Gehrig's American League record. Greenberg's lifetime home run total when he retired after the 1947 season was the fifth greatest in major league history, and he had been awarded a pair of most valuable player awards. Even Greenberg's career batting average, .313, was two points higher than Robinson's. Robinson's record was impressive in its own right. It included one year when he got over 200 hits, six seasons when he scored more than 100 runs, six campaigns when he batted over .300, a batting championship, two stolen base titles, and an MVP crown of his own. Robinson helped lead his Brooklyn Dodgers to six National League pennants and their only World Series championship when the Boys of Summer finally defeated the New York Yankees in the 1955 Fall Classic. Greenberg's Detroit Tigers won four pennants and a pair of World Series, in 1935 and 1945.

Both men, along with their teams, undoubtedly would have accomplished even more on the baseball diamond but for fate and the circumstances they faced. Because of injuries and extended military service, Greenberg effectively played major league ball for only nine-and-a-half years. His 1936 season was all but aborted due to a broken wrist, while World War II pulled him away from the ballpark for four-and-a-half years when he was at the pinnacle of his game. Robinson, another military veteran and one who suffered a court-martial because of his refusal to accept Jim Crow practices, did not sign a contract with the Dodgers general manager Branch Rickey until he was twenty-six years old. He entered the majors almost two years later. The color barrier had kept out Robinson, as it had so many other stellar African American ballplayers. At the same time its presence in other sports, including professional football and professional basketball, ironically enough compelled Robinson to become a racial pathfinder in organized baseball. Had pro football not contained racial strictures of its own, Robinson, a star tailback at UCLA, undoubtedly would have been drafted by a National Football League team. If the American Basketball League and the National Basketball League, predecessors to the Basketball Association of America (which itself evolved into the National Basketball Association in 1949, following a merger with the National Basketball League), had not closed their doors to black players, Robinson, a two-time college conference scoring champion, could have played professional basketball. With a foot in the NFL or a professional basketball league, he likely never would have entered major league baseball—baseball was hardly his favorite sport—or even played with the Kansas City Monarchs of the Negro National League, as he did for a season before signing with Brooklyn.

The two men's paths literally crossed during the epochal 1947 season—Robinson's first and Greenberg's last in the major leagues—when they collided during a close play at first base in the midst of a game in Pittsburgh. The encounter resulted in a mutual display of respect rather than the abuse and slurs that each frequently suffered from other players and fans. Robinson later recalled Greenberg's offering "the first real words of encouragement I received from a player on an opposing team." Greenberg later wrote that he "identified with Jackie Robinson . . . because they had treated me the same way."[1] The black player never forgot the civility that Greenberg exemplified. Hank admired Jackie's dogged determination to overcome historic obstacles to make his mark in the game they both loved. Robinson later told sports columnist Bob Considine "that Hank Greenberg did more to smooth his path than anybody else in baseball."[2]

Nine years after that collision at first base, Greenberg was inducted into the National Baseball Hall of Fame in Cooperstown, New York. Robinson joined him six years later. But the athletic prowess of the two men, as considerable at it was, was overshadowed by what they experienced and represented. Throughout much of the period in which Greenberg starred in the American League, anti-Semitism flourished as never before, even considering its lengthy history. Greenberg joined the Tigers lineup as the 1933 season began, just months after Adolf Hitler became chancellor of Germany. Five years later Greenberg ended the 1938 season, having failed to homer in any of the Tigers' last five games in a futile attempt to match Ruth's single season home run record. On November 9, 1938, the Nazis conducted *Kristallnacht*, the "night of the broken glass," a pogrom against Jewish shops and synagogues in Germany and Austria, when scores of Jews were killed and tens of thousands sent to concentration camps. As the German blitzkrieg continued to rain on Europe, the then thirty-one-year-old Greenberg, who had just led the Tigers to another pennant and been named the 1940 American League MVP, entered the U.S. Army. Demobilized in early December 1941, Greenberg quickly reenlisted following the Japanese attack on Pearl Harbor, remaining in uniform for the next three-and-a-half years. The defeat of Hitler in the spring of 1945 resulted in the unveiling of the death camps where millions of Jews had been slaughtered. Germany's surrender enabled Greenberg to be released from military service. He returned home, slammed a homer in his first game back, and rapped a ninth-inning grand slam to enable Detroit to win the pennant on the final day of the 1945 season; his pair of home runs and seven RBIs helped the Tigers capture the World Series title.

Through it all Greenberg had to ignore or deflect religious slurs that demonstrated that his own nation was hardly immune to anti-Semitism. While Hitler's American supporters remained few in number and were generally viewed with disdain, the easy aspersions that came the way of Greenberg and many other Jews in America abounded. Cries of "kike," "sheenie," and "Christ killer" were heard repeatedly by Jews on playing fields and elsewhere. Jews also encountered more subtle means designed to keep them in their place, such as restrictive covenants in real estate transactions or quotas involving university admissions.

African Americans during the same era remained beset by Jim Crow laws, discriminatory treatment, and violence meted out in the form of beatings, lynchings, and race riots. Robinson grew up in a period when the Ku Klux Klan was gathering strength; most significant was the appeal of the KKK in the Deep South, where he was born. There, signs remained in place that prevented blacks from using the same toilets, water fountains, restaurants, hotels, theaters, or swimming pools as whites did. Outside the South some of the same "no colored" markings could be seen or slurs like "nigger" and "coon" heard. While a growing middle class could be found in the African American community, most blacks remained mired in low-paying jobs, with many relegated to domestic or janitorial work; one was Mack Robinson, Jackie's older brother and a star athlete in his own right who had captured a silver medal in the 200-meter dash at the 1936 Olympic Games. Still, the advent during the 1920s of the so-called New Negro, proud and racially assertive, afforded a new role model. So too did organizations like the National Urban League, the Negro leagues, and the National Association for the Advancement of Colored People, which continues its legal assault on segregation.

During the 1930s and 1940s, Hank Greenberg and Jackie Robinson, in their own fashion, served as role models for Jews and African Americans—

both long ostracized—in the United States. Greenberg and Robinson made their initial and enduring marks on the playing fields, which helped to recast the image of the groups they represented in the minds of many others. They did not set out to become pioneers or pathfinders, yet that was what they proved to be. A proud, nonreligious Jew who refused to consider changing his last name to make it appear less Jewish, Greenberg called into question the anti-Semitic ideas of a "master race" in the very era when they flourished most horrifically overseas, culminating in the unprecedented calamity of the Holocaust. Robinson followed in the path Greenberg had carved out. He contested racial notions regarding the supposed inferiority of people of African ancestry when African states remained under the yoke of European imperialism and segregationists proved determined to maintain racial barriers in the United States. In the end the two baseball superstars became important figures in the civil rights crusade, showing that all Americans, no matter their religion or race, were entitled to equality of opportunity. This was no small accomplishment, and one that should not soon be forgotten.

Greenberg's entrance into the big leagues remained largely singular in the sense that few Jews followed in his footsteps. Only Sandy Koufax, initially a struggling young southpaw with the Brooklyn Dodgers but eventually a brilliant pitcher for the Los Angeles Dodgers, achieved stardom comparable to or even beyond what Greenberg attained. The 1953 American League MVP, Al Rosen of the Cleveland Indians, and Shawn Green, who delivered forty-nine homers for the Los Angeles Dodgers in 2001, also starred in the major leagues, as does the 2011 National League MVP, Milwaukee Brewers outfielder Ryan Braun presently, but not quite at the level of Greenberg and Koufax. By contrast Jackie Robinson helped transform the national pastime altogether. Robinson came first, but then Don Newcombe, Roy Campanella, Larry Doby, Willie Mays, Hank Aaron, Ernie Banks, and Frank Robinson, along with many other black stars of the Negro leagues, arrived in the big leagues as well. The dramatic impact made by African American players opened the doors for others, including Latin American players from Puerto Rico, the Dominican Republic, and Venezuela, and eventually Japanese and

Korean athletes as well. Six decades after Robinson broke the color barrier in organized baseball, the polyglot nature of the game was more apparent than ever, with players from the Caribbean, South America, and Asia among the most celebrated.

The impact of Greenberg and Robinson, whose public personae were hardly dampened by the fact that each was movie-star handsome, proved larger still in other ways. Greenberg became an American Jewish icon in the shadow of Nazi Germany. His 6'4", 200-plus-pound physique and his accomplishments on the baseball diamond refuted long-held stereotypes about physically weak Jews unable to compete in the athletic realm and in many other arenas too. The 5'11", broad-shouldered, muscular Robinson served as a role model for African Americans, who suffered verbal and physical abuse while the educational, economic, and professional shackles of Jim Crow remained in place. An American system of apartheid proved crippling to the vast majority of black citizens while at the same time buttressing perceptions about supposed racial inferiority. Greenberg and Robinson perhaps necessarily became torchbearers for their religious and racial kin. They opened doors for many others and helped bring to fruition certain ideals associated with American democracy. They set the stage for other great sports figures, including Jim Brown, Red Auerbach, Sandy Koufax, Muhammad Ali, Mark Spitz, Michael Jordan, and Tiger Woods, who were able to surmount religious or racial barriers and recast images about what constituted an American. It is hardly an exaggeration to suggest that Hank Greenberg and Jackie Robinson also helped to open the doors in other venues, including the realm of politics, where Jewish and black politicians have thrived in recent decades. In that sense it was not only Willie Mays, Hank Aaron, Al Rosen, and Red Holzman who followed their lead but also politicians like Abraham Ribicoff, Willie Brown, Paul Wellstone, Rahm Emanuel, and Barack Obama. In the process the American nation underwent further changes suggesting at least the possibility that a new, brighter day awaited in which the "politics of hope" might surmount ancient prejudices, just as Greenberg and Robinson once shattered long-standing biases because of their individual courage, dedication, and athletic brilliance.

1

Discrimination and the National Pastime

It was 1868, three years after the end of the Civil War, fought over the future of slavery in the United States. In 1865 the 13th Amendment to the U.S. Constitution had formally abolished that institution. Reconstruction was supposed to put the country back together and transform the South. The federally orchestrated Freedmen's Bureau attempted to improve the lot of blacks as well as poor whites but encountered bitter resistance. Of little help was the mind-set displayed in a *Brooklyn Daily Eagle* newspaper ad, trumpeting a NOTICE TO FIRST BASEMEN. The National Club of Washington needed a first baseman, and the organization had unsuccessfully sought one in Brooklyn. Promised was a "first-rate position in the Treasury Department." Terms of the proposed contract required the successful applicant to work at the government post until mid-afternoon "and then practise [*sic*] at base ball until dark." But the advertisement read, "No Irish need apply."[1] The newly formed National Association of Base Ball Players (NABBP) had recently delivered its own edict, refusing admission to teams "composed of one of more colored persons."[2]

A small number of black players did manage to enter the ranks of organized baseball by the early 1880s. These included pitcher-infielder John "Bud" Fowler, catcher Moses Fleetwood "Fleet" Walker, second baseman Frank Grant, and pitcher George Stovey. Not all were pleased by this turn of events, especially the great first baseman and Chicago White Sox manager Cap

1

Anson. By contrast, Irish baseball players had come to be accepted in the game that Henry Chadwick called the "national pastime" and Mark Twain viewed as symbolizing late–nineteenth-century America.[3] Michael "King" Kelly was the best-known baseball star of the period, whose fame was ensured when his contract was sold to the Boston Beaneaters for a record $10,000 following the 1886 season.

White ethnics increasingly played and watched the game with no restrictions. Meanwhile blatant racial discrimination rained on African American athletes as Jim Crow practices intensified in many parts of the country. Responding to the racial prejudices afflicting organized baseball, black players formed leagues of their own. An editorial dated April 13, 1887, in *Sporting Life*, one of the leading sports publications of the day, discussed the emergence of the Colored League, which was said to be attracting "considerable interest." "Prominent colored base ball clubs" had appeared previously, but this was the first attempt to form such a circuit. The Colored League hoped to acquire the backing of the National Agreement that governed organized baseball. The editorial suggested that "this consent should be obtainable." After all, the Colored League did not intend to compete with the white clubs and was unlikely to threaten them financially. But even if such support were lacking, the new league could make a go of it. The National Agreement protected the white teams by ensuring "undisturbed possession" of players. Black clubs would not soon confront such a problem, for "there is not likely to be much of a scramble for colored players." Only two black players were on professional white teams, and "that number [was] not likely to be ever materially increased owing to the high standard of play required and to the popular prejudice against any considerable mixture of races."[4] *Sporting Life* vividly underscored the major obstacles confronting black athletes: the easy belief that they were unable to compete with whites and the refusal to allow them to do so.

Cap Anson actively fought to keep African Americans out of the game. He refused in 1887 to let his team take the field against Newark until its two African American players, star pitcher Stovey and catcher Walker, were pulled from the lineup. The next year Anson again threatened to call off a game until Syracuse benched Walker. *Sporting Life* reported Anson's insistence that he "will never pit the Chicagos against a team containing colored players." The paper subsequently related how Toledo temporarily bested Anson by threatening to withhold Chicago's share of the gate.[5]

In its March 23, 1889, edition, *The Sporting News* offered that no more than a handful of African American ballplayers had achieved recognition on the baseball diamond. "What fame they have won has been made in the face of very disheartening circumstances," the publication acknowledged, for "race prejudice exists in professional base ball ranks to a marked degree, and the unfortunate son of Africa who makes his living as a member of a team of white professionals has a rocky road to travel." His teammates refused to deal with him socially, and many strove "to 'job him' out of the business." Coaching tips were invariably wrongheaded, and scoring decisions saddled him with as many errors as possible.[6]

A handful of African American players had performed in the International League despite confronting considerable prejudice. One player admitted to such feelings himself but pitied "some of the poor black fellows." Bud Fowler "used to play second base with the lower part of his legs encased in wooden guards," realizing that opponents attempting to steal the bag "had it in for him, and would, if possible, throw the spikes into him." Although Fowler was "a good player," he shied away from second base whenever a close play loomed. The confession continued with the ballplayer revealing, "I have seen him muff balls intentionally, so that he would not have to try to touch runners, fearing that they might injure him. Grant was the same way."[7]

Thanks to the insistence of Anson and like-minded players, managers, and executives, racial lines in organized baseball hardened, paralleling the solidifying of segregation throughout the American South and beyond. The end of the nineteenth century was characterized by a collapse of the dreams spawned by the Reconstruction-era amendments abolishing slavery and providing for due process of the law, equal protection, and the right of African Americans to vote. Political disfranchisement, social discrimination, economic entrapment, and the legal embedding of segregation proceeded apace.

The threat of racially charged violence against African Americans and anyone who attempted to improve their lot buttressed the Jim Crow system.
During the first years of the twentieth century, black and white players did
compete against one another in barnstorming tours, with the legendary,
dark-skinned Andrew "Rube" Foster guiding a number of squads against
stars from the major and minor leagues. *Sol White's History of Colored Base
Ball*, published in 1907, insisted that if racial barriers fell, "there would be
a score or more colored ball players cavorting around the National League
or American League diamonds at the present time." Foster contended in the
Indianapolis Freeman on April 16, 1910, that "we have players who are
classed with the best in the land."[8]

Throughout the following decade Foster, Ben Taylor, and C. I. Taylor
struggled mightily to ensure the success of black baseball in the face of Jim
Crow laws. Black players continued to barnstorm on occasion against
organized baseball's top competitors. Some of baseball's greatest players still
remained locked out of the major and minor leagues, including Foster, José
Méndez, and Smokey Joe Williams, pitchers believed to be as skilled as even
the best big leaguers; shortstop John Henry Lloyd, the "black Honus
Wagner"; second baseman Charlie Grant; and outfielder Pete Hill.
Discrimination and war soon imperiled black baseball altogether.

In the December 1918 issue of *Baseball Magazine*, editor F. C. Lane felt
compelled to ask, "Where, oh where, have the colored ball clubs gone? What
has become of the dusky entertainers whose antics—and genuine playing
skill—erstwhile sent thrills of joy through the breasts of white and negro gathering?" Lane acknowledged that black ball clubs had "played some of the best
ball anyone could ask to see." He also recognized that "the whole game . . .
conducted African-fashion" had "been richly enjoyable for many reasons."
Lane continued, "The agile coons . . . have been as good as their white rivals,
but credit has never been given them for their skill." Indeed "numerous
American negroes have for years been ranked as topnotchers." Lane referred
to major leaguers who admitted that "only the color-line kept these men from
standing at the summit of their profession." He also praised the good-natured
black athlete for having "known his place."[9]

Organized baseball was not afflicted with a color barrier alone. Pitcher Ed Corey appeared in one game for the Chicago White Sox during the 1918 major league season. His widow later indicated that her husband changed his name from Abraham Simon Cohen because of ethnic slurs involving Jews. A few fans raucously hounded Corey during a game in the Midwest League. They "loudly and continuously derided [him] about his ethnic background."[10] A small number of Jews had played in the majors, starting with outfielder Lipman Pike back in the 1870s. Jews owned big league teams, beginning in the 1880s, including the Baltimore Orioles, Cincinnati Reds, Louisville Colonels, New York Giants, and Pittsburgh Pirates. Nevertheless, stereotypes confronted Jewish players and those who hung around the game. As suspicions emerged about the performance of the Chicago White Sox during the 1919 World Series; *The Sporting News* worried that "there are no lengths to which the crop of lean-faced and long-nosed gamblers of these degenerate days will go."[11]

The founding of the Negro National League in February 1920 elicited no immediate comment from leading sports publications across the country. *Baseball Magazine* spoke of purported efforts by Andy Lawson, organizer of the short-lived Continental League, "to give the colored ball player a chance." Lane delivered the following editorial comment in mid-1921: "The brand of Cain rests heavily on the Negro in this country. Through no fault of his own, life for him is beset with heavy handicaps. In this land of vaunted freedom he finds only the shadow of the substance." Nowhere did fewer opportunities exist "than in professional sport." The black fighter confronted "a crushing handicap" while "in organized baseball that handicap becomes an impossibility." Lane referred to a statement delivered earlier by Washington Senators owner Clark Griffith that a black ball player—undoubtedly John Henry Lloyd—was as gifted as Pittsburgh's star shortstop Honus Wagner. Had Lloyd been white, Lane wrote, "sixteen major league ball clubs would have fallen over one another in a mad scramble to claim him. As it was, he couldn't have forced his way to any major league roster with a load of dynamite." Lane noted that strong teams of the semi-professional Negro National League performed well against top white players. Lane then went on to question the campaign by the Continental League to integrate baseball: "Through all the ages the effort to mix oil with water has failed. In this country at least all efforts to mix black and white have also failed." The sportswriter still praised Lawson. "We cannot but sympathize, however, with the attempt of the Continental League to give the colored ball player a show. He has never had a decent chance before."[12]

Anti-Semitism, too, continued to shape perceptions about the impact certain players, fans, and illicit actions (which had culminated in the 1919 World Series fix) might have on the game. In the September 1921 issue of his anti-Semitic newspaper, the *Dearborn Independent*, Henry Ford offered two scathing essays by the journalist W. J. Cameron blaming Jews for having corrupted American baseball. Some warned that baseball had "received its death wound," Cameron wrote. Others suggested the game could be saved by "a clean sweep . . . of the Jewish influence" that had "dragged" baseball "through a period of bitter shame and demoralization." To Cameron "its Jewish character" most imperiled the sport, which might devolve into "cheap-jack entertainment." He charged that Jews were not sportsmen, which might or might not suggest a character defect but was a fact that even "discriminating Jews" readily acknowledged. The fault perhaps lay with "their dislike of unnecessary physical action, or their serious cast of mind," but the Jew was "not naturally an out-of-door sportsman." The Jew presently did not despoil sport as a participant but rather as "an exploiter and corrupter," Cameron insisted. The Jews sought the opportunity to financially benefit through the weakness of others. This had been borne out as several members of the Chicago White Sox, paid by Jewish gamblers (including the notorious Arnold Rothstein), had agreed to throw the 1919 World Series to the Cincinnati Reds. Cameron pointedly stated, "If fans wish to know the trouble with American baseball, they have it in three words—too much Jew," as the sport had become yet "another Jewish monopoly."[13]

Cameron asserted that all baseball managers in the United States, other than Jews, feared "what the Jews are doing to baseball" and what they would do if the managers complained. He proceeded to blame Jews for the "rowdyism" afflicting the game, which suffered from umpires being abused, bottles tossed, and profanities hurled, as well as attempts by Jewish gamblers to bribe players and to tamper with gate receipts. Jews had already moved into other sports, operating as gangsters, insisting on the sure thing. In similar fashion, Jewish lightweight boxing champion Benny Leonard (considered by many one of the two top lightweight fighters of all time), unlike other pugilists, remained "unscarred," purportedly refusing to let anyone hit him. In wrestling, Jews dominated and barred the way for the "real wrestler." Baseball too was heading down the path of vaudeville-styled entertainment offered in the afternoon. The decline of the game had been evidenced in the Chicago trial involving the 1919 World Series fix. That fiasco featured a "curious medley of Jewish defendants, witnesses, lawyers and judge" with the players acting as "Gentile boobs." The indicted players, the "dupes," had heeded the imploring of Jews, who suffered little retribution. Happily baseball's new commissioner, federal judge Kenesaw Mountain Landis, had been "one of the few judges" never to "quail before Chicago meat packers and Jewish bootleggers." He always dealt forthrightly with "the numerous cases of Jewish business crookedness" that came before his court. To save baseball required eradicating the disease "caused by the Jewish characteristic which spoils everything by ruthless commercial exploitation," Cameron bristled.[14]

On May 31, 1924, Orval W. Baylor, minister of the Richmond Street Christian Church in Cincinnati and a member of the Ku Klux Klan, the group ill disposed to Jews, blacks, Catholics, and immigrants, wrote to August Herrmann, president of the Cincinnati Reds. Baylor asked if Sunday, July 20, could be set aside as Klan Day at Redland Field when the New York Giants came to town. The Klan hoped to deliver special bouquets to Giant manager John McGraw and Reds skipper Jack Hendricks. Similar bouquets were to be presented to the players. The Klan possessed 100,000 members in Cincinnati and nearby communities. Most of these "were loyal Red fans and your club benefits by their patronage from day to day," Baylor suggested. Herrmann expressed a willingness to talk to Baylor about his request, but the date in question was unavailable, because Sunday games against the Giants were always sold out well in advance.[15]

In June 1925 Henry Montor of the news service Seven Arts Feature Syndicate in Manhattan sent a copy of a sports column by Harry Conzell discussing anti-Semitism to major league owners and twenty-five top publications in the United States. AN OPEN LETTER TO THE BASEBALL MAGNATES pointed to "rumors among Jewish baseball fans that Jewish baseball players are being discriminated against in the major leagues." Conzell reported that he had received numerous letters from across the country posing the same query: "Where are the Jewish ballplayers?" Conzell then noted,

> Claims are put forward that baseball magnates do not care to carry Jewish names on their club rosters, that players with Jewish names are indirectly forced to change them, that team managers are opposed to Jewish players, on the ground that the other members of the team would object, that these discriminations are well known to the semiprofessional ranks, and that the Jewish college or semi-professional players are therefore not even trying to break into the big leagues, knowing that it is a hopeless task.[16]

The sports columnist insisted that he tended to view such charges "as childish and unfounded." He remembered that Giants manager John McGraw had long sought out a Jewish ballplayer "because he considered it a very good proposition to attract the Jewish fans to the park." Conzell felt that the big leagues "should rather welcome Jewish players as assets." He pointedly concluded, "I believe that it is up to you gentlemen to solve the puzzle of 'Where are the Jewish ball players.' The floor is yours." Sportswriter Ford Frick also discussed the issue of anti-Semitism in organized baseball: "There must be at least half a hundred Jews in the game but we'll never know their real names. During the early days of this century the Jewish boys had tough sledding in the majors and many of them changed their names."[17]

F. Scott Fitzgerald's novel *The Great Gatsby* appeared in 1925, with its protagonist, Jay Gatsby, possessing a murky past that included a longtime association with the Jewish gambler Wolfsheim, a character obviously patterned after Arnold Rothstein. Gatsby informs the book's narrator Nick Carraway that Wolfsheim is "quite a character around New York—a denizen of Broadway." He explained that his acquaintance is a gambler, then "added coolly: 'He's the man who fixed the World Series back in 1919.'" Carraway is simply "staggered" by the very notion "that one man could start to play with the faith of fifty million people—with the single-mindedness of a burglar blowing a safe." Carraway asks, "How did he happen to do that?" Gatsby responds, "He just saw the opportunity." Carraway wonders, "Why isn't he in jail?" Gatsby answers, "They can't get him, old sport. He's a smart man."[18]

In the January 1926 issue of *Baseball Magazine*, editor F. C. Lane posed a question similar to the one he had earlier asked about blacks, "Why Not More Jewish Ball Players?" Former Chicago Cubs star pitcher Ed Reulbach charged that baseball owners lacked business acumen. "If I were a magnate, in Greater New York at least, I would send scouts all over the United States and Canada in an effort to locate some hook-nosed youngster who could bat and field. Then I would ballyhoo him in all the papers." Reulbach explained, "The Jewish people are great spenders and they could be made excellent fans. You could sell out your boxes and your reserved seats any time in Greater New York, if you had a Jewish star on your ball club." Following Reulbach's lead, Lane agreed that "it has always been remarkable that a game as cosmopolitan as baseball has developed so few Jewish players." He disavowed the notion that Jews were not naturally athletic, pointing to the boxing realm, where "some of the greatest of champions have been Jews." As Lane saw matters, only Cincinnati second baseman Samuel Bohne presently rivaled former pitcher Erskine Mayer, a two-time twenty-game winner with the Philadelphia Phillies, as "a sensational regular" in major league ranks. For his part, Bohne suggested that Jews were more inclined to "some other line of business and are not willing to thus apply themselves" to the sport. Bohne declared, "Jews as a race have certain qualities which should make them proficient in baseball," including "keen and active minds and that is what counts decisively in baseball."[19]

While some worried about the way that Jews might be influencing the national pastime and others hoped that more might aspire to the big leagues, still others wondered about the plight of black players. The May 1929 issue of *Baseball Magazine* contained an article by Oliver S. Arata titled, "The Colored Athlete in Professional Baseball." Arata explored the dilemma faced by African American ballplayers. "The negro has his proper place in the game. And many an athlete with a dusky skin has developed marked abilities in the field, at bat and on the hurling mound that would assure him fame and fortune on the Big League diamond. But here, the color line intercedes." Kept out of organized baseball, African Americans, led by Chicago American Giants manager Rube Foster, had founded the Negro National League nine years earlier. The game offered by that league was "usually a thriller" as "the players have the habit of pulling the unexpected." Contests were "exceptionally fast. Baseball there has not fallen into a rut. Something unexpected crops up in almost every ball game. Bunting a third strike is common, if the third baseman plays too far back." Players used their intelligence and were "not restrained by respect for any rigid system." Willie Wells performed like Honus Wagner at his peak, George "Mule" Suttles exhibited power in the manner of Babe Ruth, and Cool Papa Bell was perhaps the fastest player anywhere to be found.[20]

The Negro National League appeared to be thriving despite lacking the minor league clubs that organized baseball possessed. The league still boasted "numerous stars who would be stars anywhere, were it not for their dusky skins." And "the quality of play on the circuit is of a high order." Negro leaguers who competed against major leaguers held their own.[21] However, the unfolding of the Great Depression, coupled with the deaths of Rube Foster and C. I. Taylor, proved crippling to the Negro National League, which suspended operations altogether in 1932. The league, led by the Pittsburgh Crawfords' Gus Greenlee, reemerged within a year. Organized baseball remained as segregated as ever although some journalists and newspapers began challenging its Jim Crow makeup. On February 1, 1933, the *New York Daily News* criticized "the color line . . . in the big leagues," bemoaning the fact that "good colored ballplayers aren't eligible."

The *Daily News* referred to the economic implications of this practice: "There must be a lot of possible fans in Harlem who don't step over to the Stadium or the Polo Grounds to baseball games." Just four days later, the *New York World-Telegram* columnist Heywood Broun, speaking before a gathering of the Baseball Writers Association of America (BBWAA), expressed his disapproval of organized baseball's segregation practices. He could "see no reason why Negro should not come into the American and National Leagues. The race possesses a high talent for the game." Moreover "there is no set rule for barring Negroes, it is merely a tacit agreement, or possibly custom."[22]

On February 8, 1933, Jimmy Powers, the top sportswriter with the *Daily News*, opened his column with the statement, "I would like to make a case for the colored baseball player." He referred to other top black athletes, including football stars Duke Slater, Fritz Pollard, and Paul Robeson; track-and-field performers Eddie Tolan, Ralph Metcalfe, and Phil Edwards; and boxing greats Joe Gans, Sam Langford, Joe Walcott, and Tiger Flowers. Only tennis, golf, and baseball continued to snub black players. At a recent BBWAA dinner, Powers heard the St. Louis Cardinals president Branch Rickey, National League chieftain John Heydler, Yankees owner Jacob Ruppert, and major leaguers Frankie Frisch, Herb Pennock, and Lou Gehrig express "a refreshing open mindedness" about integrating organized baseball. Powers concluded, "I believe it is only a question of time before the colored player is admitted into the big leagues." This was due to the fact that the contemporary ballplayer was both "more intelligent-and liberal" than his predecessors.[23]

Top black newspapers quickly followed the lead of the New York dailies in exploring the possibility that baseball's color barrier might evaporate. The *Chicago Defender* reported White Sox president J. Louis Comiskey's insistence he would "never refuse to hire a great athlete simply" due to considerations of race if "the bar you tell me is against them is lifted." At the same time, Comiskey admitted he had never explored the issue. He also acknowledged that Negro League left-handed pitcher Willie Foster, the half-brother of the recently deceased Rube Foster, would likely attract thousands of spectators. The *Defender* still credited the White Sox with having hired at least twenty black employees and for avoiding overt Jim Crow practices at Comiskey Park, beyond the playing field.[24]

Chicago White Sox president Comiskey proclaimed in early March 1933 that his team was "not opposed to admitting Race players into the American league." Interviewed by the *Defender*, Comiskey insisted, "Oh, yes, the Sox want color," referring to the recent purchase of outfielder Al Simmons from the Philadelphia Athletics. One reporter then interjected, "Yes, Mr. Comiskey, but we are talking about Colored players on your ball team." Comiskey responded, "Well, now. I have never had reason to think of that." That journalist countered, "But that's why we are here today. The question has come up in the East and we wish to know how you stand." The White Sox boss dissembled: "The question of Colored men in baseball has never crossed my mind. Had some good player come along and my manager refused to sign him because he was Negro I am sure I would have taken action or attempted to, although it isn't up to me to change what must be." He continued, "I cannot say that I would have insisted on hiring the player over the protest of my manager, but at least I would have taken some steps—just what steps I cannot say, for the simple reason that the question has never confronted me." [25]

The *Defender* viewed Comiskey's response favorably, far more so than the one attributed to John McGraw, who had recently stepped aside as the New York Giants manager. McGraw now expressed doubts that organized baseball could be integrated. The White Sox had already demonstrated a more positive attitude about "the Race question," the *Defender* noted. Art Ballard, an African American, had served as chief assistant to the club president for over two decades, and Bill Buckner had been the club trainer for nearly as long. The *Defender* indicated that Comiskey's declaration was a hopeful sign, demonstrating recognition that "there are many good Race players within striking distance of his ball park." The *Defender* only hoped that Comiskey would begin "wondering why some of them aren't mentioned for trial on his own club."[26] In August 1933, the *Daily Worker*'s Ben Field commented about Jim Crow baseball at Ebbets Field, the home of the Brooklyn Dodgers. "A Negro rushes about with a whisk-broom curry-ing you down. He's got to earn a few cents. He chants: 'Anything at all. Nothing is too small.' You spot a few Negro fans. Negro workers make good athletes. But where are the Negroes on the field?" Field queried. The major leagues, he continued, "will not admit Negro players. This is something else to chalk up against capitalist-controlled sports."[27]

On August 11, 1933, with the Negro Leagues about to hold their first All-Star contest, the *Pittsburgh Courier* reported that Babe Ruth and former Pittsburgh Pirate great Honus Wagner had spoken favorably about black players. Home run king Ruth acknowledged, "The colorfulness of Negroes in baseball and their sparkling brilliance on the field would have a tendency to increase attendance at games."[28] The Negro Leagues held their long awaited All-Star Game that month, leading the *Courier* to assert that base-ball "is looking at a 'fading' color line. For years there has been agitation about added color in the big leagues. Fans have been wanting to see new color, and they've wanted that color to be dark." The *Courier* quoted major league owners like the Pittsburgh Pirates' William Benswanger as lauding black stars. Some Negro Leaguers were "worthy of the highest in baseball," Benswanger declared. Such praise "will probably re-open the eternal question about whether or not Negro baseball super-stars are of big league calibre [*sic*]," the *Courier* wrote.[29]

On February 3, 1934, Al Monroe, a columnist for the *Defender*, indi-cated that *The Sporting News*, the top baseball publication, considered discussion of the major leagues' Jim Crow practices "to be news." Monroe chortled, "Now, ain't that something!" In referring to *The Sporting News*'s acknowledgement "that Race players have ability commensurate with the white stars of the game," Monroe stated, "One might scream better late than never and again we may chronicle the cloudy side and say it took 'em a long time to come around." Monroe elaborated that his employer should be pleased that "baseball's official organ" was at last "speaking on a subject that this paper has fostered single-handed for so long." It was not. It did applaud "those Race fans" who fired off letters to major league owners and baseball commissioner Landis "demanding a showdown." Despite initiating "a crusade against Jim Crowism in baseball," the *Defender* little anticipated that such a campaign "would put Race boys in the major leagues." The plan was actually concocted with the expectation that "mass action" would be required to bring results.[30]

Something of a furor occurred in 1935 when organized baseball confronted the case of Edwin "Alabama" Pitts, who, while serving a sentence in Sing Sing for armed robbery, had displayed athletic prowess for the prison's baseball and football squads. Pitts was granted early release after serving five years and planned to play for the Albany Senators of the minor-league International League. William G. Bramham, president of the National Association of Professional Baseball Leagues (NAPBL), refused to allow Pitts to join Albany, worrying the arrangement would reflect badly on professional baseball. As public support for Pitts grew, Commissioner Landis ruled he could play in organized baseball. After batting only .233 for Albany, Pitts left baseball but soon appeared in a Philadelphia Eagles football uniform. Supporters of baseball's integration were appalled by Landis's willingness to admit a felon like Pitts while continuing to exclude black athletes. The absurdity of organized baseball's position was further underscored in the mid-thirties when Joe Louis contended for the heavyweight crown and, at the 1936 Berlin Olympics, where Jesse Owens captured four gold medals through track-and-field performances that refuted Nazi theories regarding racial supremacy.

The *Daily Worker* initiated its own drumbeat for integration of the national pastime, delivering a banner headline on August 16, 1936, "Fans Ask End of Jim Crow Baseball." The communist newspaper pointed to the sensational performance at the Berlin Olympics by black athletes, including Owens and sprinter Mack Robinson, as drawing "attention to the un-American barrier" that marred the "National game." The *Daily Worker* exclaimed, "Baseball is the people's game. It is everyone's game. Negroes are among its most enthusiastic supporters." The publication compared pitcher Satchel Paige to Dizzy Dean and slugger Josh Gibson to Lou Gehrig. It bemoaned "the invisible barrier of race prejudices that keeps the Negro ball players on the sidelines." Noting that both sportswriters and

African Americans wanted the sport integrated, the *Daily Worker* charged that there was little difference between Adolf Hitler, whom the communist paper wrongly accused of having cravenly avoided shaking Owens's hand, and the American who refused to afford equal opportunities for blacks. When asked to speak about the issue of Jim Crow baseball, an obviously embarrassed Gehrig replied, "Sorry, but I can't talk," while Yankees general manager Ed Barrow also declined to discuss the matter. *New York Daily News* columnist Jimmy Powers stated forthrightly, "Negroes belong in big league baseball competition," and suggested that major league baseball "would gain added sparkle" by the inclusion of the finest black players. Sportswriter Lester Rodney of the *Sunday Worker* contended that the admission of outstanding Negro Leaguers would improve major league ball. He urged spectators to demand baseball's integration. "Fans, it's up to you! Tell the big league magnates that you're sick of the poor pitching in the American League."[31]

In the August 23, 1936, edition of the *Sunday Worker*, Fred Farrell suggested that "Southern boys" like Mel Ott, Travis Jackson, and Bill Terry would have no difficulty playing alongside black teammates. "It isn't their fault that Charleston and Satchell [*sic*] Paige and Josh Gibson aren't out there with Johnny Mize and Luke Appling and Lou Gehrig." Farrell instead blamed wealthy baseball magnates like the Tigers' Walter Briggs, the Reds' Powel Crosley Jr., the Red Sox's Tom Yawkey, and the Indians' Alva Bradley.[32] In the same issue, Ted Benson related a discussion in which National League president Ford Frick denied that an unwritten law existed to prevent black players' entrance into the major leagues. Frick declared, "I do not recall one instance where baseball had allowed either race, creed or color to enter into the question of the selection of its players." Frick nevertheless dismissed the notion that he possessed any authority to deliver "an official opinion" about the issue. He offered that "the whole subject is a sociological problem, something society, not the big leagues, must solve." Yawkey acknowledged that he had "never given any thought to [the] matter," the pat answer for those unwilling to contest baseball's Jim Crow makeup.[33] In mid-January Mike Kantor of the *Daily Worker* revealed that Dodger president Stephen

McKeever stood ready to sign Negro League star pitcher Satchel Paige. "Yes, I know that Satchell [*sic*] Paige is a great pitcher and would do the Brooklyns a lot of good," McKeever stated before declaring that such a decision was up to manager Burleigh Grimes. When asked about such a possibility, Grimes hedged his bets by declaring that he would "do what the others did," although the decision resided with National League president Frick.[34]

On September 13, 1937, only the *Daily Worker* reported Joe DiMaggio's answer to the question of "who was the best pitcher he ever faced." The Yankee Clipper readily responded, "Satchell [sic] Paige." The *Daily Worker* featured the headline "DiMaggio Calls Negro Greatest Pitcher" while once more condemning organized baseball's "un-American race discrimination." The paper again blamed wealthy owners for refusing to allow "a member of a supposedly inferior race [to show] his ability in the glare of the American sports page." Referring to black stars in other sports, such as Joe Louis and college football star Homer Harris of the University of Iowa, the *Daily Worker* claimed that "only big league baseball holds the discredited fort of Jim Crow in athletics."[35]

In December 1937 Sam Lacy of the *Washington Tribune* met with Clark Griffith, president of the Washington Senators, urging him to add players from the Negro leagues to revitalize his struggling ball club. Griffith acknowledged that the Negro leagues contained "some mighty good players" and stated that most major league owners recognized integration of organized baseball would soon occur, perhaps through admission of a strong black league. William Benswanger informed reporters from the *Courier* he was "heartily in favor" of integrating the sport. He too offered that organized baseball might add a black league. Benswanger declared, "I firmly believe that just as Negroes have their rights in anything else, they should have a chance in organized baseball."[36] Frank "Fay" Young of the *Defender* reported the acknowlegment by former major leaguers in March 1938 that several Negro leaguers, including Paige, Gibson, Hilton Smith, Mule Suttles, and Willie Wells, could readily compete in organized baseball. One former Yankee said Ray Dandridge "is easily as good as Mel Ott at his best." An ex-Dodger favorably compared Fats Jenkins with DiMaggio.[37]

On July 29, 1938, Chicago White Sox broadcaster Bob Elson interviewed New York Yankee reserve outfielder Jake Powell on his pregame radio program. Powell indicated that he served as a policeman during the offseason. He then delivered a bombshell: "I crack niggers on the head."[38] Calls immediately inundated the radio station protesting Powell's statement. Commissioner Landis suspended the ballplayer for ten days, deeming Powell's action more careless than intentional. The black press applauded the suspension. Al Monroe of the *Defender* appreciated the fact that finally "professional baseball was forced to sit up and take notice of the Race's power. This could not and would not have happened ten years ago."[39]

In the July 15, 1939, edition of the *Courier*, the young African American sportswriter Wendell Smith initiated his own campaign to integrate organized baseball. Smith referred to baseball as "the great American game" and declared the United States "a baseball-mad nation." He charged that a "ghastly discloring" marred "this fascinating American portrait." Organized baseball had long "unjustly branded the Negro baseball player as an undesirable and refused to allow him his place on its canvas of countless colors." This continued during the very period when world war threatened to erupt. Referring to baseball's segregation policy as "the great American tragedy," Smith condemned the gentleman's agreement that allowed for the exclusion of "the sepia player." This remained the case despite concerted efforts by leading sportswriters like Jimmy Powers and Shirley Povich. They and Smith's own paper had taken the lead in questioning major league officials about their exclusionary policy. Baseball moguls responded by declaring that managers and players alike would revolt if black athletes were admitted. Determined to find out how authentic the claim was, Smith interviewed forty top National Leaguers and eight managers, beginning with representatives from the Cincinnati Reds. Referring to a game against the Philadelphia Stars, Cincinnati pitcher Johnny Vander Meer stated, "They had some of the best ball players I've ever seen." He also revealed, "I certainly wouldn't object to a good Negro ball player on our team."[40] Five of the managers interviewed indicated that they would add black players if allowed to. The Cardinals' Ray Blades, the Giants' Bill Terry, and the Braves'

Casey Stengel expressed reservations. Terry stated outright, "I do not think that Negro players will ever be admitted in the majors!" but his top player, Mel Ott, termed Gibson "one of the greatest backstops in the history of baseball."[41]

Bill McKechnie, who would guide the Reds to the 1939 National League pennant, asserted, "Some of the greatest ball players I have ever seen were Negroes," and mentioned Charles "Bullet Joe" Rogan, Oscar Charleston, Satchel Paige, Judy Gans, and Josh Gibson. Skipper James Thompson "Doc" Protho of the Philadelphia Phillies called Paige "good enough for any big league team in the country." Paige "has a world of stuff, and he certainly knows how to use it. His fast ball, I would say, is the best I've ever seen," Protho revealed.[42] Brooklyn manager Leo Durocher revealed that there were "plenty of colored boys who could make the grade in the majors."[43] Pitcher Dizzy Dean called Gibson "one of the best catchers that ever caught a ball," agreeing with Walter Johnson's assessment that Gibson was worth $200,000 to a major league squad. Dean also stated that Gibson "could hit a ball a mile" and "didn't have a weakness."[44] Boston Bees manager Casey Stengel said, "Most Negro players are what we call naturals. They can hit, run and throw exceptionally well." When asked which Negro Leaguers could play in the majors, Stengel stated, "Any number."[45]

Wendell Smith wrote that major league owners had "misinformed the public" in insisting that white managers and players refused to compete alongside black athletes. Smith then pointedly stated, "Negro ball players deserve a place in big league baseball." He insisted "this undemocratic custom of barring Negro players" be "smashed forever." Then Smith remarked, "Open your doors, Mr. Owner. The time has come."[46] For his part, Fay Young of the *Defender* explicitly questioned the worth of Smith's endeavor. "All the interviews with the big league players don't amount to the space it takes to print them for the reason these players have nothing to do with the question."[47] However, the *Daily Worker* conducted its own survey of major leaguers, coming up responses similar to those obtained by Smith.

The *Daily Worker* in September 1939 offered an article by Dave Farrell that referred to Jackie Robinson as "little short of sensational." The next month,

Dave Farrell further suggested that UCLA athletic star Robinson might be a prime candidate to break organized baseball's colored barrier. The following year, the *Daily Worker* praised Robinson yet again while including a photograph with a caption referring to him as a "sensational running back." The newspaper went on to say, "The Pacific Coast [Conference] . . . is sure to boast one of the country's greatest [college athletes] in Jackie Robinson of UCLA, one of the most amazing athletes in the land. Rated ready to equal or surpass the great Kenny [Washington] as a back, the twenty-year-old Jackie also was the leading scorer on the Coast in basketball, as well as a shortstop of big league caliber and a track ace."[48] Lester Rodney reported Brooklyn Dodgers manager Leo Durocher's observation that he would sign black players "in a minute, if I got permission from the big shots." Rodney also indicated that Durocher "got into hot water for saying that. They told him to shut up and not say another word about it."[49] Thus even as World War II approached, organized baseball remained segregated, refusing to admit some of the nation's finest athletes, including players as skilled as Robinson or UCLA teammate Kenny Washington.

2

Anti-Semitism and a
Detroit Tiger

Anti-Semitism had long flourished in the United States side-by-side racism, and not just in the athletic realm. Despite innumerable incidents of anti-Semitism, America was nevertheless viewed as a haven for many whose ancestors had suffered through the diaspora. At the midpoint of the nineteenth century, German Jews, many well educated, came to the United States. During the Civil War, Gen. Ulysses S. Grant issued a directive, General Order #11, expelling Jews from his military district, blaming them for pervasive smuggling and speculation that caused a spike in cotton prices. Responding to protests from Jews, President Abraham Lincoln rescinded Grant's order, although the blight of religious intolerance scarcely abated. Beginning in the 1880s, millions of Jews from Russia and Eastern Europe emigrated across the ocean seeking religious freedom and economic opportunity. German-American Jews now comprised something of an elite group within American Jewry, haughtily looking down on their brethren from Russia, Poland, and other parts of Eastern Europe. White Anglo-Saxon Protestant Americans, fueled by nativist sentiments, regarded these new immigrants and millions of Catholic émigrés with considerable disdain. Cries rang out for immigration restrictions to prevent the "polluting" of the nation's bloodstream. Matters threatened to come to a head during World War I when Madison Grant published his scathing indictment of recent immigration patterns, *The Passing of the Great Race*, which argued that the vast influx of new immigrants threatened American democracy itself.

Perhaps no single individual focused more stridently on the peril supposedly posed by the infusion of Jews into the United States during the first stages of the twentieth century than auto magnate, presidential aspirant, and Detroit resident Henry Ford, who was linked to a pamphlet produced in London titled "The Jewish Peril." In mid-1919 Ford exclaimed to the *New York World*, "International financiers are behind all war . . . they are what is called the international Jew." He insisted that the Jew "is a threat." Ford's own newspaper, the *Dearborn Independent*, which appeared weekly and circulated widely across the nation with a readership of several hundred thousand, ran a series of articles condemning Jews. The paper became, as historian Sidney M. Bolkosky indicates, the most "virulent anti-Jewish publication" in the country.[1] While the articles in the newspaper were unsigned, the Dearborn Publishing Company boasted Henry Ford as president, his wife Clara Ford as vice president, and their son Edsel Ford as secretary-treasurer. They in turn admitted to "full responsibility" for the newspaper, which included articles such as "The International Jew: The World's Problem," "Germany's Reaction Against the Jews," and "The Jew in the United States." These articles, most penned by the journalist William J. Cameron, sought to demonstrate that "the vengeful Jews of the world are united to capture and govern the world." At present, Cameron contended, that vengeance purportedly had resulted in the communist state in Russia, where "every commissar is a Jew," and had afflicted Germany, where Jews supposedly possessed an abundance of power. "The main source of the sickness of the German national body is charged to the influence of the Jews," the *Dearborn Independent* insisted. "Jewish intrigue and purpose" had purportedly led to the disarray and attempted revolution that Germany suffered following World War I. The author of "Germany's Reaction Against the Jew" stated that "thoughtful Germans hold that it is impossible for the Jew to be a patriot."[2] Jews back home sought to control leading American institutions with a cabal seeking to dominate the national economy, the *Dearborn Independent* alleged. Dismissing concerns about anti-Semitism,

Ford claimed he was merely seeking to "awake the Gentile world to an understanding of what is going on." This was necessary, for "the Jew is a mere huckster."[3] Ford's anti-Semitic offerings helped strengthen the Ku Klux Klan in Michigan, which boasted almost 900,000 members in 1921, more than in any other state.

The denigrating of Jews hardly lessened as reports of a fix of the previous year's World Series broke near the end of the 1920 major league season. Among the most prominent figures blamed for the scandal involving eight members of the 1919 American League champion Chicago White Sox were the New York gambler-racketeer Arnold Rothstein and former featherweight champion Abe "The Little Hebrew" Attell. As news of the Black Sox scandal unfolded and the *Dearborn Independent* continued its run of anti-Semitic rants, leading publications in the United States turned to *The Protocols of the Elders of Zion*—believed to have been devised by the Russian czar's secret police at the beginning of the twentieth century—a book that purportedly unveiled a Jewish plot to rule the world. The wholly fraudulent documents neatly matched prevailing anti-Semitic stereotypes. Ford expressed belief in the *Protocols* despite being informed that they were fabricated.

In his autobiography, *My Life and Work*, published by Doubleday in 1922, Ford again downplayed concerns regarding anti-Semitism. He insisted that "the question is wholly in the Jews' hands." He wrote, "If they are as wise as they claim to be, they will labor to make Jews American, instead of America Jewish." Time would demonstrate "that we are better friends to the Jews' interests than those who praise them to their faces and criticize them behind their backs."[4] A drive to put Ford in the White House evidently induced him to temporarily discard his anti-Semitic efforts. Others proved determined to maintain the campaign.

The journalist Lewis S. Gannett grappled with the question of whether the United States was anti-Semitic in the March 21, 1923, issue of *The Nation*. Anti-Semitism in America was in keeping with "a long Anglo-Saxon tradition of dislike of the newer arrival," Gannett explained. The latest edition of the Ku Klux Klan flowed naturally from Anglo-Saxon Protestantism. This version was "anti-Catholic, anti-Negro, anti-Jew. It is 100-per-cent white, Gentile, and Protestant." The determination of Jews to succeed stoked already existing prejudices. Entering college a full generation or more before other immigrant groups ensured that "there are in fact more dirty Jews and tactless Jews in college than dirty and tactless Italians, Armenians, or Slovaks." They seemed to believe that "membership in the Chosen People" resulted in intellectual superiority.[5]

During the very period when both opportunities and disdain beckoned for Jews in America, Henry Benjamin Greenberg grew up in New York City, where his immigrant parents had met. He was born on Perry Street, located in Greenwich Village, on January 1, 1911. His father, David, came from Roman, Romania, while his mother, Sarah, had been raised in Fălticeni, only seventy miles away. David and Sarah were Yiddish-speaking Orthodox Jews who were determined that their boys have bar mitzvah ceremonies, but religious strictures hardly stuck. Greenwich Village, with its lovely townhouses and wide streets, was something of an oasis within the lower sector of New York City, which contained large slum areas, many teeming with Jewish immigrants. The Greenbergs lived comfortably thanks to David's work in the textile industry. Nevertheless the area was riven with ethnic rivalries, including those pitting Irish and Italian kids against Jewish ones. As Greenberg later reflected, "Kids down in the Village thought the national pastime was beating up kids of other nationalities."[6] Hank was big for his age and thus able to hold his own in the street wars that sometimes filtered into the neighborhood.

The New York City neighborhood where the Greenbergs lived was deteriorating and hardly proved immune to anti-Semitic incidents, which led many Jewish families to move away. David's business fortunately prospered, enabling the family to relocate to the Bronx, where the Greenbergs acquired a rambling, sixteen-room house in the East Tremont section on Crotona Park North, or East 174th Street. Crotona Park was across the street, and to Hank's delight, a playing field was a block away. Known to his friends as Bruggy Greenberg, Hank became hooked on baseball after his father took him to a Sunday doubleheader at the Polo Grounds, which housed both the New York Giants and the New York Yankees until the start of the 1923 major league season. Giants second baseman Frankie Frisch banged out seven hits in the two-game set against the Philadelphia Phillies.

Hank Greenberg's parents viewed his love of baseball with disdain and bewilderment. Their attitude was in keeping with the sentiments expressed in a letter from an immigrant that appeared in the *Jewish Daily Forward*, a mainstay for many Jews who had migrated to the United States around the turn of the century. The letter read:

> It makes sense to teach a child to play dominoes or chess. But what is the point of a crazy game like baseball? The children can get crippled. When I was a boy we played rabbit, chasing each other, hide and seek. Later we stopped. If a grown boy played rabbit in Russia, they would think he had lost his mind. Here in educated America adults play baseball. They run after a leather ball like children. I want my boy to grow up to be a mensch, not a wild American runner. But he cries his head off.

Abraham Cahan, editor of the *Forward*, had responded with this sage advice: "Let your boys play baseball and play it well, as long as it does not interfere with their education or get them into bad company. Half the parents in the Jewish quarter have this problem. Chess is good, but the body needs to develop also. . . . Baseball develops the arms, legs, and eyesight." Kids should not "grow up foreigners in their own country," Cahan warned.[7]

The Greenbergs' neighbors in the Bronx understood the parents' concerns perfectly. They could be heard to say, "Mrs. Greenberg has such nice children. Too bad one of them has to be a bum." David Greenberg now ran the Acme Textile Shrinking Works in New York City; his financial success enabled the family to adopt a comfortable middle-class lifestyle. Both he and his wife were continually perplexed by their middle son. Hank's mother would ask him, "Why are you wasting your time playing baseball? It's a bum's game." His father hollered that Hank would never amount to anything. Ignoring such admonitions, Hank invariably grabbed his bat and glove and headed for the sandlot.[8]

Greenberg played on his first organized baseball team at grammar school PS 44 in the Bronx. Much of the rest of the time away from school found him playing pickup games at Crotona Park, where each kid batted until he made three outs. This suited Greenberg perfectly, although he was forced to bat last, for he belted the ball further than any of his companions. "Here comes big Bruggy!" his friends cried out. "Make him get out in the field first. He'll hit all day if you let him!" Greenberg attained varsity letters in basketball, football, and baseball at James Monroe High School, was a member of the swimming and soccer teams, and threw the shot put.[9]

But the tall and lanky Greenberg—he was 6'3" by the age of thirteen—worked particularly hard at baseball, which did not come easily to him. As he later acknowledged,

I didn't *play* ball when I was a kid, I *worked* at it. I'd play pepper by the hour, for example, to improve my fielding. Guys would hit or bunt the ball to me and I'd catch it. Over and over again. I'd count how many balls I'd fielded without an error, and then after I missed one I'd start counting all over again. To improve my hitting, I'd get friends and kids hanging around the park to pitch to me and to shag balls for me.

His high school coach Irwin Dickstein also indicated that "Hank never played games: he worked at them. He wasn't the natural athlete. His reactions were slow and he had trouble coordinating his big body. He couldn't run a lick because of his flat feet." Greenberg's awkwardness made him self-conscious, and the fact that other kids laughed at him hardly helped. Determined not to look ridiculous, he put in up to eight hours a day practicing at Crotona Park from the spring until the end of fall. During summers, he worked for Acme Textile (helping out on a delivery truck) then raced home to play ball.[10]

Greenberg admitted that a sense of insecurity fed his determination to become a good baseball player. He often "felt out of place" because he lacked grace, was forced to cram his oversized body behind a student desk, and suffered from a bad case of adolescent acne. It was "the event of the day" when he got called to the blackboard, with the other students chortling as he towered over the teacher. Greenberg was constantly asked on school days, "How's the air up there?" Visitors to the Greenberg home exclaimed, "My God, look how much he's grown! He's grown two feet in a week!"[11]

While he was in high school, Greenberg began to dream about the possibility of playing major league baseball. Paul Krichell, a top scout with the New York Yankees (then loaded with sluggers Babe Ruth, Lou Gehrig, and Bob Meusel), expressed an interest. Krichell attended one of James Monroe High School's games in 1928 to check out a pitcher. The scout proved little impressed with the pitcher, but Greenberg, then a "gangling" junior but boasting "powerful shoulders," caught his eye. Krichell introduced himself to both Greenberg and Hank's family. He purportedly sought to ingratiate himself with David and Sarah Greenberg by gorging "on gefultefish (*sic*) and herring."[12] That summer Greenberg landed a spot with the semipro Bay Parkways, who were based in Brooklyn. He belted two home runs in a game against the House of David, a touring team with bearded ballplayers. Krichell and other major league scouts also tracked Greenberg's progress as he played for the East Douglas squad of the Blackstone Valley League in Massachusetts.

Discussion of "the Jewish problem" in the United States had dramatically lessened during the mid-1920s. However, social commentators again began exploring that very issue as the decade neared an end, perhaps in response to the heightening of anti-Semitism abroad, particularly in Central Europe. The August 7, 1929, issue of *Outlook and Independent* referred to the fact that a quarter-century previously, an American woman on a visit to Germany had been startled by the level of anti-Semitism. Now "Americans are beginning to rival Europe in their hatred of Jews." The publication suggested that this was due to "characteristics of the Jewish race," including an "astonishing driving power and intelligence" and "neglect of certain social graces." *Outlook and Independent* still insisted, "The American conscience must recoil from hatred of the Jew."[13]

Baseball moguls were at least willing to look at Jewish prospects in contrast to African American players, who remained wholly locked out of the minor and major leagues. At a tryout with the Washington Senators, Hank

Greenberg went against recently retired Walter Johnson, who had won 417 games as a fireballing pitcher and was now the Senators manager. Johnson could still throw a heater that jumped, and Greenberg was unable to get around on any of the pitches. One team that refused to even consider Greenberg was the New York Giants. Their fiery little manager, John McGraw, declined to give Greenberg a look after receiving a report that Hank was clumsy and uncoordinated. A business acquaintance of David Greenberg reportedly asked McGraw, who had long sought a Jewish star to play for his National League powerhouse, why he displayed no interest in Hank. McGraw indicated that one of his scouts had declared that Greenberg would "never make it."[14] The great skipper thus passed on the opportunity to even scout Greenberg, baseball's greatest Jewish star in the first half of the twentieth century. The general sentiment about Hank back in the Greenberg neighborhood remained little better than that expressed by McGraw's scout. Greenberg later recalled, "Jewish women on my block in the Bronx would point me out as a good-for-nothing, a loafer, and a bum who always wanted to play baseball rather than go to school. . . . I was Mrs. Greenberg's disgrace."[15]

Hoping to attend Princeton University, Greenberg worked hard to maintain his grades, graduating from high school in early 1929. That summer Krichell introduced Greenberg to the Yankees general manager, Ed Barrow, at the team's office, located at 42nd Street and Sixth Avenue. Barrow asked, "How'd you like to play with the Yankees?" Greenberg managed to respond, "I'd like to very much." Barrow handed him four general admission tickets to watch the Yankees in action. Krichell invited Greenberg to a game at the stadium on the final day of the 1929 season. That act of generosity came back to haunt the Yankees, who, like the Giants, never got around to featuring a topflight Jewish ballplayer able to appeal to the city's large Jewish population. In this particular instance, Krichell's baseball acumen, which had led to his earlier signing of Lou Gehrig, also worked against the Bronx Bombers landing another great slugger. Greenberg simply did not believe he could displace Gehrig at first base.[16]

Greenberg watched intently as the great first baseman entered the on-deck circle during the Yankees' half of the first inning. The Yankees scout and his young guest were seated nearby in a first-row box near the home team's dugout. Krichell indicated to Greenberg that Gehrig was "all washed up. In a few years you'll be the Yankees' first baseman." But Greenberg was overwhelmed by Gehrig. "His shoulders were a yard wide and his legs looked like mighty oak trees. I'd never seen such sheer brute strength. 'No way I'm going to sign with this team. Not with *him* playing first base,'" Greenberg told himself. He responded to Krichell, "That Lou Gehrig looks like he's got a lot of years left." Krichell then countered, "Look at how his batting average has slipped," referring to the fact that Gehrig was then batting just under .300, although he ended the season at that mark. Greenberg proved perceptive. Gehrig went on to play every Yankees game for the next nine seasons before the crippling disease that took his name drove him from the game.[17]

Both the Yankees and the Senators offered Greenberg $10,000—a sizable bonus for that era—to sign. The Pittsburgh Pirates and the Detroit Tigers, in whom he was increasingly interested, also pursued him. The Tigers offered less than some other teams but came up with a creative package that appealed to David and Sarah Greenberg. Hank was to receive $3,000 up front and then another $6,000 after he completed his first year of college. Hank discussed the various proposals with his father. "Pop, are you against baseball as a career?" he asked. His father indicated that he was, but Hank informed him of the Tigers' offer. "$9,000?" a bemused Mr. Greenberg queried. "You mean they want to give you that kind of money just to go out and play baseball?" When Hank answered affirmatively, his father then asked, "And they'll let you finish college first?" That appeared to cinch matters for David Greenberg. "I thought baseball was a game," he said. "But it's a business—apparently a very good business. Take the money."[18]

Greenberg told the Detroit scout, Jean Dubuc, that he did not think he could sign with the Tigers. Hank declared that he intended to go to college, having received a scholarship to New York University. Dubuc then proposed to deliver $6,000 up front after Greenberg inked the deal, and then hand over an additional $3,000 when Hank joined the major league squad. Krichell sought to one-up the Tigers, but Greenberg, recalling the Yankee behemoth at first base, turned him down. In early 1930 Greenberg joined the Tigers in Tampa, Florida, for spring training. After he belted a homer in his first exhibition game, a Detroit newspaper reported, "Henry Greenberg, the prize rookie, stole the show. He made a couple of sensational plays at first base . . . and his trip to the plate resulted in a home run and Babe Ruth never hit a ball harder."[19] Al Lang, the former mayor of St. Petersburg, told Col. Jake Ruppert, co-owner of the Yankees, "I saw the greatest hitter since Ruth," referring to Greenberg. Ruppert asked Krichell, "Didn't we have a chance to sign that boy? What happened to him?"[20] Although called "the greatest prospect in years," Greenberg soon proved overmatched by big league pitchers and was sent down to Hartford, the Tigers' Class-A franchise in the Eastern League. Despite smacking a homer in his final game there, the nineteen-year-old Greenberg's struggles worsened as he batted a mere .214 and soon dropped down to Raleigh in the Class-C Piedmont League. After again flailing away at the plate, Greenberg rebounded, hitting .314 and knocking out nineteen homers. He also encountered something that recurred throughout his baseball career: expressions of amazement that a Jew was playing baseball. At one point, Greenberg asked a gawking Jo-Jo White, "What're you looking at?" His teammate replied, "Nothing. I've never seen a Jew before. I'm just looking." Greenberg responded, "See anything interesting?" The fellow admitted, "I don't understand it. You look just like anybody else." "Thanks," Greenberg countered, thereby terminating the conversation. Later, Greenberg recalled Atlanta native White admitting, "Hell, I thought all those Jews had horns."[21]

Greenberg returned to the Tigers for the major league campaign's final few weeks near the close of his first season in organized baseball. In his lone plate appearance, he popped up to Yankees second baseman Tony Lazzeri. At the tail end of the season, Tigers manager Bucky Harris, who had scarcely spoken to Greenberg, ordered him to go play first base. The strong-willed Greenberg blurted out, "I ain't gonna play for this team" and headed for the clubhouse.[22] The next season saw Greenberg play for Evansville in the 3-I League. There he batted .318 with 15 homers and a league-leading

41 doubles. He also committed a league-high 25 errors at first base before appearing as a pinch hitter in three games for Beaumont of the Texas League. He rejoined Beaumont in 1932, becoming the league's most valuable player by hitting 39 homers and driving in 131 runs. Notwithstanding his success, both seasons hardly unfolded without controversy as riots occurred on the baseball diamond in Decatur, Illinois, and in Dallas, Texas. Anti-Semitic slurs played a major part in both instances, with Greenberg angrily responding to an opposing player's verbal assault and a barrage of abuse emanating from the grandstands in Decatur. The police had to escort him out of the ballpark. Following the disturbance in Dallas, the ensuing newspaper coverage resulted in everything being "focused on that dirty Jew" as the following day's game took place.

Events occurred overseas that winter that drew Greenberg's attention and that of other American Jews. On January 30, 1933, German president Paul von Hindenburg appointed Adolf Hitler chancellor of the national government. Following the burning of the Reichstag, which the Nazis blamed on the communists, Hitler pressed for suspension of civil liberties and the beginning of his totalitarian state. The Nazis quashed all political opposition and set up concentration camps, the first in Dachau, just outside Munich, to warehouse dissidents. Nazi storm troopers threatened all foes as a bill was proposed to establish Hitler's dictatorship. They chanted, "Full powers—or else! We want the bill—or fire and murder!" Membership in the Nazi Party soared following easy passage of the bill.

That season the Detroit Tigers landed in the second division for the fifth straight year, coming in fifth, 29½ games behind the world champion New York Yankees. The Tiger franchise remained, nevertheless, one of baseball's most storied, thanks to former stars like Ty Cobb, Sam Crawford, Hughie Jennings, and Harry Heilmann. The Tigers had captured three straight American League pennants from 1907–1909 but had come up short in the World Series each time. Bucky Harris remained the Tigers skipper as the 1933 season opened. Harris was the former "boy wonder" who as playing manager had led the Washington Senators to consecutive pennants and a World Series title during the middle of the previous decade. His star player was second baseman Charlie Gehringer, considered so smooth and consistent he was known as "the Mechanical Man."

During spring training Harris informed Greenberg, who was paid $3,300 for 1933, that he was going to be the Tigers' third baseman, but Hank was unable to play that position. Lacking any confidence that he could do so, Greenberg muttered, "They'll bunt me to death." Teammates suggested he work hard to remain in shape so that he might get the opportunity to play first base. Greenberg fretted, "I'll get fat sitting on the bench, and my baseball career will be over before it really started."[23] He finally replaced the slick-fielding but light-hitting Harry Davis at first base two months into the season. Greenberg worked diligently to overcome his initial awkwardness in the field. He appeared at the ballpark before anyone else. He practiced after no else remained. He attempted to glean any useful hints from his manager, coaches, or other ballplayers. He experimented with different gloves, but it was obvious that his bat would determine whether he remained in the majors. Despite missing almost forty games, he ended the campaign having smacked his first dozen major league home runs and having compiled eighty-seven RBIs while batting .301. He did so while proudly sporting his family surname. Greenberg evidently never considering the possibility of changing his name, which former sportswriter-turned–major league publicist (and later National League president and baseball commissioner) Ford Frick had suggested and many other ballplayers had earlier done. The addition of Greenberg to the Tigers lineup unfortunately failed to alter their position in the league standings as they again finished fifth with a slightly poorer record than the previous season.

3

A Major League Star

The Tigers' 1933 performance hardly lifted the spirits of the residents of Detroit, as it remained more economically destitute than any major American city. Detroit had experienced dramatic transformations during the previous three decades. Its population mushroomed from 265,000 at the turn of the century to over 1.5 million by the beginning of the 1930s. Previously referred to as the "Paris of the Midwest" due to its boulevards, Detroit had increasingly taken on a blue-collar feel in line with its role as the world's automotive capital. By 1929 Detroit was producing over 5 million automobiles a year. The downtown area featured the forty-seven-story Penobscot Building, one of the world's largest skyscrapers, complete with Art Deco shadings. The just-completed thirty-story-tall Fisher Building, located in the city's New Center, led the *Detroit Times* to suggest that it would represent the city as the Eiffel Tower did Paris. But it was hardly surprising that the nation's economic downturn took the glow off the metropolitan area with its impressive skyscrapers and the commercial prosperity associated most of all with Henry Ford. Car production plummeted by 2 million in 1930 as unemployment skyrocketed and gang warfare escalated. Vendors sold apples on downtown street corners. Shelters attempted to take care of the rapidly growing number of jobless. Restaurants provided free lunches on Christmas Day. Auto production slid to 1.3 million in 1931, and relief drives mounted. Many more families were evicted the following year by landlords who had not received rent for several months. Meanwhile 225,000 city residents were out of work. Approximately 3,000 individuals participated in the Ford Hunger March from Detroit to Dearborn. The peaceful march ended with tear-gassing by police, the killing of four organizers, and the wounding of scores of other marchers. By 1933 the Great Depression had crippled the nation's industrial and agrarian sectors, resulting in massive numbers of collapsed businesses, failed banks, and more and more unemployed workers in Detroit and around the country. Recalling her introduction to Detroit at the beginning of the decade, one settlement worker reported, "I have never encountered such misery on the zero day of my arrival."[1]

Desperate conditions in Detroit helped lead to the growing appeal of fascist-styled influences during this period. The KKK proved influential in certain circles, as did the paramilitary Black Legion, which sprang out of the Klan in 1933, had about 20,000–30,000 members in Michigan at its peak, and was centered in Detroit. The Black Legion despised immigrants, blacks, Jews, Catholics, communists, labor activists, and farm cooperatives. Promising to defend "Protestantism, Americanism and Womanhood," the founders of the Black Legion devised a pledge through which a would-be member, with a gun pointed at his heart, promised his readiness to "be torn limb from limb and scattered to the carrion" should he betray the organization's secrets. Black Legionnaires subscribed to "the tenets of the Christian religion, the maintenance of white supremacy, and principles of pure Americanism."

Detroit's three most prominent residents at the beginning of the 1930s were auto magnate Henry Ford, Father Charles Coughlin, and Mayor Frank Murphy, a trio alternately celebrated and reviled. Applying the scientific management techniques of Frederick Taylor to the assembly line, Ford had recast American industry, becoming something of a folk hero in the process. His Model T automobile, or Tin Lizzie, proved to be the most popular among American consumers. His method of production, referred to as Fordism, provided a model that other industrialists, both in the United States and abroad, attempted to replicate. Ford's fame spread even to the

Soviet Union, while the radical author John Dos Passos included a biographical sketch on him in *The Big Money*. During the 1910s Ford had wanted to make his cars affordable and ensure that his own workers could purchase them, paying a then-generous five-dollar daily wage for an eight-hour workday. He offered various amenities in the workplace while hoping to stave off union efforts. Praise poured forth with Ford called "the new Messiah." [2] Ford's popularity continued to surge as many urged him to run for the presidency. Ford's fame spread beyond his own industrial plants, exemplified by the attention his Peace Ship received during World War I. The controversial Peace Ship transported Ford and nearly two hundred peace activists to Europe in 1915 as war raged. More troublesome was Ford's weekly newspaper, the *Dearborn Independent*, which republished *The Protocols of the Elders of Zion* and spewed anti-Semitic tirades. Then in 1922, Ford published *The International Jew: The World's Foremost Problem*, a four-volume series of pamphlets that were later discovered in Adolf Hitler's library.

A libel action against Ford resulted in a mistrial, but the auto magnate seemed determined to abandon his anti-Semitic operations. In a letter dated July 8, 1927, Ford informed Arthur Brisbane, a top columnist with the *New York Evening Journal*, of that decision. Ford expressed regrets that Jews viewed him "as their enemy," and he apologized "for resurrecting exploded fictions," stating that he now recognized that the *Protocols* contained "gross forgeries." He also distanced himself from earlier charges that Jews were engaged in a sweeping conspiracy to control the world, asserting instead that he fully recognized "the virtues of the Jewish people as a whole." He applauded their industry, "sobriety and diligence . . . benevolence, and their unselfish interest in the public welfare." Ford thus sought "to make amends for the wrong done to the Jews as fellow-men and brothers." The *Detroit News*, in its December 31, 1931, edition, nevertheless reported Adolf Hitler as asserting, "I regard Henry Ford as my inspiration. I am imbued with his philosophy that many small units yield a better return than a few large ones." [3] Eleven months after Hitler came to power, twenty-nine editions of *The International Jew* had been published in Germany, containing prefaces lauding Ford's "great service" in condemning Jews. [4] It would be another four years before Ford denied any connection to the German publication of his booklets.

Born in Ontario, Canada, in 1891, Father Charles Coughlin of the Roman Catholic Church received his ordination in Toronto in 1916 and moved to Detroit seven years later. Beginning in 1926, when he helped establish a new church in Royal Oak, Michigan, located twelve miles from downtown Detroit, Coughlin delivered weekly sermons on a Detroit radio station. Influenced by the social gospel movement that involved the Church in the campaign to foster economic justice, Coughlin attacked the Ku Klux Klan, which had resurfaced in the 1920s. During the early stages of the Great Depression, Coughlin delivered radio addresses transmitted by the Columbia Broadcasting System, condemning communism, socialism, and "predatory capitalism." He insisted that "Christ and Christianity are the only active, unassailable forces which today have compassion on the multitudes." He appeared before a House subcommittee, chaired by Hamilton Fish Jr., that explored the issue of domestic subversion. Coughlin reported, "The greatest force in the movement to internationalize labor throughout the world is Henry Ford." The auto magnate and other industrialists, Coughlin charged, were pushing workers in the direction of socialism. CBS failed to renew his contract due to concerns about the political makeup of Coughlin's messages, but he soon established his own radio network, which acquired a national audience. He also befriended both Detroit mayor Frank Murphy and newly elected president Franklin Delano Roosevelt. Coughlin repeatedly blasted the incumbent Republican chief executive Herbert Hoover during the 1932 presidential campaign. At first Coughlin resoundingly praised FDR. He asserted, "Roosevelt or Ruin!" and "The New Deal is Christ's Deal."[5] Roosevelt soon expressed disdain for Coughlin, who began to castigate the president's relief efforts, First Lady Eleanor Roosevelt, and FDR himself.

Detroit's third leading public figure, Frank Murphy, a native of Harbor Beach, Michigan, worked his way through the University of Michigan, where he received a law degree, before serving in France with American Expeditionary Forces during World War I. He campaigned for a position on the Recorder's Court in Detroit after working in the U.S. attorney general's office. He contended that the powers-that-be were in league with profiteers and those who exploited the poor. Murphy presided over the trial of Ossian Sweet, an African American physician indicted for murder, along with ten other family members and friends, after a member of a mob was killed during an attempt to drive Sweet out of his home. Angry whites had gathered shortly following Sweet's purchase of a house in a previously all-white Detroit neighborhood. Famed trial attorneys Arthur Garfield Hays and Clarence Darrow headed the defense team. Darrow later noted that Murphy was "a judge who not only seemed human, but who proved to be the kindliest and most understanding man I have ever happened to meet on the bench."[6] The jury failed to deliver a verdict despite deliberating for forty-six hours, and the prosecution eventually dropped all charges. Murphy put together a working-class coalition that included blacks, whites, Catholics, Protestants, and Jews, and was elected mayor of Detroit in 1930. He subsequently supported Roosevelt's bid for the presidency, and FDR in turn named Murphy, whom he considered young and idealistic, governor-general of the Philippines.

In the very period when Ford, Coughlin, and Murphy remained Detroit's most celebrated residents, a much younger man began competing for the allegiance of city dwellers. As the decade continued, baseball slugger Hank Greenberg eventually supplanted them all in popularity, particularly as Ford's often violent opposition to labor unions became more obvious, Coughlin's anti–New Deal and anti-Semitic rants proved more pronounced, and Murphy's pro-labor stance while serving as governor of Michigan cost him political support. Greenberg's rookie season in 1933, which occurred at the height of the Great Depression and during the opening stages of the New Deal, merely foreshadowed his eventual impact on major league baseball, particularly in economically distraught Detroit.

By the early 1930s, a number of Jewish athletes had made their mark in various sports, particularly boxing, basketball, and football. Benny Leonard held the world lightweight crown from 1917 to 1925, the longest reign in the division's history. After dropping his first professional bout, Leonard won eighty-eight straight fights, including sixty-eight by knockout. Having retired from the ring a wealthy man, Leonard fought once again, albeit unsuccessfully, after suffering a financial shellacking due to the stock market crash. In 1933 Barney Ross captured both the world lightweight and junior welterweight titles, and the next year he took the welterweight crown. Heavyweight Max Baer, whose father was a non-practicing Jew, first sported trunks embroidered with a Star of David during a match at Yankee Stadium in June 1933 against the German Max Schmeling. The following year, Baer won the heavyweight crown.

Basketball's greatest star during the 1920s, Nat Holman, coached at City College of New York and played professional basketball on the weekends. Through much of the decade, Holman led the New York Celtics, guiding them to a remarkable 531-28 record over eight seasons. In 1927 Abe Saperstein founded the Harlem Globetrotters basketball squad, which he owned and coached. The all-black Globetrotters offered a fast-paced comedic brand of basketball that delighted fans. Benny Friedman was a two-time All-American quarterback at the University of Michigan in the 1920s before starring with the New York Giants of the National Football League. In 1928, his second year in the NFL, Friedman was the circuit's top passer and rusher, the only player ever to accomplish that feat.

No Jewish athlete of comparable skills had played in the major leagues. A small number of Jews had played big-league ball, including Buddy Myer, an infielder with the Washington Senators and Boston Red Sox who was a consistent .300 hitter and stolen base artist and who became a regular during the 1926 campaign. Andy Cohen played two full seasons in the majors at the close of the decade but never became the star that John McGraw long envisioned, batting only .281 with only fourteen home runs during a shortened career. Cohen did inspire a poem by Frank Getty titled "Cohen at Bat," after he helped lead the New York Giants to an opening day victory.

Far less accomplished on the baseball diamond but noteworthy in other regards was catcher Moe Berg, who bounced around with a series of major league teams, seldom as an everyday player. The multilingual Berg was a graduate of Princeton University, the Sorbonne, and Columbia Law School.

He also batted a mere .185 during the just-concluded 1933 season while making only sixty-five plate appearances in forty games.

The next major league campaign was Hank Greenberg's first great season and the finest a Jewish player had yet delivered in organized baseball. Greenberg continued to be referred to as the "Pants Presser" or "the youngster with the noodle."[7] Displaying far more pop than he had during his rookie campaign, Greenberg, now earning $5,000 with the promise of an additional $500 if his team finished among the top three spots in the American League, helped to keep the Detroit Tigers in the pennant chase. The Tigers were much improved over the previous season. They had added player-manager Mickey Cochrane, the great catcher purchased from the Philadelphia Athletics, where he had played on three pennant- and two World Series–winning teams, and outfielder Goose Goslin, a former batting champion traded by the Washington Senators. Greenberg, Goslin, and second baseman Charlie Gehringer made up Detroit's version of the G-men (as government agents were called), all hard-hitting sluggers. Cochrane skillfully guided the Tigers while compiling a .320 batting average on the way to an MVP selection. Goslin batted .305 with 100 RBIs, and Gehringer hit .356 (second only to Lou Gehrig's .363 mark), belted 11 homers, drove in 127 runs, led the league in scoring with 134 runs and 214 hits, and finished second in the tabulations for the league MVP, only two votes behind Cochrane. Greenberg, who came in sixth in the MVP count, blossomed in his second full year in the majors, batting .339 (the fifth-best average in the American League), hitting 26 homers, and driving in 139 runs. He also scored 118 runs, had a .600 slugging average, and led the league in doubles with 63, at the time the third-highest total in major league history. Also spurring the Tigers were 22-game winner Tommy Bridges and 24-game winner Schoolboy Rowe. The rookie sensation Rowe won 16 games in succession, tying the American League record held by Walter Johnson, Joe Wood, and Lefty Grove. Both Elden Auker and Firpo Marberry added 15 wins.

One unhappy moment occurred during preseason when Greenberg verbally tussled with Rip Sewell, a young pitcher who had played with Hank in Beaumont and hoped to make it with the Tigers. The incident took place on a bus when Greenberg raised a window, which Sewell asked him to lower. Greenberg purportedly responded by calling Sewell "a rookie fresh Southern son of a bitch." Sewell retorted, "Well, you big Jew bastard." The two threatened to fight when they reached Lakeland where Detroit was training. Greenberg started "pummeling" Sewell when they got off the bus. After listening to Sewell's account of what happened, Cochrane responded, "Okay, Rip, you're going to the minor leagues."[8] Greenberg continued to have anti-Semitic epithets hurled at him on the playing field. Tiger backstop Birdie Tebbetts would later declare, "I think Hank . . . was abused more than any other white ballplayer or any other ethnic player except Jackie Robinson."[9] Greenberg believed that the anti-Semitism he encountered actually made him a better competitor. As he put it, "I was a very sensitive, fired-up ballplayer, and when they got on me that way, it brought out the best in me. I played all the harder."[10]

The Tigers vied with the New York Yankees for the top spot in the American League during the season's early months. Just past the midseason mark, Harry Salsinger, sports editor of the *Detroit News*, sang the praises of Greenberg, rapidly moving into the first rank of major league players. Salsinger wrote:

The development of Greenberg is one of the most amazing features of an amazing baseball season. He was a good hitter last year and a long one, but today he is one of the most powerful sluggers who has come along in years. All at once he gained the confidence. . . . The unusual feature of Greenberg's development is that Greenberg's fielding has improved with his hitting. He was probably the weakest fielder among the first basemen of the American League last season but today his defensive work is as good as you will see.

The reporter went on to say that Greenberg was "an ideal kind of player. He is of the winning type, the ultra-aggressive competitor with loads of courage and at his best in the tight spots. The boy Greenberg has grown into quite a baseball player."[11]

The American League race remained tight, with the Yankees—led by Triple Crown winner Lou Gehrig, a fading Babe Ruth, and the circuit's top pitcher, Lefty Gomez—battling into September. The *Detroit Free Press* on September 9 prominently featured a photograph of Greenberg at the plate with the headline, "Rosh Hashanah," in both English and Hebrew. A caption read, "And, so to you, Mr. Greenberg, the Tiger fans say: '*Leshono tovo tikosayyu!*' which means 'Happy New Year.'" Greenberg was referred to as "the great Jewish slugger of the Tigers."[12] He drove in the winning run that day against the Boston Red Sox in the bottom of the 10th inning at Navin Field, enabling the Tigers to maintain a four-game lead over New York.

Greenberg wondered that night whether he should play the next day when Jews would celebrate Rosh Hashanah. "Like Jacob of old, he spent the night wrestling with the angels," reporter Charles P. Ward indicated.[13] Reporters in Detroit spoke to local rabbis to determine whether Greenberg should play. One rabbi—possibly Jacob Thumin of the Orthodox synagogue Beth Abraham; Dr. Leo M. Franklin of Temple Beth El, the oldest Jewish congregation in the state and a leading Reform synagogue; or Abraham M. Hershman of Congregation Shaarey Zedek, a Conservative synagogue—informed Greenberg that the Talmud indicated "the start of a new year was supposed to be a happy day." As Greenberg reported, "He found that Jews in history had played games on that day; so he felt it would be perfectly all right for me to play baseball." Other rabbis favored a stricter interpretation. They suggested Greenberg could play but only if no Orthodox Jews purchased tickets on Rosh Hashanah, no smoking took place at the game, and only kosher refreshments were sold.[14]

On the morning of Rosh Hashanah, Greenberg attended services at Congregation Shaarey Zedek, the large Conservative synagogue located at 2900 Chicago Boulevard in Detroit. Greenberg went to the ballpark still undecided about whether he would be in the lineup. He asked Cochrane if he had to play. Mickey responded that he badly wanted him to but was uncertain as to what Hank's religion required. Greenberg worried that the pennant race might come down to this one game. He feared his absence might keep Detroit out of its first World Series in over two decades. Hank finally informed Cochrane that he was going to be in the lineup. Greenberg had a game that would become part of major league and Jewish American folklore. Cochrane got a double and a single, and Marv Owen managed a single. The rest of the Tiger lineup was shut down by Red Sox hurler Gordon Rhodes. The Red Sox themselves eked out only three singles and a first-inning run against Auker. But Greenberg belted a "towering" homer that flew over the scoreboard in the bottom of seventh to tie the score. He then delivered a walk-off smash in the last of the ninth.[15]

The next day's edition of the *Free Press* prominently displayed Greenberg nearing home plate after the game-winning homer. The headline blared out, "A Happy New Year for Everybody."[16] Reporter Ward reported how fans "swarmed around" Greenberg as he approached home plate after hitting his second home run. Greenberg "had waged a terrific battle with himself" during the twenty-four hours before game time. One report had Greenberg experience relief upon receiving a supportive message from Dr. Franklin of Temple Beth El. "I guess, I didn't do the wrong thing after all. Tonight I'm going home and pray to God and thank him for those home runs."[17] Historian William M. Simons considers the statement purportedly issued by Rabbi Franklin more "ambiguous" than Greenberg evidently did.

In the Jewish faith there is no power granted to the rabbi to give dispensation to anyone for doing anything which reads contrary to this own conscientious convictions—indeed we insist upon the doctrine of personal responsibility. In such a case as this, Mr. Greenberg, who is a conscientious Jew, must decide for himself whether he ought to play or not. From the standpoint of Orthodox Judaism the fact that ballplaying is his means of livelihood would argue against his participation in the Monday game. On the other hand, it might be argued quite consistently, that his taking part in the game would mean something not only to himself but to his fellow players, and in fact at this time, to the community of Detroit. But in the last analysis, no rabbi is authorized to give or withhold permission for him to do so.[18]

Other accounts indicated that Greenberg felt considerable pressure from other ballplayers and civic leaders to put on his uniform.

Reporter Jack Cravath discussed Greenberg's decision to play in the game, saying it was made "strictly on his conscience." Greenberg later revealed in the Tiger clubhouse, "I did a lot of praying before the game and I am going to do a lot of it after, but certainly the Good Lord did not let me down today." Admitting that he worried about getting brushed back during the game, Greenberg said, "Once I was in there, I had only one thing to do—keep swinging. I guess I did pretty well and the Lord was with me." Cravath applauded Greenberg's performance. He declared that "Ruth at this best, never hit a baseball to more effect or never won a ball game more dramatically than the big, conscience-stricken youngster from the Bronx did."[19] The *Free Press* columnist known as Iffy the Dopester (who was actually the paper's editor Malcolm Bingay), declared Greenberg's Rosh Hashanah homers "strictly kosher," no matter what "the priests of the synagog [*sic*]" said.[20] Bud Shaver of the *Times* reported that "there was more than the mighty bone and sinew of Hank Greenberg behind those two home runs which went whistling out of Navin Field." Rather "they were propelled by a force born on desperation and pride of a young Jew who turned his back on the ancient ways of his race and creed and helped his teammates." Greenberg considered the hits an indication "the good Lord did not let [him] down, but nevertheless later revealed having been villified by both fellow parishioners and certain rabbis."[21]

His decision only strengthened the affection felt for Greenberg by the vast majority of Jews in Detroit and New York City. Appreciated too was the obvious discomfort he, a non-practicing Jew, confronted in wrestling with twin responsibilities to his teammates and his fellow American Jews.

By the mid-1930s, around ninety thousand Jews, the sixth-largest number in the United States, resided in Detroit, making up almost 4 percent of the metropolitan population. Just over 50 percent of Jewish workers in Detroit were involved in "trade," with a good number operating as "proprietors, managers, and officials," most in "dry goods or clothing stores, food stores, junk, or rags," with another 8 percent pursuing careers in law, medicine, or dentistry, Sidney Bolkosky reports. Detroit Jews belonged to Reform, Conservative, or Orthodox synagogues, or adopted a wholly secular lifestyle. As was true in other American communities where relatively large numbers of their religious brethren were found, Detroit Jews could join socialist, Zionist, or anti-Zionist groups. Beginning in 1932, Harry Weinberg presented *Weinberg's Yiddish Radio Hour* each Sunday morning for ninety minutes. Education was considered of paramount importance, and the synagogues operated schools of their own, while independent Jewish educational programs were readily available. Jewish relief agencies, including the Jewish Welfare Federation, provided assistance for downtrodden Jews in the city. Sports and Jewish athletic stars provided a venue whereby religious, political, ideological, and ethnic divisions could be surmounted, however temporarily. No figure loomed larger in that regard than Hank Greenberg.[22]

The week following his decision to play on Rosh Hashanah, with the Tigers now seven-and-a-half games ahead of the Yankees with only eleven regular season contests left, Greenberg chose to sit out the game against the St. Louis Browns on Yom Kippur, the Jewish Day of Atonement. David Greenberg, informed the *New York Evening Post* that his son agreed not to play. "Yom Kippur was different," David stated. "I put my foot down and Henry obeyed." Iffy the Dopester applauded the decision, which meant that for the first and only time all season, Greenberg, Gehringer, shortstop Billy Rogell, and third baseman Marv Owen did not make up the Tiger infield. As Greenberg walked into Shaarey Zedek to attend the Yom Kippur service, the congregants gave him a standing ovation in the midst of the rabbi's davening. One fan remembered seeing Greenberg at the synagogue and telling himself, "My God, nobody ever saw a Jew that big." The *News's* Bud Shaver contended that "the qualities which make [Greenberg] an appealing figure are the direct heritage of race and creed. His fine intelligence, independence of thought, courage and his driving ambition have won him the respect and admiration of his teammates, baseball writers, and the fans at large. . . . He feels and acknowledges his responsibility as a representative of the Jews in the field of a great national sport and the Jewish people could have no finer representative."[23] The *News*'s sports editor, H. G. Salsinger, praised Greenberg as "the greatest player the Jews have contributed to baseball" and as "an illustrious torch bearer of his people" who was a "fierce competitor" with "a keen eye, a fighting heart," "set purpose," and "humility."[24]

The popular poet Edgar Guest, who resided in Detroit, responded by delivering a tribute, "Speaking of Greenberg."

> *The Irish didn't like it when they heard of Greenberg's fame.*
> *For they thought a good first baseman should possess an Irish name;*
> *And the Murphys and Mulrooneys said they never dreamed they'd see*
> *A Jewish boy from Bronxville out where Casey used to be.*
> *In the early days of April not a Dugan tipped his hat*
> *Or prayed to see a "double" when Hank Greenberg came to bat.*
> *In July the Irish wondered where he'd ever learned to play.*
> *"He makes me think of Casey!" Old Man Murphy dared to say;*
> *And with fifty-seven doubles and a score of homers made*
> *The respect they had for Greenberg was being openly displayed.*
> *But on the Jewish New Year when Hank Greenberg came to bat*
> *And made two home runs off Pitcher Rhodes—they cheered like mad*
> *   for that.*
>
> *Came Yom Kippur—holy fast day world wide over to the Jew—*
> *And Hank Greenberg to his teaching and the old tradition true*
> *Spent the day among his people and he didn't come to play*
> *Said Murphy to Mulrooney, "We shall lose the game today!*
> *We shall miss him on the infield and shall miss him at the bat,*
> *But he's true to his religion—and I honor him for that!"*

The Tigers went on to clinch the pennant, winning 101 contests, seven games in front of the Yankees. The World Series against the St. Louis Cardinals went the full seven games, with the Tigers holding a 3–2 lead after game five. The Gashouse Gang, as the Cardinals, led by Pepper

Martin, Joe Medwick, and Dizzy Dean, were known, took the sixth game, 4–3, and routed the Tigers in game seven, 11–0. The last two games were played in Detroit, and irate Tiger fans threatened a riot in the decisive meeting. Dizzy and his brother, Paul, each won two games, while the Tigers fell notwithstanding Gehringer's .379 batting average, which resulted from eleven hits, and Greenberg's .321 mark. Despite hitting one homer and driving in seven RBIs, Hank stranded several men on base, struck out nine times, and might have been perceived as the Series goat.

Near the beginning of the following season, a full-length article titled "Hank Greenberg the 'Local' Hero" appeared in the April 12, 1935, edition of the *Detroit Jewish Chronicle and the Legal Chronicle*. The story only burnished the ballplayer's heroic image. The essay by Morris Weiner indicated that Greenberg was now "the boy who made good. The lad who is bringing game and credit to the Jewish people." Following the close of the previous year's World Series, Greenberg was afforded "the biggest reception and ovation by the Jews in the Bronx that New York had ever seen." In fact, "Hank Greenberg owned the town." Jewish mothers in the New York borough seemed to view him differently than before and made certain that their children headed to play sandlot baseball after school. It appears as though each kid in the Bronx who could wield a bat was "an embryo 'Bruggy' Greenberg."[25]

Detroit Tigers manager Mickey Cochrane credited Greenberg's slugging with carrying the Tigers to the 1934 American League pennant. Weiner referred to Greenberg and teammates Gehringer and Goslin as "the famous 'G' trio . . . the most feared trio in the American circuit these days." A veritable "slugging unit," the trio "wreaked havoc . . . with their fancy stick wielding." Weiner predicted that Greenberg would prove as good, if not better than, the great Lou Gehrig, and the Tiger star likely had fifteen years of baseball life left. Calling Greenberg "one of the outstanding Jewish athletes" in America, Weiner pointed out that Hank, Olympic speed skating champion Irving Jaffee, and U.S. Maccabi Association executive director Dave White spent a good deal of time during the winter months speaking for that organization in promoting activities by Jewish athletes. Greenberg proved to be the tour's "main center of attention."[26]

The 1935 season began slowly for the Tigers, who were temporarily stuck in the cellar. They bounced back to take a commanding lead in the race for the American League pennant by early September. Detroit featured the same everyday lineup, with Cochrane again making the All-Star team and batting .319; Gehringer hitting .330, with 201 hits, 123 runs scored, 109 RBIs, and 19 homers; and Goslin batting .292 with 109 runs scored. Bridges won 21 games and Rowe 19 to head the Tiger pitching staff, with Bridges leading the league in strikeouts and his teammate coming in second. Elden Auker contributed 18 victories, and Alvin Crowder won 16. But the Tiger star of 1935 was clearly Hank Greenberg, who tied Jimmie Foxx for the home run title with 36 apiece, six more than Gehrig; delivered 170 RBIs, a whopping 51 more than runner-up Gehrig; and produced 389 total bases, 49 more than Foxx. Greenberg produced the second best slugging percentage, .628, a mere eight points behind Foxx; rapped out 46 doubles and 16 triples, while compiling a .328 batting average, scoring 121 runs, and knocking out 203 hits. The league's batting champion was Washington's Buddy Myer, another Jewish player.

Greenberg received a letter from a thirteen-year-old girl in July, expressing her grave disappointment that former heavyweight champion Max Baer had dropped a recent title bout to Jimmy Braddock. Consequently she and "thousands of little boys and girls like her" were counting on Greenberg. *Free Press* reporter Charles Ward informed Greenberg, "You have an immense responsibility," and he gravely replied, "Yes, I have."[27]

The sports section of the September 12, 1935, edition of the *Free Press* headlined a recent Tiger loss that left Detroit with a comfortable seven-and-a-half-game lead over the Yankees. It also displayed a photograph topped by the heading, "Number One G-Man Shows Mickey's G-Men How It's Done," featuring FBI director J. Edgar Hoover, Cochrane, Gehringer, Goslin, and Greenberg, with rifles in place.[28]

The Sporting News that same day contained a lengthy article by Frederick G. Lieb titled "Oi, Oi, Oh, Boy! Hail that Long-Sought Hebrew Star," with the subheading, "Hank Greenberg, Greatest Jewish Player, Touted as A.L.'s Most Valuable." A companion pair of drawings of Greenberg referred to him as "The Greatest Jewish Ball Player of All Time!!" After indicating that Jews made good boxers, Lieb wondered, "Why they don't make better ball players?" It was the question that had been asked of him a hundred times during his career. Jews were "great sports fans" with a special fondness for baseball throughout the New York City area, Lieb reminded his readers. He then suggested that Jews had been denied the opportunity to excel at the sport. They frequently lacked the necessary size and could be pushed aside on playgrounds by larger boys boasting Irish, German, or Scandinavian ancestry. Jews also lacked the tradition of sport that the Irish, for instance, possessed. Now "the big bat of Hefty Hank Greenberg" shattered old stereotypes, as did his fellow major leaguers Harry Danning, Buddy Myer, Moe Berg, Milt Galatzer, and Phil Weintraub. Lieb referred to John McGraw's long search for a great Jewish star and his frequent declaration, "An outstanding Jewish ball player in New York would be worth his weight in gold." McGraw did hire Mose Solomon, Jack Levy, Harry Rosenberg, and Andy Cohen, but none came close to performing at the level he envisioned. Meanwhile "the greatest Jewish ball player of all time sat in his distant center field bleachers. He was a tall, skinny kid from the Bronx, who would have given his right eye to see the Giants win."[29]

Lieb related how the three New York City teams failed to sign "this Bronxian clubber" to a baseball contract. Greenberg went unnoticed by sportswriters like Lieb, in contrast to schoolboy phenoms Lou Gehrig and Waite Hoyt. Lieb had never heard of Greenberg until around 1930, when a Detroit baseball writer, Harry Bullion, spoke of the Tigers training camp in Tampa, Florida. Bullion said, "We have a high-school kid from New York with us that hits a ball farther than any kid I ever saw. The distance he can get is amazing. His name is Hank Greenberg. Do you know him?" Since that time, Lieb had indeed gotten to know Greenberg and recognized that he was "getting better and better." After a fine season in 1934, he was "moving forward by leaps and bounds," leading the majors in both homers and RBIs and with a shot at the batting crown.[30]

A week later, Iffy the Dopester referred to "Homer Hank, the big Greenberg boy," as "the league sensation" who was only twenty-four years old and still learning how to hit. Greenberg would be batting .400 within two years, Iffy predicted. "He can't help it. Great as he looks now, he is just starting. Hank hits at more bad balls than any great hitter that ever flashed across the horizon and lets more good ones go." He was guessing less and learning to use the whole field more rather than simply swinging for the fences. Iffy continued, "Right now he reminds me of nothing so much as a beautifully built champion racing car just getting underway with its power apparent but not as yet hitting on all its cylinders." The columnist predicted that if Greenberg listened to his manager, "He will rank with Pop Anson, Ed Delahanty and Babe Ruth as one of the greatest sluggers of all history."[31]

Baseball Magazine offered a lengthy article on the sport's "new sensation . . . the outstanding player of the year." Editor F. C. Lane referred to Greenberg's "terrific hitting," especially in the clutch, that had "smashed down all opposition" and steered the Tigers to "an assured new pennant." Lane indicated that Greenberg had accomplished still more. He had "led his ancestral race into a new promised land, the field of major league baseball, a field where they have been comparative strangers." It seemed right that baseball would boast "players of all racial strands and stocks" because the United States served as "the melting pot of all nations." Irish players had been highly visible early in the game's history. Then German players arrived, followed more recently by Italians, Poles, Lithuanians, and Hungarians. There were Spaniards, Portuguese, Greeks, and even a few Frenchmen. Native Americans had made the majors, and Chinese players had appeared in the minor leagues. "And our colored population has developed many great players," Lane wrote. Jews had been little represented until recently, despite their success in other sports, especially boxing.[32]

Greenberg "is not only the greatest of Jewish ballplayers" but was rapidly becoming one of the finest players in the game, Lane continued. His performance during the 1935 season had "verged upon the sensational" as he joined Jimmie Foxx and Lou Gehrig at the forefront of the post-Ruthian era of major league sluggers. Lane found this remarkable because Greenberg was fundamentally a line-drive hitter, albeit a hard-hitting one. Still, rather than swing for the fences, Greenberg sought to drive in runs. On a lesser team, mired in the second division, he might be swinging for the fences, Greenberg admitted. That was not his role with the pennant chasing Tigers. The 6'4", 215-pound Greenberg acknowledged that his size—"I am tall and heavy and reasonably strong"—assisted him in swatting a baseball considerable distances. He was a "guess" batter and could "look pretty bad" when he made the wrong call. Greenberg asked his supporters to wait until he had that kind of breakout campaign when asked if he ever thought about topping Babe Ruth's single-season home run mark. Then he denied having any expectations along those lines. Instead he saw himself as the kind of player who merely wanted to help his team win. Greenberg also sought to play down comparisons with the era's other greatest sluggers. "It's a mistake to compare me with either Foxx or Gehrig," he declared. "They are veterans with years of service. I am only a beginner."[33]

The Tigers' record stood at 93–58 at season's end, three games better than the Yankees. The National League champion Chicago Cubs, managed by Charlie Grimm and led by pitchers Bill Lee and Lon Warneke, along with second baseman Billy Herman and outfield Augie Galan, produced the year's best mark, 100–54, four games ahead of the defending World Series champion Cardinals. The Cubs rang up a 21-game winning streak on their way to the pennant and were favored to take the world title. In the second inning of the first contest, umpire George Moriarty warned the players on the Cubs bench to stop razzing Greenberg. The Cubs kept hurling insults, including several of an anti-Semitic variety, at the Tigers first baseman. Moriarty—who later declared that the Cubs "crucif[ied] Hank Greenberg for being a Jew" and tagged Dolly Stark, a Jewish umpire, as a "Christ-killer"—stopped the game in an effort to curb the rhetorical abuse. For his troubles, baseball commissioner Kenesaw Mountain Landis fined Moriarty $250 for holding up the game.[34] After dropping game one, 3–0, the Tigers came back the next day to win 8–3 behind Greenberg's two-run homer and Bridges's solid pitching. Greenberg broke his wrist during a collision with Gabby Hartnett at home plate, but Detroit prevailed in six games to win its first World Series championship. Game six ironically fell on Yom Kippur, which would have caused another conflict for Greenberg, but his wrist injury kept him on the bench. He received word on October 20 that he had unanimously been named American League MVP. Buddy Myer came in fourth.

Greenberg was undoubtedly aware of events taking place overseas affecting European Jewry, particularly those in Central Europe. As the 1935 regular season entered its final weeks, the Congress of the National Socialist German Workers' Party (Nazi Party) gathered in Nuremberg, Germany. On September 15, 1935, it passed a series of measures referred to as the Nuremberg Laws, purportedly designed to provide a scientific basis to discriminate against Jews. The laws forbade marriages and extramarital intercourse between Jews and non-Jews, the hiring by Jews of German females under the age of forty-five as domestic workers, and the display of the Reich and national flag by Jews. Those violating such measures were to be subjected to punishment involving hard labor, imprisonment, or fines. The Reich Citizenship Law stripped those considered to be non-Germans, including German Jews, of citizenship. Anyone with at least three Jewish grandparents was considered a Jew.

During the mid-1930s, the anti-Semitic Black Legion remained influential in certain circles in still economically depressed Michigan. The state's Black Legion commander concocted a plan to detonate bombs in every American synagogue across the United States on Yom Kippur, hoping to kill one million Jews. In May 1936, fifty members of the organization, sporting robes and hoods, agreed in Detroit to beat and murder thirty-two-year-old Charles Poole, who was employed by the Works Progress Administration and was said to have battered his wife. Although hoping to hang Poole, the Black Legionnaires decided to shoot him instead. A congressional investigation of the Black Legion soon followed, along with the criminal prosecution of leaders of the organization on charges of criminal syndicalism, with the indictment alleging a conspiracy to wage an armed uprising against the U.S. government.

Someone as intelligent as Hank Greenberg would likely have been aware of the Poole murder and other disturbing incidents involving the Black Legion in Michigan. These included night "ridings" resulting in beatings, kidnappings, political assassinations, and the killing of "Negroes for a 'Thrill.'"[35] Meanwhile, Greenberg had to await the healing of his broken wrist and conduct contract negotiations with the Detroit Tigers management. After initially holding out, Greenberg somewhat reluctantly agreed to a contract estimated to be in the range of $20,000 for the 1936 season. Only twelve games into the season, during which he batted .348 with 16 RBIs, Greenberg collided with Yankees outfielder Jake Powell at first base, again breaking his wrist. This led to speculation that Greenberg's career might be over. Some accused Powell of deliberately going after Greenberg. The Tigers struggled to an 83–71 mark, despite fine seasons by Gehringer, who hit .354, and Bridges, who led the league in wins and strikeouts. Detroit finished second behind the resurgent New York Yankees, who, led by Lou Gehrig and the sensational rookie center fielder Joe DiMaggio, won the American League pennant by nineteen-and-a-half games.

In the midst of the 1936 season, Germany held the Berlin Olympics, during which the Nazi regime appeared to soften its attack on Jews. "Jews Unwelcome" signs were removed from certain public places, and newspapers moderated their virulent attacks on Jews as Hitler attempted to improve his image before an international audience. Still, Jewish athletes, including American Jews, were discouraged from competing in the Games, although the German team included Helene Mayer, who won a silver medal in women's individual fencing. Despite evident hostility from U.S. Olympic team head Avery Brundage, seven Jewish athletes from the United States went to Berlin. Black participants, led by Jesse Owens of the United States, showed up, with the track star capturing four gold medals. Immediately following the Olympics, the Nazis again intensified their campaign, demanding the registration of property and "Aryanizing" of Jewish enterprises, the firing of Jewish workers and managers, and placement of those businesses in the hands of non-Jews. Jewish physicians could no longer have non-Jews as clients. Jewish attorneys were not allowed to practice their profession. The German government now required Jews to carry identity cards stamped with a red "J" and containing middle names for Jews who lacked first names easily recognizable as Jewish. Males were referred to as "Israel" and females as "Sarah."

In 1937 Greenberg initially signed a contract for $1, which was torn up after he went through spring training and proved that he was healthy enough to play at a top level once again. With Greenberg's return to the lineup, the Tigers improved to an 89–73 record but again finished well back of the Yankees, thirteen games short this time. The season was badly marred by the skull fracture player-manager Cochrane suffered in a game against the Yankees on May 25. After belting his second homer of the season, Cochrane was hit in the head with a pitch from Bump Hadley, resulting in a concussion and a triple skull fracture. The thirty-four-year-old Cochrane, a .320 lifetime hitter, never again played in the major leagues. His star second baseman, Gehringer, had another spectacular season, leading the American League with a .371 batting average, and rookie infielder Rudy York belted 35 homers, including a record 18 in August, in only 375 official plate appearances, while Roxie Lawson, Auker, and Bridges won 18, 17, and 15 games, respectively. Greenberg had one of the greatest slugging years in major league history and the season he considered his finest. He batted .337, scored 137 runs, walked 102 times, produced an on-base percentage of .436, and smacked 49 doubles, 14 triples, and 40 homers, second to DiMaggio's 46. One early season homer over the center field fence was called the longest four-bagger ever hit at Fenway Park. Another homer in Yankee Stadium was the first belted into the center field stands. Hank compiled a .668 slugging percentage and 397 total bases, both marks second again to DiMaggio, and he drove in 183 runs, only one behind Gehrig's league record, set six years earlier. His failure to top Gehrig proved disappointing because "runs batted in were my obsession," not home runs, Greenberg remembered. "I've always believed that the most important aspect of hitting is driving in runs. . . . That's what wins ball games: driving runs across the plate."[36] Gehringer ended up as league MVP, just nipping out DiMaggio, while Greenberg came in third in the voting, ahead of Gehrig.

The next season was yet again mediocre for the Detroit Tigers, but another spectacular one for Greenberg. The team ended up in fourth place, with an 84–70 record, sixteen games behind the front-running Yankees, and Cochrane got fired mid-season. Gehringer was an All-Star for the sixth

straight year, with a career-high 20 homers and 107 RBIs, although his batting average slid to .306. Like Greenberg earlier, York avoided the infamous
sophomore jinx, knocking out 33 round trippers while driving in 127 runs.
Greenberg hit .315, had a career-best slugging percentage of .683 and .438
on-base percentage, drove in 146 runs, walked a league-best 119 times, and
compiled 380 total bases. He also scored more runs than anyone in major
league baseball (144) and crushed 58 homers, tying Jimmie Foxx for the
most ever produced by a right-handed hitter. One homer in late May was
the first to end up in the center field bleachers at Comiskey Park. On July
27 Greenberg belted homers during his first two trips to the plate, after
having hit two in his last two times at bat in the previous game; this tied a
major league record of four straight homers. Sportswriters and fans alike
tracked his quest to better Babe Ruth's single-season record, particularly in
the final weeks of the campaign when the Yankees appeared to have already
clinched the pennant. The *Free Press* applauded Greenberg's fifty-fifth and
fifty-sixth homers, delivered against Earl Whitehill of the Cleveland Indians
with nine games left in the season. Greenberg had now hit two or more
homers in one game ten times during the 1938 season, breaking Foxx's just-
established record.

Two additional homers, hit in the second game of a doubleheader, gave
Greenberg fifty-eight with five games to play, with Bud Shaver of the *Times*
comparing his accomplishment with unsavory developments occurring in
Germany. "There is no shuffle of marching feet, no roar of armored tanks
down well-paved streets . . . [no] frightening banners of war and all its
ghastly consequences. But in Detroit at least the question still is, 'Can he
make it?'"[37] Greenberg for the first time thought he might break Ruth's
record. In his autobiography, Greenberg discussed the added weight of his
religious affiliation: "How the hell could you get up to home plate every
day and have some son of a bitch call you . . . a sheenie and get on your
ass without feeling the pressure?" Opponents hurled invectives at him, and
so too did fans. "I used to get frustrated as hell," Greenberg later admitted. "Sometimes I wanted to go up in the stands and beat the shit out of
them." Well aware that he was the most celebrated Jewish baseball player

in major league history, Greenberg felt he possessed "a special responsibility," representing 2 million Jews in a nation of at least sixty times that number of gentiles. He "was always in the spotlight" as he was large and prone to errors and strikeouts. Yet, "I was there every day, and if I had a bad day, every son of a bitch was calling me names so that I had to make good. I just had to show them that a Jew could play ball," Greenberg remembered.[38] Throughout the season, drunken fans occasionally hurled epithets, calling Greenberg "Jew bastard and kike," and he stormed into the clubhouse after games and unloaded. Sportswriters refused to print anything about Greenberg's tirades in keeping with standard journalistic practices of the era.[39] *Baseball Magazine* instead referred to the "determined assault" on Ruth's record by "hammering Hank," who was said to have "made a gallant attempt."[40]

Any number of individuals contended that opposing pitchers refused to pitch to Greenberg during the last several days of the 1938 to ensure that a Jew did not become the single-season home run champ. Greenberg received a few walks in those contests. He also got a number of hittable pitches but was unable to drive any more out of the park. He denied that anti-Semitism came into play, arguing instead that pressure, the size of the ballparks he competed in, and the quality of his opponents, including Indian fireballer Bob Feller on the last day of the season, stymied him. Feller set a major league record of eighteen strikeouts, with Greenberg fanning twice, in the first game of a doubleheader. Greenberg managed to drive a ball off the fence in left center field during the second contest, but the fading sun compelled umpire George Moriarty to explain, "I'm sorry, Hank, this is as far as I can go." Greenberg replied, "That's all right, George, this is as far as I can go too." Greenberg later reflected, "Mainly it was the pressure. Not only was the pressure on me; it was on the pitchers, too." He asked, "What is pressure? It's the tension. You fear time is running out. You become impatient. You become paralyzed at the plate. You're so fearful that you're going to swing at a bad pitch, you wind up taking a good one. Then you become so disgusted with yourself you start swinging at the bad pitches."[41] Greenberg hardly compared himself to Ruth as a slugger, and he did belt far more homers in 1938 than in any of his other seasons in the majors. Yet he was obviously one of the greatest home run hitters of his or any other era, compiling impressive numbers in what would prove to be an abbreviated big-league career.

Fans and sportswriters alike now deemed Greenberg, Joe DiMaggio of the New York Yankees, and Jimmie Foxx of the Boston Red Sox as organized baseball's top right-handed sluggers. Because the sport continued to be viewed as the national pastime, this was a matter of some significance, as was the fact that Greenberg was baseball's first great Jewish star. His stature matched in its own fashion that of luminaries in other endeavors who had overcome various prejudices and obstacles, ranging from stark anti-Semitism to quotas. Henry Morgenthau Jr. served as secretary of the treasury. The U.S. Supreme Court included justices Louis D. Brandeis and Benjamin Cardozo. Harvard professor Felix Frankfurter soon replaced Brandeis on the court. Reform Rabbi Stephen S. Wise, a strong Zionist, was one of the most respected religious leaders in the country. American literature boasted numerous Jewish writers, such as playwrights Clifford Odets and Lillian Hellman, along with novelists Edna Ferber, Tess Slesinger, Michael Gold, Henry Roth, and Nathanael West. Among the nation's leading intellectuals were Sidney Hook, Lionel Trilling, Waldo Frank, and Lewis Mumford. They were soon joined by a younger group of New York intellectuals like Irving Howe, Irving Kristol, Daniel Bell, and Alfred Kazin. Hollywood featured motion pictures moguls like Samuel Goldwyn, Louis B. Mayer, and the Warner brothers, and stars on the order of George Burns, John Garfield, and Paulette Goddard. The entertainment world also included Eddie Cantor, Al Jolson, Irving Berlin, and Benny Goodman. Sidney Hillman and David Dubinsky remained powerful labor leaders. The Guggenheims were among the wealthiest families in the country. Jews ran the Yellow Cab Company, Macy's, and Gimbels. Jews continued to advance into the ranks of the middle class and the professions.

Greenberg had to have been aware of certain tragic events overseas that increasingly involved his religious brethren. German troops flooded into Austria in March 1938 to force the Anschluss, or the annexation of Austria (which already boasted rampant anti-Semitism), into Greater Germany. Many Austrians, particularly those of German ancestry, welcomed the Anschluss, while opponents would soon be silenced. Hitler continued to pressure Czech leaders to cede land to Germany but found time in July to honor an old favorite, Henry Ford. On July 30, 1938, Ford's seventy-fifth birthday, Hitler sent personal congratulations for the auto magnate's receipt of the Order of the German Eagle. Initiated by Hitler the previous year, the award was now given to Ford, Italian dictator Benito Mussolini, and two other individuals. Ford ignored condemnations by Jewish groups in the United States for several months. Hitler maintained his relentless assault on Czechoslovakia and threatened wholesale military action by September. The leaders of France, Italy, and the United Kingdom agreed through the infamous Munich Pact to allow Germany to take over the rich Sudetenland from Czechoslovakia, Eastern Europe's lone democracy. The United States, led by President Franklin Delano Roosevelt, remained hamstrung by a series of neutrality laws and a disinclination to become involved in the affairs of other countries. FDR consequently sent no official representatives to Munich but supported the "agreement." Hitler's demands were hardly sated, and his determination to destroy the Czech nation continued unabated through the fall of 1938. During that same period, he awarded the Order of the German Eagle to another controversial American figure, Charles Lindbergh, who had expressed appreciation for the Nazi regime.

On the night of November 10, 1938, Nazis and those they encouraged stormed through German and Austrian cities and towns, breaking the store windows of Jewish shops, destroying Jewish houses and apartments, and setting afire or ransacking almost two thousand synagogues. A number of Jews were beaten, nearly one hundred were murdered, tens of thousands were arrested, and thirty thousand were taken away to concentration camps, as Kristallnacht (Night of Broken Glass) continued. Hugh Carleton Greene, a correspondent for the *London Daily Telegraph*, traced developments in Germany, condemning mob rule and the horrific levels of violence directed against Jews that had been applauded by well-dressed women with babies in hand. This modern pogrom occurred following the shooting of a German embassy official, purportedly by a seventeen-year-old Polish Jew, in Paris three days earlier.

In an essay that appeared in his journal, *Social Justice*, only days after Kristallnacht, Father Charles Coughlin, who started in the mid-thirties to refer to the New Deal as the "Jew Deal," now displayed a more overt brand of anti-Semitism while implicitly linking godless communism with "atheistic Jews." Claiming that he was "not ignorant of Jewish . . . glories . . . its glorious sons" and its "keen intellectuality," Coughlin charged that Nazism would be not terminated "until the religious Jews in high places" attacked communism.[42] *Social Justice* defended Henry Ford against charges of anti-Semitism. It reported his conviction that if any persecution were occurring in Germany, it was being "overplayed in the press" and was due to the actions of "war mongers" and "international financiers," not the German people.[43] Early the following month, Coughlin asked if the world had to suffer war for six hundred thousand German Jews. While Coughlin's views were extreme, they were hardly out of line with those of many Americans, including various members of Congress, which proved little inclined to admit larger numbers of Jewish refugees notwithstanding the rapidly deteriorating situation in Europe. Coughlin soon denied that he would ever join a fascist movement or "assail Jewry in general" but promised to "distinguish between the good, religious Jews and the irreligious, atheistic Jews."[44]

Meanwhile the Black Legion, notwithstanding the prosecution of several of its leaders, continued to spew out invectives of an anti-Semitic nature. Stickers appeared at automobile plants warning, "Jews Keep Off These Stairs," "Jews Teach Communism, Jews Destroy Christianity, Jews Control Money." Legionnaires established the Detroit National Workers League in 1938, seeking "legal establishment of clean racial standards in the United States of America," along with "legal reduction of Jewish influence in American public life to the minority position which they are entitled [*sic*]." The League denied "most emphatically" being anti-Semitic, as its members "neither oppose all Jews, nor most Semites." At the same time the organization celebrated fascism and Nazism.[45]

4

Baseball in a Time of War

Drumbeats threatened during the winter of 1938–1939. The Spanish Civil War, which originally pitted a democratically elected, left-tilted government against Gen. Francisco Franco and the fascist-rooted Falangists, ground to a close. Begun in 1936, the Spanish Civil War was viewed by many at the time as the initial battleground for a second world war. The Spanish Republicans, or Loyalists (backers of the Spanish government), received support from the Soviet Union and the International Brigades, made up of leftist volunteers from across the globe, including the English socialist George Orwell and the French writer André Malraux, both of whom fought on the Republican side. Franco and the Falangists, championed by the Spanish military, large landowners, and the Catholic Church, obtained money and war matériel from Germany and Italy, which also sent planes, pilots, and support from their own, smaller international contingent of rightists. In February 1939 the Spanish Republic was crushed; Franco's repressive regime continued to target those who had fought against him. Germany dismembered Czechoslovakia the following month.

Demands for a hands-off approach to European affairs scarcely lessened back in the United States. Many Americans believed that their country had become involved in World War I because of the so-called merchants of death or arms merchants, and big moneyed interests headed by J. Pierpont Morgan. They consequently insisted, as did several of their political representatives, that the American nation not be fooled again into participating in a European bloodbath. They also continued to grapple with the economic and social dislocations caused by the Great Depression, which displayed few signs of fully dissipating as the decade neared an end.

To alleviate stress and take their minds off domestic and international developments, Americans continued to enjoy their favorite pastimes, including syndicated radio programs, big band music, Hollywood films, and major league baseball, which had reduced operations during World War I. During the 1939 season, the New York Yankees swept to their fourth straight American League pennant and World Series championship. Led by Joe DiMaggio, who flirted all season long with batting .400 until vision problems and possibly stress hampered his performance, New York finished seventeen games in front of second-place Boston, while Detroit limped into fifth place, 26½ games back. The Yankees rolled along without Lou Gehrig, who in early May failed to appear in the lineup for the first time in 2,131 games. Gehrig soon announced his retirement. The Iron Horse was afflicted with amyotrophic lateral sclerosis, the infamous Lou Gehrig's disease that soon took his life. Speaking at Yankee Stadium on July 4 before more than 61,000 fans, including Babe Ruth, from whom he had earlier been estranged, Gehrig tearfully declared, "I consider myself the luckiest man on the face of the earth."[1] The Yankees retired his uniform number 4, the first major leaguer to achieve that honor. Gehrig was elected to the Baseball Hall of Fame later in the year, thanks to suspension of the rule requiring that a player be retired for five years before achieving such a distinction.

The 1939 Tigers had one twenty-game winner, Bobo Newsom, and a seventeen-game winner, Tommy Bridges, while Charlie Gehringer hit a robust .325. Somewhat less consistent that season—suffering, in fact, a temporary benching due to a slump—Hank Greenberg still hit .312, drove in and scored 112 runs, rapped out 42 doubles, and delivered 33 homers, only 2 behind Jimmie Foxx's league-best total, along with a .622 slugging percentage. Boston Red Sox rookie Ted Williams, soon linked with Greenberg and DiMaggio as the top three American League sluggers, quickly recognized that "Hank was smarter than most players. He was a great guy, a *great* guy, and I wouldn't say that if I didn't mean it. Shit, he was ab-so-lutely terrific." Williams went on to say that new players in the league idolized a small number of their peers, including Foxx, DiMaggio, and Greenberg. As for Hank, Williams remembered, "He was so outgoing with me and when we'd get the chance to talk he'd want to talk about the pitchers, and he was listening with keen ears as to what I had to say, and I know I was listening very close to what he thought was going on." Williams recalled Greenberg's holding his bat high at the plate, swinging with "a nice rhythmic-y cut, not too hard," and then belting the ball into the upper deck. Greenberg "was great."[2]

Greenberg was paid $35,000, reportedly the highest salary in the game, for the 1939 season. Only Babe Ruth had ever received a larger one, having peaked at $80,000. Perhaps Greenberg felt added pressure during the 1939 season because of events overseas. Such news now made "being Jewish carry with it special responsibility," as he later remembered. For he had come "to feel that if I, as a Jew, hit a home run I was hitting one against Hitler."[3] The December 1939 issue of *Baseball Magazine* discussed Detroit's big hitters in an article titled "Tiger Claws": Charlie Gehringer; Earl Averill, a fading slugger brought over during the season from the Cleveland Indians; and Greenberg. Hank was said to possess "less natural skill than Gehringer," but he had turned himself into a star athlete through hard work. Greenberg believed any wholly determined boy with the proper physical skills could become a major leaguer.[4]

Late in the season, Philip Slomovitz, editor of the *Jewish News*, published in Detroit, wrote to Frank Murphy, now serving as the attorney general of the United States, regarding the rightwing Detroit National Workers League. Slomovitz referred to a public gathering held by the League that helped trigger "an organized movement to incite a riot against the Jewish people" in his city; he also warned about a recent rally in which the League adopted the rhetoric of Fritz Kuhn, leader of the pro-Nazi German-American Bund.[5]

World War II began in earnest that fall, shortly following the carving out of an alliance between Nazi Germany and the Soviet Union. The announcement of that agreement on August 23, 1939, astonished many around the world, shaking up communist parties and their allies. The German and Soviet armies were soon on the march, penetrating into Poland, resulting in a declaration of war against Germany by the United Kingdom, France, Australia, New Zealand, and Canada. The United Kingdom and Germany nevertheless refrained from attacking one another during the period of the so-called Phoney War. The United States proclaimed neutrality. The Soviets meanwhile attacked Finland, while both the Soviet Union and Nazi Germany continued decimating Poland. The Nazi regime initiated a campaign of euthanasia against the infirm and the disabled in Germany. German bombers attacked a naval base near Scotland by the following spring, and German soldiers headed into Denmark and Norway. Invasions of France, Belgium, Luxembourg, and Holland followed. Germany initiated the Battle of Britain by the summer, with London targeted for aerial assault. The Soviets swept into the Baltic republics. The Italians took over British Somaliland and invaded Egypt.

On a far less momentous note, the off-season had nevertheless threatened to become a trying one for Greenberg. Tigers management attempted to cut his salary by $5,000, contending that he had not performed as well as anticipated in 1939. He expressed displeasure with the city of Detroit during an interview. Despite his generally fine performance the previous season, Detroit fans hollered at him, he complained. Charged with being a quitter, Greenberg seriously considered refusing to play. Hank wondered how much he could take, as he was on the receiving end of brickbats in every American League city except for his hometown of New York.

Also troubling to Greenberg was the determination of the Detroit front office to convince him to allow Rudy York, a struggling outfielder and catcher, to take over at first base. Greenberg delivered his own proposal after stewing over the matter. He would resign for the same contract he had just worked under and attempt to learn how to play left field. The Tigers would have to pay him a $10,000 bonus if that endeavor worked out, but if it did not, he would return to first base. To Greenberg's surprise, Tigers general manager Jack Zeller agreed to the proposition. As he headed out to left field for the first time, Greenberg complained, "I hope I don't get my brains knocked out by a fly ball."[6] By working hard throughout spring training and with the assistance of coach Bing Miller, who shot fungo after fungo his way, Greenberg slowly began to learn the tricks of playing the outfield. On opening day, April 16, 1940, Greenberg stood in left field against the St. Louis Browns at Tiger Stadium. He found that playing the outfield was much easier than being stationed at first base, and, as an added bonus, bench jockeys were harder to hear. Greenberg later headed into the Tiger front office to receive a $10,000 check from Zeller. That day also witnessed the only official opening day no-hitter in the majors, tossed by Bob Feller against the Chicago White Sox at Comiskey Park. The experiment in left field still proved difficult for a time, as Greenberg did not know where to position himself. His inexperience resulted in a number of errant tosses, while lack of activity in the outfield led him to force plays too often. Greenberg improved in the field as the season progressed, helped by his ability to track the ball and a strong throwing arm; all the while, he shone at the plate.

Greenberg and York kept Detroit in a three-way pennant race with Cleveland and New York. Newsom had a fine campaign of his own, winning 21 games, and Gehringer had his last .300 season. But the sluggers were the unquestioned stars of the Tigers, with York hitting 33 homers, smacking 46 doubles, and driving in 134 runs. Greenberg came close to winning the Triple Crown, batting .340, a dozen points behind DiMaggio, and once again taking both the home run and RBI titles. His batch of 41 long balls was five better than Foxx's, and his 150 RBIs were 16 more than York's total. Greenberg also led the league in doubles with 50, in slugging average with a .670 mark, and in total bases with 384. With 8 triples, Hank had 99 extra-base hits during the 1940 season, another league best. Greenberg was just behind Ted Williams in on-base percentage, with a .433 mark, and in runs scored, with 129. He also performed competently if not gracefully in the field, with 14 assists.[7]

Most important, remaining one of major league baseball's greatest clutch players, Greenberg, like York, went on a tear late in the season during the thick of the three-team pennant race. Tigers manager Del Baker, standing along the third-base coaching line, helped his hitters out by stealing signs, enabling them to know if a fastball or a curve were coming. Greenberg refused to take the sign when facing Bob Feller, worrying that he could "get killed" if he mistakenly awaited a curveball only to step into the Indian ace's blazing fastball. Hank smacked fifteen homers in September and made several fine plays in the field as the Tigers eked out their third pennant during his tenure, nipping the Indians by one game and the Yankees by two, ending New York's title run at four years. St. Louis Browns manager Fred Haney said, "Greenberg puts more thought, effort and conscientiousness into his work than any other player in the league and to my mind he's the greatest competitor in the league."[8] Longtime slugger Al Simmons sang Greenberg's praises as the Tigers readied to battle the National League champion Cincinnati Reds in the World Series. "There is no one on the Cincinnati pitching staff who can stop Greenberg, and if the Reds can't stop Greenberg they can't stop the Tigers," predicted Simmons. "I never saw anybody hit the ball the way Greenberg has. Whew!"[9]

In a tightly waged World Series, Detroit took an early lead in the decisive game seven before falling 2–1, after Cincinnati scored twice in the bottom of the seventh. Batting .357 in the series, Greenberg had 10 hits, 1 homer, 6 RBIs, and 5 runs scored, and played a flawless outfield. Receiving his second MVP award in late October to beat out twenty-seven–game winner Feller, Greenberg became the first player to win the honor for a second time when playing a different position that he had in an earlier MVP season. *Baseball Magazine* announced in December that Greenberg had been chosen its player of the year. Sportswriter Daniel M. Daniel declared that the Tigers slugger "won the pennant" for his ball club, which "could not possibly have finished in the first division without him." Daniel continued, "Not since the palmy days of Babe Ruth had there been so thorough a one-man job. In fact, come to think of it, not even Ruth ever stood out in a pennant victory with the prominence that went to Hank's 1940 achievement."[10] Clearly at the peak of his career, Greenberg soon signed a contract for the 1941 season for $55,000, again the top salary in the majors.

Major league moguls undoubtedly readied with some trepidation for the upcoming season. On September 16, 1940, President Roosevelt had signed the Selective Training and Service Act, which required all American men between the ages of twenty-one and thirty-six to register for twelve months of military service. This was intended "to ensure the independence and freedom of the United States." In late September, Germany, Italy, and Japan completed the Tripartite Pact, an alliance of the leading right-wing states. German forces rolled into Romania the following month, and Italy invaded Greece. German pilots attacked Coventry, England, in November, while Hungary and Romania joined the Axis powers. Germany conducted fierce bombing runs over London in late December. British forces made advances in Northern and Eastern Africa by early 1941 and soon headed into Greece. President Roosevelt signed the Lend-Lease Act, providing a vitally important economic pipeline to Great Britain. Pro-Nazi elements took control of the Iraqi regime. Germany attacked both Greece and Yugoslavia, with Greece soon falling.

Greenberg had registered for the draft right after the World Series, indicating that he resided in a hotel in Detroit. One newspaper referred to Hank's "case," noting that it "has made baseball conscription conscious." Journalists tracked his draft status. As it appeared increasingly likely he would be called up, there was talk that Greenberg might attempt to avoid military service. References were made to his flat feet. "Overtones of anti-Semitism" flavored the "mockery" heaped on the Tigers slugger, writer Robert Creamer charges. The *Detroit Free Press*, for its part, suggested that Greenberg's role on the Tigers, at least through the 1941 season, would be "in the community interest." Ben Shepard, who headed Greenberg's draft board, denied talk that the ballplayer sought an occupational deferment, stating, "I don't think he's asking [for a] deferment on any grounds." Shepard soon reported, "I thought there might be something going on in the board that I didn't know about, but there wasn't. This is all a tempest in a teapot. Greenberg just filed his questionnaire and that's all there is to it." Reporters continued tracking the story of Greenberg and the draft. Greenberg denied that he was seeking a deferment, indicating that when his number was called, "I'll be ready. I have no intention of trying to get out of military training." His draft board categorized Greenberg so that he could be called up for military training provided he passed his physical. A report floated that one member of his draft board revealed Greenberg had sought a six-month deferment, purportedly contending that his playing career was limited and that time away from baseball would reduce his earning capacity.[11]

On arriving at New York City Municipal Airport, also referred to as LaGuardia Field, Greenberg encountered reporters posed to ask more questions about the draft. "What's all this fuss about?" he queried them. "You'd think I was the only guy going into the army." Asked if he were seeking a deferment, Greenberg sarcastically replied, "I don't know a thing about it, boys. You'd better see the draft board. They're making a statement every day." Regarding the questionnaire, Hank said, "Questionnaires are supposed to be confidential," and also stated that "there have been all sorts of stories" about a deferment. "All I'm going to say is that when my number is up, I'm going. My number is 621 and they've reached about 300 out there. All this publicity isn't doing me any good, you know. If there are many more stories about it, you guys will have me in the army next week." A physical in Lakeland, Florida, revealed that Greenberg suffered from "second degree bilateral pes planus," or flat feet, as more rumors surfaced about his draft status. Greenberg reiterated, "When they want me, I'm ready." A medical advisory board in Detroit declared him fit for regular military duty, classifying him 1A.[12]

Amid all the draft controversies, Greenberg's 1941 major league campaign began somewhat slowly before abruptly ending after only 19 games. He had driven in 12 runs and batted only .269 with but 2 home runs, belted against the Yankees' Tiny Bonham in the last game Greenberg played before entering the service. Greenberg angrily refused to field questions from reporters following the game. He blurted out, "I don't want the papers to think I'm a good guy, because I'm not. I think the papers are horseshit." Later that day, he said, "I guess my attitude is kind of silly, but I'm bitter. Not about going into the army. I expected that. What I'm sore about is the way the papers hammered away at me, printing untruths and making a heel out of me. I'll be glad when this day is over and I'll be glad to get into the army. This has been an awful strain." He then predicted, "It's not as if I'm through with baseball for life. I'll be back next year and there's no reason why I shouldn't be as good as I ever was."[13]

On May 7, Greenberg was inducted into the U.S. Army, the first American Leaguer drafted. Philadelphia Philly pitcher Hugh Mulcahy, who had lost twenty-two games in the 1940 season, had been inducted two months earlier. "Never before has our American civilization been in such danger as now," Mulcahy declared.[14] Several members of the Fifth Division, stationed at Fort Custer in Battle Creek, Michigan, appeared at the train station to greet Greenberg as he arrived for basic training. He informed *The Sporting News* that he intended to be a good soldier. Greenberg completed his basic training at Fort Custer, Michigan, receiving pay of $50 a month. Greenberg indicated to a reporter for *Life* magazine that he really was not making much of a sacrifice, as taxes took most of his $50,000 salary. He had never asked for a deferment and stood prepared to go when called. His country was most important.

During a visit to the Washington Senators camp during spring training in 1941, Greenberg stated, "In the early years I used to look around and see which ball players I'd have to fight some day, which bastards made one remark too many. That wouldn't bother me now. I've been hiking and sleeping on the ground for weeks, and I'm leaner and harder and stronger than I've ever been, and I'd pity any S.O.B. who gets in my way."[15] Walter Matthau, who came from the Lower East Side in New York City, later recalled a story involving Greenberg and an inebriated soldier who shouted out, "Anybody here named Goldberg or Ginsberg? I'll kick the livin' daylights out of him." The 6'4" tall, broad-shouldered ballplayer stood up and declared, "My name is Greenberg, soldier." The drunkard looked at Hank and responded, "Well, I said nothin' about Greenberg, I said Goldberg or Ginsberg." Greenberg denied that the event ever took place.[16]

Isolationists led by Charles Lindbergh, the first individual to undertake a solo transatlantic flight, suggested that Jews were agitating for a fight in Europe. Speaking in Des Moines, Iowa, on September 11, 1941, to an America First crowd, Lindbergh addressed the question of who were the war agitators. He warned against the machinations of "foreign interests" and "a small minority of our own people" who had carried the United States to the brink of war. Lindbergh particularly blamed the British, the Roosevelt administration, and Jews. He understood the desire of the latter to overthrow Hitler's regime, as "the persecution they suffered in Germany would be sufficient to make bitter enemies of any race." Lindbergh claimed that "no person with a sense of the dignity of mankind can condone the persecution of the Jewish race in Germany." But he warned that American Jews should be opposing the war "for they will be among the first to feel its consequences." War, after all, lessened tolerance. Affirming that he admired both "the Jewish" and "the British people," Lindbergh insisted that their leaders, "for reasons which are as understandable from their viewpoint as they are inadvisable from ours, for reasons which are not American, wish to involve us in the war." He continued, "We cannot blame them for looking out for what they believe to be their own interests, but we also must look out for ours. We cannot allow the natural passions and prejudices of other peoples to lead our country to destruction."[17]

Meanwhile, the nation's most famous Jewish athlete joined an anti-tank gunnery that conducted maneuvers in Tennessee. The *New York Times* displayed a photograph of Hank Greenberg in uniform shaking hands with Joe Louis. The heavyweight champion had just boxed with a number of sparring partners at Fort Custer, where Greenberg was stationed. Greenberg rode in a gun carrier in a parade involving thousands of cheering city residents in Detroit on Armistice Day. He then served until December 5, having reached the rank of sergeant, as the U.S. Army had decided to release all men over the age of twenty-eight. The front page of the *Free Press*, dated December 6, 1941, reported that Greenberg, who would remain in the Army Reserves, was just itching to get back on the baseball diamond. His commanding officer, Col. Isaac Gill, stated, "The Army is losing a good soldier."[18] The *Times* presented an article on Greenberg's return to baseball and a photograph of the slugger's departure from Fort Custer. Still attired in Army fatigues, Greenberg expressed his readiness "to make myself ready to take over the old job with the Detroit Tigers." Greenberg planned to head for his home in New York City. "After that, it's baseball," he stated.

Expressing his eagerness to play ball once again, Greenberg admitted, "Since I've been in the Army there hasn't been a chance even to think about baseball." He expressed pride in having served in the U.S. Army and indicated that he had kept in shape by playing handball regularly.[19]

The following day, Japanese pilots bombarded the U.S. naval base at Pearl Harbor. The United States issued a declaration of war on December 8. The *Free Press* indicated that Greenberg's furlough might be at an end. The paper soon reported that Greenberg was preparing for a return to the Army. He stated, "I'm going back in. We are in trouble and there is only one thing to do—return to the service."[20] Greenberg declared, "I have not been called back. I am going back of my own accord." In a statement undoubtedly tinged with sadness, he continued, "Baseball is out the window as far as I'm concerned. I don't know if I'll ever return to baseball. If I do, all right. If not, well, that's all right, too."[21]

J. G. Taylor Spink of *The Sporting News* applauded Greenberg's determination to reenlist shortly following Pearl Harbor. After that "dastardly attack," Spink wrote, "Greenberg made up his mind. He was not going back to baseball." He "was returning to the Army . . . ready to go wherever his country needs him in this struggle of the seven seas." Greenberg stated, "This doubtless means I am finished with baseball, and it would be silly for me to say I do not leave it without a pang." However, "all of us are confronted with a terrible task—the defense of our country and the fight for our lives." Spink referred to Greenberg's immigrant parents and the fact that they had prospered in the United States. "Their son had an equal opportunity with the sons of all other people in this country, and achieved a notable position in a notable profession." Spink asserted that fans across the nation did "salute" Greenberg for his decision to return to military service.[22] Greenberg headed to Officers Training School in Miami Beach, Florida, receiving a commission as a first lieutenant. Cleveland Indian pitching ace Bob Feller quickly enlisted in the U.S. Navy, where he served as a chief petty officer aboard a battleship in the Pacific theater of the war.

In a message delivered to the United Press on January 2, 1942, Greenberg revealed that he had reenlisted two weeks earlier. "I am definitely through with baseball for the duration," Greenberg reported. Detroit Tigers officials expressed surprised at Greenberg's announcement, as he had failed to inform team management that he planned to return to military service. The *Times* indicated that Greenberg had remained on reserve duty and would likely have been called back, even had he not chosen to reenlist.[23]

Writing in *Baseball Magazine*, James M. Gould referred to the fact that war now menaced "the most truly NATIONAL sport in the world—BASEBALL." In the same fashion as had occurred during WWI, baseball offered "its honor, its men, its courage and its resources" in pursuit of victory. While uncertain on how the war would affect the sport, Gould insisted, "BASEBALL AS EVER, WILL DO ITS FULL DUTY!" The New York Giants' Eddie Grant had died on the battlefield of France during WWI. Stars Grover Cleveland Alexander, Eddie Collins, Christy Mathewson, Chief Meyers, Tris Speaker, Ty Cobb, Rube Marquard, and Rabbit Maranville had joined the American Armed Forces as the war in Europe continued. Gould predicted that top athletes would again place the needs of their nation first. Baseball bosses, led by Commissioner Landis and league presidents Will Harridge and Ford Frick, pledged full cooperation with the U.S. government almost immediately after the latest declaration of war.[24]

Gould believed that baseball would provide necessary "diversion and recreation" for millions during a time of war. The sportswriter nevertheless remained uncertain whether organized baseball would continue in 1942. Gould quoted from the late Billy Sunday, the former big league player turned evangelist who had made the following observation during World War I: "The idea that baseball is a luxury that ought to be postponed until the war is over is ridiculous." Sunday declared the game useful to both spectators and soldiers and predicted that baseball would not suffer irreparably because of the war. Sunday asserted, "Nothing can really hurt baseball. It is too big a game. It is too deeply imbedded in the love of the people." He insisted, "Baseball is A WAR GAME. We need it now more than ever."[25]

Commissioner Landis wrote to President Roosevelt on January 14, 1942, indicating that major league squads and minor league teams, "in ordinary conditions," would be readying for spring training. Acknowledging that "these are not ordinary times," Landis asked FDR "what you have in mind as to whether professional baseball should continue to operate." Landis underscored the fact that his query did not apply to individual members of organized baseball whose military status was determined by law.[26] Responding to Landis's inquiry the very next day, the president stated that the commissioner and the baseball owners would make "the final decision" regarding the new season. Roosevelt even indicated that his observations were wholly "personal . . . not an official point of view," but his next statement obviously carried great weight with baseball magnates. He affirmed, "I honestly feel that it would be best for the country to keep baseball going." Roosevelt offered that fewer people would remain unemployed during the war and American workers would toil "long hours and harder than ever before." He consequently believed they should "have a chance for recreation and for taking their minds off their work even more than before." Then the president noted that baseball games provided recreation lasting two-and-a-half hours at most, and at minimal cost. Roosevelt also envisioned more night contests, which workers could attend on occasion. The president indicated that he believed, as he was sure Landis did, that those of eligible age should join the military "without question." FDR reasoned that the sport's appeal would not be diminished even if the quality of play suffered accordingly.[27]

Sportswriter Gould declared Roosevelt's response to have been "heard and applauded around the baseball universe." Gould continued, "It was, indeed, a heartening thing for the national game" that Roosevelt had indicated "that the game should 'carry on.'" Organized baseball could help to maintain American morale, as Roosevelt suggested. In fact it appeared as though "baseball is due to play a star part" in supplying needed recreation. Organized baseball for its part had contributed $25,000 to purchase baseball equipment for soldiers, helping to break the monotony of camp life. The enlistment of baseball players in the U.S. military would serve as one of the sport's "best investments," as the gospel of baseball would be spread even wider, Gould indicated. He also contended that if baseball had already dug deep roots in Europe and Asia, then both world wars would have been avoided.[28]

On July 6, 1942, the All-Star game was played at the Polo Grounds. Lou Boudreau and Rudy York belted first inning homers to lead the American League to a 3–1 victory. Another All-Star game was played the next night, pitting the American League team against a squad made up of U.S. servicemen, with proceeds ending up in the Army-Navy relief fund. The military unit was managed by Mickey Cochrane, Hank Greenberg's former teammate with the Detroit Tigers who had entered the U.S. Navy, and included Bob Feller, Brooklyn Dodgers third baseman Cookie Lavagetto, and Washington Senators third sacker Cecil Travis. The American League All-Stars shut out Cochrane's team, 5–0. The two games resulted in over $159,000 in relief funds.

Greenberg performed tasks similar to those carried out by several other athletes in military uniform during his first months back in the army. He took charge of athletics at MacDill Field in Florida, even making a few appearances on the baseball field. The army assigned Greenberg to direct a series of physical fitness programs during the summer of 1942. He traveled across the country over the next several months, frequently working with other big league players while helping to train combat-ready soldiers.

In late June 1942, the *Times*, drawing on reports in the *London Daily Telegraph*, indicated that the Nazis had killed more than one million Jews. On November 24, 1942, Undersecretary of State Sumner Welles informed Rabbi Stephen Wise of Temple Emanuel in New York City and president of the World Jewish Congress, "I regret to tell you, Dr. Wise, that these [documents] confirm and justify your deepest fears" regarding the destruction of European Jewry. In a press conference that evening orchestrated by the American Jewish Conference, Rabbi Wise revealed the existence of Nazi extermination camps. Wise indicated that the Nazis were shipping Jews to Poland for mass slaughter, and he confirmed that two million Jews had already been murdered. The *Times* in a page ten account the following day quoted Wise as declaring, "The State Department finally made available today the documents which have confirmed the stories and rumors of Jewish extermination in all Hitler-ruled Europe."[29]

When asked in February 1943 what the upcoming major league season would be like, baseball's greatest Jewish star responded that he had to help provide physical training for air corpsmen and was unable to track baseball closely. On August 26, 1943, Greenberg played in one of the few organized baseball games he participated in during his military service. The game was held at the Polo Grounds, home of the New York Giants, and was intended to sell war bonds. Other major leaguers appearing in the contest included St. Louis Cardinals outfielder Enos Slaughter and Washington Senators pitcher Sid Hudson, both of whom would lose three years of their playing career to military service.

Captain Greenberg studied at the U.S. Army's program for special services, held at Washington and Lee University in Lexington, Virginia, in February. He later asked to be sent into combat. Greenberg consequently was part of the initial group of B-29 bomber squadrons to head overseas. He led a B-29 bomber unit in the China-Burma-India theater that flew five missions over the Himalayas, referred to as the Hump. This proved to be "a pretty nerve-racking experience," as Greenberg informed Arthur Daley of the *Times*. Weather concerns were always paramount, as was the possibility of crashing into a mountain peak. He told Daley about his first mission out of Japan:

> I drove out to the field in a jeep with General Blondy Saunders who led the strike, and took my place in the control tower. Those monsters went *off*, one after the other, with clocklike precision. Then we spotted one fellow in trouble. The pilot saw he wasn't going to clear the runway, tried to throttle down, but the plane went over on its nose at the end of the field. Father Stack, our padre, and myself raced over to the burning plane to see if we could help rescue anyone. As we were running, there was a blast when the gas tanks blew and we were only about thirty yards away when a bomb went off. It knocked us right into a drainage ditch alongside the rice paddies while pieces of metal floated down out of the air.

Stunned and unable to speak or hear for the next couple of days, Greenberg was otherwise unscathed. As he recalled, "The miraculous part of it all . . . was that the entire crew escaped. Some of them were pretty well banged up but no one was killed. That was an occasion, I can assure you, when I didn't wonder whether or not I'd be able to return to baseball. I was quite satisfied just to be alive." Still, to his disappointment, he "never made it all the way to the front."[30] Recalled to the States in mid-1944, Greenberg joined an outfit in New York City that sent combat veterans out to speak in war plants in an effort to boost morale. He was sent to Richmond, Virginia, later that year.

Lacking its biggest star in 1941, and facing the loss of Charlie Gehringer to retirement and rookies Pat Mullin, a promising outfielder, and Fred Hutchinson, a future pitching star, to the military, the defending World Series champion Detroit Tigers had slipped into fourth place, winning less than half their games and finishing 26 games back of the Yankees. That year in baseball is best remembered for Joe DiMaggio's 56-game hitting streak and Ted Williams's .406 batting average. The Yankees defeated the Brooklyn Dodgers in their initial World Series matchup. The next season saw the St. Louis Cardinals hand the Yankees their first World Series setback in sixteen years, while the Tigers, led by new manager Steve O'Neill, slid to fifth in the American League, 30 games back, with a 73–81 mark. The Yankees rebounded in a repeat encounter against the Cardinals in the 1943 Fall Classic. The Tigers, now without pitcher Al Benton, outfielder Barney McCosky, catcher George "Birdie" Tebbetts, outfielder Walter "Hoot" Evers, infielder Billy Hitchcock, and third baseman Mike "Pinky" Higgins, again finished fifth, this time 20 games behind the obviously less-powerful Yankees.

Detroit continued to be afflicted by "bitter resentment toward minority groups, especially Jews," according to a government survey, with many viewing Jews, notwithstanding the well-publicized exploits of Hank Greenberg, as "draft dodgers" or "economic exploiters." The war brought unwanted changes for many in the city as more than 500,000 people migrated to Detroit by mid-1943 in hopes of obtaining employment. Many were whites and blacks from the South, who came to reside in the city's southern and eastern sectors, setting the stage for a racial cauldron. African

Americans made up about ten percent of the more than 2 million city residents but increasingly chafed at racially discriminatory practices involving housing, restaurants, and the police. Clashes between whites and blacks occurred in defense plants, residential areas, and recreational spots. *Life* magazine had warned several months earlier, "Detroit is Dynamite," declaring "Detroit can either blow up Hitler or it can blow up the U.S."[31]

Detroit indeed suffered a race riot during the summer of 1943 in which thirty-four people, including twenty-five blacks, were killed, nearly seven hundred experienced serious injuries, almost two thousand were arrested, and millions of dollars of property damage occurred.[32] A riot began at Belle Isle, the city's largest municipal recreational center, on June 20 and spread from there, continuing until June 22. During the explosion, angry black mobs deliberately targeted Jewish-owned stores on Hastings Street to loot and burn. The Central Conference of American Rabbis denounced the urban disturbance as amounting to a "triumph of Hitlerism."[33] The Hastings Street riot induced blacks and Jews to establish "unity committees" in Detroit and at the state level to explore race relations. Black leaders soon lauded Jewish merchants in Detroit for forming the East Side Merchants Association, which provided assistance to poor families, and for helping African American defense plant workers obtain public housing, previously denied them.

Major league baseball was clearly weakened by 1944 due to the departure of many players into the ranks of the U.S. military. The Cardinals returned to the sport's summit, defeating the St. Louis Browns, winners of the only pennant in their history, in the World Series. Having lost pitchers Virgil Trucks, Hal White, and Tommy Bridges, along with second baseman Jimmy Bloodworth and outfielder Dick Wakefield, Detroit fought hard throughout the season, ending up only a game behind the Browns. Leading the Tigers were pitchers Hal Newhouser and Dizzy Trout, who won twenty-nine and twenty-seven games, respectively. Newhouser, who had volunteered for military service back in 1942 but been turned down because of a heart murmur, was named the American League MVP.

5

Racism and the Making
of a Sports Star

The United States, led by President Franklin D. Roosevelt, waged World
War II against Nazi Germany, fascist Italy, and militarist Japan in ideological fashion. Closely aligned with Great Britain (guided by Prime Minister
Winston Churchill) and the Soviet Union (spearheaded by Joseph Stalin),
the United States conducted the war as an anti-fascist fight, promising to
foster democracy throughout the globe. The Grand Alliance, made up of
the three often-uneasy partners, possessed inherent contradictions because
of British colonialism, Soviet communism, and the continued presence of
Jim Crow in the world's greatest democracy. But ironies and paradoxes had
long characterized the newest of the three nations that comprised that
wartime alliance.

During the first half of the nineteenth century, democracy flowered in
the still fledgling United States, but it was democracy of a peculiar, limited
variety. Americans, from the Founding Fathers to common laborers and
farmers, drew from the egalitarian principles enunciated in the Declaration
of Independence, the participatory engagement by common citizens in the
revolutionary struggle against Great Britain, and the political battles resulting in the nation's first political parties. Reform movements, including abo-
litionism, thrived in the antebellum period. The defeat of the Confederacy
ensured the demise of slavery, the "peculiar institution." However, even con-
stitutional amendments that eradicated slavery, safeguarded the privileges

and immunities of citizens, demanded equal protection and due process of the laws, and shielded the right of former slaves to vote failed to wholly eradicate the determination of some to continue treating others like chattel. Black codes, social segregation, economic restrictions, educational impediments, and violence sustained the discrimination through which people of color were subjugated once again. Jim Crow edicts and prejudicial treatment solidified. The federal government, during the administration of the progressive Democratic president, Woodrow Wilson, actually strengthened its own Jim Crow strictures, to the chagrin of champions of racial equality, such as members of the newly formed National Association for the Advancement of Colored People (NAACP) and the National Urban League (NUL).

Scientific racism came into vogue in both Europe and the United States during the last half of the nineteenth century and the first decades of the twentieth. The American lawyer Madison Grant, a champion of eugenics, published *The Passing of the Great Race* in 1916. Grant subscribed to the idea of the Nordic race, idealizing "Homo europaeus, the white man par excellence," characterized by fair skin, light hair, blue eyes, a straight nose, considerable physical stature, and an abundant crop of hair.[1] Grant expressed grave concerns about mounting emigration from Eastern and Southern Europe to the United States and also pointed to the movement of African Americans into the nation's northern cities. He urged restricting immigration from both Southern Europe and Asia and called for purifying the nation's populace through selective breeding. The advent of World War I first temporarily halted, and then after the United States entered the war, intensified the immigration restriction movement, which challenged notions about the great American melting pot.

American participation in the Great War sped up the pace of various strands of progressivism at home, including those involving efforts to influence the social and racial order. Led by President Wilson, the United States entered World War I in April 1917, helping to ensure an Allied victory. Wilson spoke often and eloquently about the meaning of the conflict. He indicated it was "the war to end all wars," "the war to vindicate national honor and the rights of humanity," and "the war to make the world safe for democracy." World War I proved to be nothing of the sort. Its destructive swath brought about social disintegration in countries ranging from Czarist Russia to the Kaiser's Germany and planted far deadlier seeds. Even in the United States, which was a belligerent for only nineteen months, President Wilson's promises generally failed to bear fruit. The war endangered American democracy itself, or so it must have seemed to the countless individuals whose rights were violated in pursuit of the Wilson administration's war aims. Government forces and vigilantes alike targeted antiwar proponents of all kinds, including conscientious objectors, socialists, cultural radicals, and Wobblies—members of the militant union, the Industrial Workers of the World. Additionally, Wilson, like former president Theodore Roosevelt (who also despised homegrown radicals), viewed so-called hyphenated Americans with suspicion. Wilson stated, "Any man who carries a hyphen about with him carries a dagger that he is ready to plunge into the vitals of this Republic whenever he gets ready," thereby casting aspersions on various groups, including particularly German Americans and Irish Americans, many of whom opposed the U.S. war effort.

By contrast, the lot of African Americans, other than those of a radical political stripe, appeared to improve during World War I, at least on the surface of race relations. In unprecedented fashion, industrial plants in the Northeast and Midwest opened their doors to black workers, both men and women, who were not called on merely to serve as strikebreakers as in days past. A. Philip Randolph, later the African American head of the Brotherhood of Sleeping Car Porters and coeditor of *The Messenger*, a socialist publication, nevertheless warned in July 1918 about the "deep and dark" causes of discontent among black Americans, including "peonage, disfranchisement, Jim-Crowism, segregation, rank civil discrimination, injustice of legislatures, courts and administrators." Randolph bemoaned the drafting of blacks both into the American military and industrial plants, part of the program to further "white democracy" thousands of miles away as racism remained rampant at home.[2] The U.S. armed forces welcomed African American enlistees and conscripts; the Harlem Hellfighters were among the most distinguished of the units to fight in the European theater.

Much as Randolph anticipated, racial advances proved short-lived. Veterans of battles in Europe and industrial veterans alike remained determined to hold onto wartime gains, whether these involved jobs, housing, or pride in self. Others proved equally committed to put blacks and other minorities "back in their place," and a series of bloody race riots ensued. Nevertheless, amid the invectives and chaos that occurred, black men and women increasingly looked to a New Negro—proud, spirited, defiant even —who appeared to have been birthed, or at least recast, during the war.

Close to six o'clock on the evening of January 31, 1919, Jack Roosevelt Robinson was born near the town of Cairo, Georgia, a short distance from the Florida border. His parents lived in a small cottage. They sharecropped on a plantation run by a white farmer. Jack—or Jackie, as he came to be called—was the fourth son and fifth child overall born to Jerry and Mallie Robinson, who added his middle name in honor of recently deceased former president Theodore Roosevelt. Georgia had proven largely inhospitable to African Americans for the past three decades, with hundreds of lynchings and terror inflicted on them, their homes, and their businesses. White supremacist ideas prevailed. The Ku Klux Klan was resurgent. All the while blacks struggled to provide for their families. For some, including Mallie's kin, education, acquiring a bit of property, and religion proved particularly important. A flagrant philanderer, Jerry frequently departed from the Robinson home, only to return again. A final clash between Mallie and Jerry in mid-1919 resulted in the family's ouster from the plantation. Her half-brother, Burton Thomas, suggested that Mallie take her children out to southern California: "If you want to get closer to heaven, visit California."[3]

More than seventy African Americans were killed in racial explosions across the nation in the last several months of 1919, the worst occurring in Chicago, where thirty-eight people were murdered, several hundred injured, and hundreds left homeless during a three-day rampage. The summer of 1919 promised to be a long, hot cauldron even before the Chicago riot. With the return of African American soldiers from overseas and the end to war-inspired economic prosperity, optimism regarding a change in the South had faded. A "sinister" tone had taken hold, the *Nation* magazine reported on June 14. Relations involving whites and blacks proved "little less than gravely alarming." A good amount of "friction and discontent" was apparent. That was most starkly exemplified by an "epidemic of lynching" and the image of "the Ku Klux Klan riding again." Whites viewed returning black soldiers as "uppity," while the soldiers resented the failure of communities to celebrate them like their white brothers-in-arms. Certain their participation in the quest to safeguard democracy abroad would translate into "some few crumbs of democracy at home," black veterans returned instead "to find their hopes dashed again." In Putnam County, Georgia, alone, five black churches, schools, and a lodge hall were burned down early one morning.[4] An editorial in the *Chicago Defender*, the nation's leading African-American newspaper, deemed the riots in Chicago and others in Washington, D.C., "a disgrace to American civilization." This behavior was hardly foreign to the United States, editor Robert S. Abbott and associate editor Alfred Anderson intoned. "America is known the world over as the land of the lyncher and of the mobocrat. . . . For years she has been sowing the wind and now she is reaping the whirlwind."[5]

In May 1920, Mallie Robinson and her brood of five, including her sixteen-month-old son Jackie, boarded a train for the West Coast. Her sister Cora Wade and her family joined the migration. Mallie considered Los Angeles "the most beautiful sight of my whole life." She managed to get a job as a maid for a white family in Pasadena, then the nation's wealthiest community. Her first employers soon left the area, but Mallie obtained a position with another family, and that job proved long lasting. The Robinsons, the Wades, and Burton Thomas shared a large house, located on a sizable plot of land in the northwestern sector of Pasadena that contained both white and black white residents.

In a speech in Birmingham, Alabama, in late 1921, President Warren G. Harding told those gathered in attendance, both white and black, "that this problem of races" was "the problem of democracy everywhere." Harding asserted that "a fundamental, eternal and inescapable difference" distinguished whites from blacks. Appealing to African Americans' "self-respect," Harding called for blacks to seek to improve themselves "as a distinct race, with a heredity, a set of traditions, an array of aspirations all its own." From such desires and pride would unfold "natural segregations, without narrowing any rights," which would satisfy "natural inclinations," the president indicated.[6] The *Boston Chronicle*, an African American newspaper, termed Harding's speech "an asinine attempt to help the negro and not offend the South." In reality, the *Chronicle* claimed, African Americans desired "the same that the Anglo-Saxon races wants—economic, political and social equality." The paper warned that across the globe, "rebellion against the unfraternal attitude of the white races abounds," with white Anglo-Saxons particularly "playing on top of the crater of a live volcano."[7]

As the attorney David E. Lilienthal recognized through his description of race relations in Detroit, the South was hardly the only part of the United States experiencing racial problems. The number of African Americans living in the Motor City had jumped sixteen-fold to almost eighty thousand during the past decade and a half, resulting in incredibly dense living circumstances. Efforts to move beyond the segregated areas seemed invariably to lead to mob action and a resulting retreat by blacks to their former communities. Dr. Alexander Turner, an African American physician, purchased a home in a previously all-white neighborhood in June 1925. After Turner and his family moved into the house, a large crowd gathered, shouted racial epithets, stoned the building, and destroyed Turner's automobile. When Turner was tricked into opening the front door, white vigilantes stormed into his house, stole the furniture, and, in the presence of policemen, compelled Turner to sell his property. No prosecution resulted.[8]

Shortly before the Turner affair, Ossian Sweet, another African American physician, also bought a home in a white neighborhood in Detroit. Some seven hundred angry whites held a mass meeting in which they established an association to stave off black residents. Dr. Sweet, having been promised police protection, moved into his new home on September 8. A large crowd maintained a noisy vigil outside the house for two-and-a-half days. Despite the presence of sixteen police officers, the crowd began hurling rocks at the house. A torrent of stones rained down on the house for approximately an hour. Someone inside fired bullets, and a member of the mob was killed.

That led to first-degree murder charges against the eleven people inside the house, including Dr. Sweet and his wife. The case became a cause célèbre across the land, with African Americans and white supporters insisting it was a classic case of self-defense. The era's greatest litigator, Clarence Darrow, delivered the closing statement for the defense, underscoring how deeply ingrained the white man's hostility was toward African Americans. The initial trial resulted in a hung jury, but a subsequent retrial of Sweet led to his acquittal.[9]

In Pasadena, California, the Robinsons and the Wades had purchased a house at 121 Pepper Street, a previously all-white block, in 1922, although within two years the Wades moved into another house just a short distance away. His sister Willa Mae watched over Jackie during the school day, placing him in a sandbox while she went to class until he was old enough to attend school. Robinson recalled his first unhappy racial incident, which occurred when he was about eight years old. While sweeping the sidewalk in front of his house, Jackie heard a neighbor girl holler, "Nigger, nigger, nigger." His older brother Mack had told him that "cracker" was considered an insult to whites, so Jackie responded by calling the little girl a cracker. Her father tore out of his house to confront Jackie, and stones flew back and forth. Robinson was evidently aware that white residents in the area had complained about his family's presence. They had even initiated petitions to drive the Robinsons out, but Mallie Robinson refused to budge.[10]

Pasadena possessed a liberal reputation, with abolitionist forefathers and civic-minded founders. And yet the city experienced racial strife of its own, as did so many American municipalities after World War I, with whites and blacks competing for jobs and living space. As Robinson's biographer Arnold Rampersad notes, Pasadena had long featured Jim Crow practices that eventually led to the formation of an NAACP chapter. All the while, white residents continued to view their city as something of a paradise. They exulted in the beginning of the Rose Bowl game, long the most significant in college football. Pasadena also boasted an impressive civic center, the nation's first freeway, the Huntington Library, and the Pasadena Community Center, which in 1928 offered the world premier of Eugene

O'Neill's *Dynamo*. At the same time, racism and discrimination hardly
proved foreign to the city. Blacks were allowed to reside only in certain dis-
tricts and were unable to get jobs as policemen, firemen, schoolteachers, or
utility workers. Unions too kept their doors closed to African Americans.
The black community remained saddled with high levels of unemployment
and poverty. Race relations across the United States, including in Pasadena,
only threatened to take a turn for the worse with the advent of the Great
Depression.

Woody Strode, later Robinson's teammate at UCLA, recalled how difficult it was for African Americans growing up in Pasadena. The Inglewood
area contained a sign declaring, "No Jews and No Coloreds Are Welcomed
in this Town!" Pasadena boasted large, affluent sectors along with less comfortable neighborhoods, including the area where the Robinsons resided.
For Strode this explained "why Jackie had a little more hate going than
the rest of us." Sports provided a necessary outlet for him, but so did gang
activity. With plenty of time on his hands, Robinson alternated between
having a paper route, cutting grass to earn extra money, running errands,
or engaging in mischief, which included pilfering from stores. Robinson
belonged to the multiracial Pepper Street Gang, with its African American,
Mexican, Asian, and white members. One of the white boys, Warren
Dorn, later went into politics, serving as mayor of Pasadena and as commissioner for Los Angeles County. The Pepper Street Gang performed various escapades at the local YMCA or at Brookside Park with its large
swimming pool. Members also tossed rocks or dirt at passing automobiles,
vandalized streetlamps and windows, and tore through orchards. Ray
Bartlett, who also later played football with Robinson at UCLA and eventually became a policeman, nevertheless recalled that the Pepper Street
Gang was relatively innocent. "There was [sic] no drugs, no smoking, no
liquor, no beating up anybody, nothing of that nature."[11] Gang activity
did inevitably lead to encounters with the police, who began to single out
Robinson as a troublemaker.

Mallie Robinson worked diligently to keep her son out of reform school.
Carl Anderson, a mechanic in town, sought to convince Jackie that he was

not suited for a gang. But Jackie remained in the Pepper Street Gang to avoid being considered "chicken." The arrival of Karl Downs, a young African American minister at the church the Robinsons attended, proved fortunate. Downs particularly reached out to those who had left the church or never attended. Encouraged by Downs, youngsters like Jackie set up dances at the church and enjoyed the badminton court the minister built. Downs played sports with the kids, but most important, as Robinson remembered, "He knew how to listen." Jackie spoke often with Downs, who offered sage advice and convinced him to teach in the church's Sunday school program.[12]

Jackie's older brothers Frank and Mack, who while overcoming a heart ailment had become something of a sports legend in local schools, influenced him even more. A state champion in the 100-yard dash in high school, Mack established national junior college records in the 100-meter and 200-meter dashes and in the broad jump. He competed in the 1936 Olympics in Berlin, leading until the final moments of the 200-meter race when he turned to check on his competition and was passed by Jesse Owens. The U.S. Olympic Committee, headed by Avery Brundage, either cravenly or willfully dropped Jewish sprinters Sam Stoller and Marty Glickman from the 400-meter relay team the day before they were supposed to compete. Having taken the silver medal in the Olympics, Mack went on to win the NCAA 220-yard title and the AAU 200-meter crown, in addition to setting a national mark for the AAU by broad jumping 25'5½", but Mack could only get a job as a street sweeper when he returned home. Even Owens was at times compelled to race against local sprinters and horses to make a living.

Like Mack, Jackie attended John Muir Technical High School, where he began to display his own athletic prowess. Despite weighing only 135 pounds, he joined the football team and also played guard on the basketball squad. Having switched from shortstop to the backstop position, Robinson was named to an all-star contingent in baseball in 1936 that included Ted Williams from San Diego and Bob Lemon from Long Beach. He competed in both the broad jump and pole vault for the school's track team. Robinson's final semester at John Muir proved more successful still, beginning with his capturing of the junior boy's singles title at the annual Pacific Coast Negro Tennis Tournament in September 1936. Robinson then quarterbacked Muir to the league championship contest (where he suffered broken ribs) before starring as a 5'11" forward in basketball and leading the team in scoring.

Following graduation from John Muir Technical High School in January 1937, the eighteen-year-old Robinson enrolled at tuition-free Pasadena Junior College, where he remained a multisport star. During his freshman year, he batted leadoff and played shortstop on the baseball team, helping the Bulldogs reach the championship game. Despite sustaining a leg injury that sidelined him for four games, Robinson starred on the football team, carrying back one interception ninety-two yards for a touchdown and running a punt back seventy-eight yards for six more points. Sportswriters sang his praises, lauding his ability to cut and accelerate on the gridiron.

Not all moments proved pleasant. During track season, when Robinson and his teammates attempted to eat at a restaurant in Sacramento, he and Jack Gordon, a light-skinned black, were denied service, something that also happening at a hotel during a football trip to Arizona. Robinson fought with a substitute player on the opposing side during a basketball game against Long Beach Junior College, leading to something of a riot involving players, coaches, and spectators alike. Shortly following that affair, Robinson landed in the Pasadena city jail after he and a friend were arrested by a policeman who was offended by their singing of "Flat Foot Floogie." Robinson subsequently received a ten-day jail sentence that the judge suspended under the condition that Jackie stay out of trouble for the next two years.

His second baseball campaign with the Pasadena Junior College Bulldogs proved even better than the first. Robinson was chosen for the All-Southland Junior College team and selected Most Valuable Player in the region. During the baseball season, Robinson also competed in track and field, leaping 25'6½" to break Mack's national junior college mark. In March he joined a team of Pasadena youngsters that played against the Chicago White Sox. Robinson belted out two hits, stole a base, and initiated a deftly turned double play. White Sox skipper Jimmy Dykes reportedly said, "Geez, if that kid was white I'd sign him now."[13] Jackie pitched for the Bulldogs for the first time, winning one game 12–1. Overall he hit .417, scored forty-three runs, and stole twenty-five bases in only twenty-four games.

That fall, the now 175-pound, muscular Robinson rushed for over 1,000 yards and scored 131 points and 17 touchdowns, including a kickoff he took back 104 yards and scoring dashes of 55, 75, and 85 yards, leading his team to 11 consecutive triumphs. He averaged 19 points a game in guiding his school to the California junior college basketball championship. Duke Snider, then a schoolboy in Southern California, closely followed Robinson's athletic feats. "Five or six of us saw him play in a baseball game, leave in the middle of it with his uniform still on to trot over to compete in the broad jump in a track meet, and then run back and finish the baseball game just as if nothing unusual had happed. That's how great and versatile he was, and how bright the fire of competition burned in him." Snider also remembered watching Robinson play football. "I was in the stands when he took a kickoff, reversed his field three times, and returned it for a touchdown. It was as dazzling a piece of broken-field running as you could ever hope to see."[14] In his autobiography, Woody Strode declared, "Jackie was probably the most sought-after athlete on the West Coast."[15]

Robinson enrolled in the Extension Division of UCLA in February 1939. Determined to make the 1940 U.S. Olympic team as a broad jumper, he informed reporters that he would only play football and compete in track and field while devoting himself to his studies. That summer delivered a crushing blow when his brother Frank was killed in a motorcycle accident. Robinson attempted to overcome his grief in competitive sports, also playing tennis, golf, and baseball. Another unhappy moment occurred in early September when Robinson was arrested after an incident in Pasadena involving him, his best friend Ray Bartlett and some other friends, and a white man who threatened to trigger an explosion by blurting out, "Niggers." Robinson pled not guilty to the charges of "hindering traffic and resisting arrest."[16] Worried that the latest arrest might lead to a jail sentence, UCLA football coach Babe Horrell and other individuals associated with the university helped prevent that from happening. With his plea changed to guilty without his knowledge, Robinson received a fifty-dollar fine, which the university paid.

Robinson enrolled at the University of California at Los Angeles in September 1939, one of only thirty blacks among the large student body; one of those black students was Tom Bradley, a star track performer and later mayor of Los Angeles. Robinson covered expenses through his athletic scholarship and by holding down a pair of part-time jobs as a janitor at the university and as a clerk at a nearby bookstore, where Bradley and football star Kenny Washington also worked. He quickly made his mark as one of nation's finest all-around athletes. An integral part of the football squad that went undefeated in 10 games but experienced 4 ties, Robinson starred in the game against Stanford, where he bolted for 52 yards on one carry and later raced 51 yards after intercepting a pass. Stanford coach Tiny Thornhill called Robinson "the greatest backfield runner I have seen in all my connection with football."[17] In the victory over Oregon, Robinson, the wingback in UCLA's single wing formation, scored the Bruins' only touchdowns, one on a pass from tailback Washington, the other on an 82-yard dash from scrimmage. He scored two other touchdowns, both against Washington State—the first on a 25-yard pass reception from Washington, the second through a 35-yard scamper into the end zone. Robinson rushed for 514 yards in only 42 carries during the season for a nation-leading mark of 12.2 yards per play. Ray Bartlett said about Robinson, "He was the greatest open-field runner I ever saw."[18] Woody Strode indicated, "Jackie Robinson was the first of the Gayle Sayers/O. J. Simpson/Eric Dickerson-type running backs. He had incredible breakaway speed coupled with an elusiveness you had to see to believe. He could change direction quicker than any back I had ever seen. Stop on a dime: boom; full speed in the other direction. They didn't have to do a lot of blocking for him because he was so instinctive. He was shifty and quick and would just out-maneuver everybody."[19] Robinson caught six passes for 145 yards, a 24.2 yard average, and led the nation with a 16.5 punt return average.

The outbreak of World War II led to cancellation of the 1940 Olympic Games. Robinson joined the Bruins basketball team instead. A top-flight passer with a terrific outside shot, Robinson led the Southern Division of the Pacific Coast Conference in scoring with an average of 12.4 points a contest (in an era when teams regularly scored only 30 or 40 points a game), and he nailed the final basket to defeat the California Bears. UCLA athletic director Wilbur Johns later stated, "If Jackie hadn't played football, he might have been the greatest of all basketball players. His timing was perfect. His rhythm was unmatched."[20] Moreover Robinson was always a team player. Teammate Ned Mathews recalled another unfortunate incident in Palo Alto when Robinson and UCLA's other black players—Washington, Strode, and Ray Bartlett—were denied service at a restaurant. Their white teammates responded by leaving too. Robinson's baseball season proved less than auspicious, despite opening on a high note when he smacked four hits; stole four bases, including home; and fielded flawlessly. He managed only two more hits during the rest of the California Intercollegiate Baseball Association season, knocking out only one homer, scoring but nine runs, and batting a meager .097 while teammate Washington hit .454. His play in the field proved little better, as Robinson committed 10 errors and ended up with a fielding percentage of .907. Following completion of the baseball season, Robinson competed in the Pacific Coast Conference track and field meet, leaping 25' to take the broad jump title, and captured the broad jump crown with a leap of 24'10¼" in the NCAA championship. He thus became the first four-sport letterman at UCLA and remains the only athlete in the school's history to attain that distinction.

In his final year at UCLA, Robinson met a lovely seventeen-year-old freshman nursing student, Rachel Isum, who had recently graduated from Manual Arts High School in Los Angeles. He eventually discovered that Rachel had watched him compete at Pasadena Junior College. She considered the star athlete "cocky, conceited, and self-centered." She was initially distrustful of him, but the two soon came to speak regularly and openly.[21] At one point in their relationship, Rachel, who was much more lightly complexioned than Jackie, heard her father ask, "What do you see in that big, ugly ape?"[22]

Robinson again starred for the football team, which suffered through a 1–9 season during his senior year at UCLA. He scored on an 87-yard punt return against SMU and completed 60- and 75-yard touchdown dashes against Washington State. He finished second in the Pacific Coast with 440 yards rushing, 435 yards passing, and 875 yards overall. He carried back 19 punts for 399 yards, averaging an NCAA-record 21.0 yards per punt return, and received honorable mention on All-American teams. Once again he led the PCC's Southern Division, averaging 11.1 points a game for a team that went 6–20. Basketball coach Wilbur Johns praised Robinson's athletic prowess, attributing it to timing, rhythm, grace under pressure, perfect physical conditioning, and the ability to be a team player, even though he was "an outstanding [individual] player."[23] Sportswriters began referring to Robinson as the "Black Jim Thorpe," thereby likening him to the great Native American football star, Olympic champion in track-and-field (whose twin gold medals were stripped because of a violation of his amateur status but restored posthumously), and major leaguer.

Following the conclusion of the basketball season, Robinson withdrew from UCLA, just a few credits shy of obtaining his degree but determined to go to work to help out his mother. He also "was convinced that no amount of education would help a black man get a job." Rather "I felt I was living in an academic and athletic dream world," he said later. Jackie hoped to become an athletic director, but his future hardly appeared bright as he left school in the spring of 1941, with the country still pulling out of the Depression.[24] President Franklin D. Roosevelt's determination to expand military production helped the nation finally leave behind the economic trauma of the past decade. Even so, Jim Crow seemed to preclude the possibility of a professional career in sports even for an athlete as gifted as Jackie Robinson.

6

Out of School and Into the Army

The Broadway Clowns (a semipro basketball team) and a Mexican base-ball team both apparently dangled offers before Robinson, albeit not terri-bly attractive ones, after he withdrew from UCLA. He instead landed a job with the National Youth Administration, a New Deal program. Thanks to NYA athletic director Pat Ahearn, Robinson got assigned to a camp in Atascadero, some 200 miles north of Los Angeles, where he worked with disadvantaged youngsters, including gang members, and starred for the camp baseball team that competed against area semipro squads. Congress soon axed the NYA, leaving him unemployed. He received an invitation to appear in the annual College All-Star Game that pitted the top senior col-legians, including many about to enter the pro ranks, against the National Football League champion Chicago Bears. The *Chicago Tribune* edition of August 16, 1941, headlined a story called "Robinson Leads All-Star Drive," about a pregame scrimmage. The article, by sportswriter Wilfrid Smith, indicated that the practice session featured "a new star, Jackie Robinson of U.C.L.A." and his 50-yard touchdown dash. Smith wrote, "The lithe, twist-ing half back, shot past the end and then plotted his own path around the would-be tacklers."[1] In another scrimmage on August 19, Robinson set up his team for the tying touchdown with a 35-yard jaunt "through a broken field," which was "the most brilliant individual exploit of the game."[2] During the contest, won by the NFL titleholders 37–13, Robinson scored on a 46-yard pass reception, came close to breaking another pair of touch-down runs, and completed one pass for 34 yards in the game played before over 98,000 fans at Soldier Field. Regarding the touchdown toss from Charley O'Rourke, Robinson indicated that his teammate "just dropped the ball in my arms and all I had to do was put on a little steam."[3] Chicago defensive player Dick Plasman declared, "That Jackie Robinson is the fastest man I've ever seen in a uniform," and admitted, "The only time I was wor-ried about the game was when Robinson was in there."[4]

Robinson next played for the semipro Los Angeles Bulldogs but lasted barely a quarter of one game before an ankle injury forced him to the side-line. He departed for Honolulu, where he played halfback for the semipro, integrated Honolulu Bears, making $100 a game. At times Robinson dis-played an electrifying brilliance. On other occasions, he suffered from an ankle injury that restricted his movements on the field. On December 5 he headed back to California, just two days before the Japanese attack on Pearl Harbor. He began working as a truck driver and played for a semipro basketball team, the Los Angeles Red Devils. He also reunited with Rachel. Robinson received a draft notice in the spring of 1942, although he believed that either a broken ankle he had suffered at Pasadena Junior College or the fact that he needed to provide financial support to his mother would keep him from military service. Rachel disagreed with that assessment. She predicted that a "huge blow up" would occur if a "big strong halfback" opted out of the draft.[5] His induction notice arrived on March 23, 1942, a few days after Robinson participated in an early but ultimately futile attempt to break baseball's color barrier.

Twenty-three-year-old Jackie Robinson and the twenty-five-year-old Negro League veteran Nate Moreland showed up at Pasadena's Brookside Park, the Chicago White Sox's spring training facility, accompanied by *Pittsburgh Courier* reporter Herman Hill. The *Daily Worker* and the *Courier* subsequently reported on the encounter, which had not been sought by the major league team. Nevertheless, the two black athletes "were greeted warmly by the big leaguers," the communist paper reported. Chicago White Sox manager Jimmy Dykes had already praised Robinson's ability when

Jackie had been on a high school squad that had competed against the White Sox. On greeting Robinson and Moreland at the White Sox training camp in Pasadena, Dykes stated, "There is no clause in the Baseball Constitution, nor is there any one in the bylaws of the major leagues which prevents Negro baseball players from participating in organized baseball. Rather, it is an unwritten law." Then, Dykes repeated the caveat delivered by other big league skippers. "The matter is out of the hands of us managers. We are powerless to act and it's strictly up to the club owners and in the first place Judge Landis to start the ball a rolling." Dykes urged the players, "Go after them." Dykes affirmed, "Personally, I would welcome Negro players on the Sox and I believe every one of the other fifteen big league managers would do likewise. As for the players, they'd all get along too." Robinson "was easily worth $50,000 to any big league ball club," Dykes acknowledged. The *Daily Worker* pointed to Robinson's stellar athletic career at UCLA and said he had been "the finest college shortstop on the coast." Robinson was "a terrific long hitter, class fielder and sparkling base runner."[6]

In an article in the *Courier*, dated March 19, 1942, Herman Hill referred to Robinson and Moreland as "intelligent college bred athletes." He called Robinson "a veritable blur on the paths, a slick shortstop, and a good hitter" who was a "versatile" player "unofficially credited with being the potential equil [*sic*] of any short-patcher in the game today." After their latest session, Dykes indicated that Robinson, despite a charley horse, "stole everything but my infielders' gloves. I'd hated to have seen him with two good legs." Hill closed his article by revealing that both Robinson and Moreland complained to Dykes about "the utter unfairness of the situation." As Moreland noted, "I can play in the Mexican National League, but I must fight to defend this country where I can't play." Hill called Robinson "a potential class 1-A draftee" who was expected to soon join the U.S. military to "fight for Democracy."[7]

A reporter in a Texas newspaper in 1942 referred to the possibility of violence erupting if black and white ballplayers competed against one another. "Fear of physical trouble on the field and race riots in the stands is frankly the most of it," Bill Cunningham wrote. "The majority of the ball players are Southerners and many of them cracker confederates. Maybe they're not right, but you try telling 'em and see how far you get."[8] In fact, black and white ballplayers had barnstormed against one another for decades. Lester Rodney of the *Daily Worker* continued his crusade to integrate baseball, damning Landis as the "MAN RESPONSIBLE FOR KEEPING JIM CROW IN OUR NATIONAL PASTIME." Landis helped to sustain "a relic of the slave market long repudiated in other American sports," Rodney charged.[9] After the *Daily Worker* quoted Leo Durocher as expressing a readiness to add black players to his team if allowed, Commissioner Landis ordered the Dodgers manager to meet with him. Durocher subsequently declared he had been misquoted, while Landis delivered a statement of his own. The commissioner disingenuously denied that he had ever issued an edict excluding blacks from organized baseball or implied that the moguls had agreed to a whites-only game. "Negroes are not barred from organized baseball by the commissioner and never have been in the 21 years that I have served. If Durocher, or any other manager, or all of them, want to sign one, or twenty-five, Negro players, it is all right with me. That is the business of the managers and the club owners. The business of the commissioner is to interpret the rules of baseball and to enforce them."[10]

The response to Landis's declaration was mixed, with the black press hoping that it might open the doors to the integration of baseball and others fearing that very possibility. The *Washington Afro-American* published the headline LANDIS CLEARS WAY FOR OWNERS TO HIRE COLORED.[11] The *Courier* and the *Chicago Defender* remained more skeptical with *Defender* columnist Fay Young declaring himself amused by the "hysteria" exhibited by some black baseball fans on hearing the commissioner's statement. The proper query to pose to Landis was, What keeps them out?, referring to black players and sportswriters alike. Young stated simply, "They are out—and they're not in." Not a single black player could be found in either the major or minor leagues. While he hoped to see the deserving black player in organized ball, "He won't get in the major leagues for sometime," Young warned.[12] The *Daily Worker* sent a reporter to speak with Landis, who finally claimed during a difficult interview, "There is no man living who wants the friendship of the Negro people more than I."[13] Washington Senators owner Clark Griffith contended that "colored people should develop their own big league baseball and challenge the best of the white major leagues." He asked, "Why take a few stars like Satchel Paige and Josh Gibson away and put them in with the whites and ruin organized colored baseball?"[14] This was more than a little hypocritical, as Griffith had earlier spoken with both Gibson and Buck Leonard about the possibility of signing with the Senators franchise.

On May 4, 1942, the *Daily Worker* published a letter from sportswriter Nat Low to New York Yankees manager Joe McCarthy, urging baseball's signature team to sign Buck Leonard to play first base, a weak spot for the Bronx Bombers since illness had befallen Lou Gehrig. The Homestead Grays star was "one of the greatest sluggers in the game" and "the nearest thing to the great Lou Gehrig that baseball has seen," Low indicated. For now Leonard was kept out of the majors "by a vicious, rotten unwritten law that says if a man's skin is black he cannot enjoy the privileges of a human being." Low demanded that skeptics ask major league barnstormers about Leonard, Paige, Gibson, Ray Brown, and "other great Negro stars." Signing Leonard to a contract was befitting, as American soldiers were "fighting throughout the world for freedom, for liberty, for equality." It would be particularly appropriate for "baseball's greatest team" to break the color barrier, Low continued.[15] Rodney reported later that month that thousands of fans appeared at Negro League games to cheer a player like Satchel Paige. Rodney asked, "CAN YOU READ, JUDGE LANDIS?" He also recalled Jimmy Dykes's admission to the "young Negro shortstop star" Jackie Robinson: "I'd love to have you on my team and so would all the other big league managers. But it's not up to us. Get after Landis."[16]

The *Daily Worker* intensified its campaign to put pressure on Judge Landis as summer approached. It reported on May 27 that the Kansas City Monarchs had just defeated a major league contingent led by Dizzy Dean, 3–1. Although the big leaguers included former American League batting champ Cecil Travis and slugger Zeke Bonura, Satchel Paige allowed them only two scratch hits. The *Chicago Herald-American*, which called Paige "the greatest pitcher Negro baseball has ever produced" and the equal of Grover Cleveland Alexander, Christy Mathewson, and Bob Feller, declared his name to be "indelibly interwoven with baseball lore and legend." Sportswriter Wayne K. Otto also praised shortstop Jesse Williams, who possessed "an arm that any major leaguer would give half his life to possess," and said first baseman Buck O'Neil would "fit in any man's club." Meanwhile, trade unions, led by the United Retail and Wholesale Employees of America, boasting over 100,000 members, called for an end to the "ban on Negro baseball players in the big league."[17] The *Daily Worker* urged readers to contact their unions, which would send telegrams to Landis demanding the lifting of organized baseball's segregation policy. Blaming Landis alone for the ban, the *Daily Worker* cried out, "END JIM CROW IN BASEBALL THIS SEASON!"[18]

On May 31, Rodney quoted Washington Senators manager Bucky Harris: "Of course there are many good Negro players who belong in the major leagues, and how some of our teams could use them this year!" Harris suggested that a matchup pitting Paige against the New York Yankees "would be quite an attraction." Rodney condemned Landis's silence regarding Jim Crow baseball, notwithstanding mounting protest that the sportswriter considered "a slap in the face of national unity." It also remained "the ugly blot on democracy and sportsmanship that it always was." Rodney saw Landis's refusal to speak out as simply "contemptuous." It insulted "every American who believes that if a man can run, hit and throw well enough he shouldn't be kept off the field because of race, color or creed." Landis, by contrast, was "not insulting Adolf Hitler, the master Jim Crower of all time."[19] The following day, Paige and the Homestead Grays again bested Dean's collection of former major league and minor league stars. In five innings, Paige struck out seven while allowing only one unearned run. The campaign to eradicate the ban against black ballplayers quickly appeared to gather momentum as Bernard J. Shell, a top Catholic bishop in Chicago, castigated the "disgrace to democracy" and the damage caused "to National Morale" by baseball's racial practices. Shell spoke to a committee, led by Judge Patrick B. Prescott Jr., which was examining the national pastime's segregation policy.[20] On June 7, Nat Low announced that his colleague Rodney was off to join the fight "to crush into the dirt the monsters of world fascism."[21]

The *Daily Worker* maintained its crusade against Jim Crow baseball. It reported on June 8, 1942, that "the greatest blow yet struck" occurred when the Greater New York Industrial Union Council, representing over 250 locals, unanimously condemned organized baseball's racial exclusivity and called on Landis to act.[22] As additional unions expressed opposition to segregated baseball, Brooklyn councilman Peter V. Cacchione, a communist labor leader, asserted that "before long Negro players will appear in big league games." Declaring baseball "a symbol of our national life," Cacchione pointed to the opportunities the "democratic game" afforded Italian Americans like Doug Camilli, Cookie Lavagetto, and the DiMaggio brothers—Joe, Vince, Dominic—all top major leaguers.[23]

Conrad Komorowski, representing the *Daily Worker*, met with Commissioner Landis in late June to discuss the possibility of black players entering organized baseball. Landis responded when pressed, "No comment on any phase of the subject." After Komorowski asked the self-proclaimed baseball czar why he refused to comment, Landis retorted, "You fellows say I am responsible." He finally attempted to blame the club moguls and posed a query of his own. "Why don't you put them on the spot?" Landis expressed concerns that black communities would blame him for failing to lift the ban and affirmed his fervent desires for the friendship of African Americans. Landis could prevent such a charge from being hurled at him by opening up organized baseball to black players, Komorowski stated, but the commissioner responded with another "no comment."[24]

The *Daily Worker* reported that the Pittsburgh Pirates owner Ben Benswanger was ready to offer tryouts to Negro leaguers Roy Campanella, Sammy T. Hughes, and Dave Barnhill. The tryouts were then cancelled. Benswanger proceeded to promise, "We will give any man—white or colored—a chance when asked. I have not changed from my original position that any player, regardless of race, will be considered for a position on the Pirates."[25] Larry MacPhail, president of the Brooklyn Dodgers, denied on July 30, 1942, that there existed any interest in black ballplayers and claimed that only a few Negro leaguers were of major league caliber.

In his column appearing in the *Defender* on July 25, 1942, Fay Young dismissed Commissioner Landis's "old worn-out" declaration that no rule existed in major league baseball precluding the hiring of black players. The *Defender* had repeatedly made that observation itself while underscoring that "the color question is and has been there for years." There clearly existed "an unwritten law" as "the buck" was being passed back-and-forth between big league managers and owners. No black player had been signed to play in organized baseball since the New York Giants' John McGraw unsuccessfully attempted to pass off the dark-hued Charlie Grant as a Native American. Young recalled great Negro leaguers like Rube Foster, Pete Hill, José Méndez, John Donaldson, Bullet Joe Rogan, and Home Run Johnson, who were never allowed to enter organized baseball. Current stars facing the unofficial ban included Buck Leonard, Buck O'Neil, Josh Gibson, Satchel Paige, and Lefty Mathis. No major league owners possessed the guts to challenge Landis, just as no professional football owners would hire black players. No African American ballplayer was playing in organized baseball "because the owners decree that he should not be and these owners hide behind such a statement which Landis dishes out," Young wrote.[26]

In his next column, Young now agreed with Commissioner Landis's declaration that major league baseball had no edict preventing the hiring of black players. Young sharply asserted that black fans hardly required Landis to apprise them of that fact. Several black sportswriters, including Ches Washington, Rollo Wilson, Ira Lewis, and Young himself, had long "waged a fight against the color barrier in the big leagues." All believed "that Landis is starting a buck-passing game." As no bar prevented blacks from playing in the majors, Landis needed to answer the simple question, "What keeps them out?" Young warned that the integration of organized baseball hardly appeared imminent. He pointed to the fact that blacks were now in the U.S. Navy but could not serve as ensigns. The American South continued to mandate segregation on trains passing through the region. It compelled blacks to eat apart from whites, sit in separate sections of auditoriums, and ride in the backs of buses. Blacks "are coming," Lewis predicted, "but we 'ain't there yet.'"[27] *The Sporting News* offered an editorial on August 6 by J. G. Taylor Spink, asserting that blacks and whites "prefer to draw their talents from their own ranks and both groups know their crowd psychology and do not care to run the risk of damaging their own game."[28]

As baseball moguls and their supporters warded off attempts to integrate the major and minor leagues, Jackie Robinson underwent the first months of an often unhappy experience in the U.S. Army, which remained segregated as the world war continued. After appearing at the National Guard Armory in Pasadena on April 3, he was driven to the induction center at Fort MacArthur, located in San Pedro, California. The induction physical resulted in a clean bill of health with no reference made to his weak ankle. He undertook three months of basic training at Fort Riley in northeastern Kansas. Receiving a character evaluation of "excellent," he also became an expert marksman after wielding an M1 rifle on the gunnery range. After being denied admission to Officer Candidate School (OCS), with no explanation provided, Robinson entered a segregated unit to undertake menial chores such as attending to horses at the camp stables. One officer, who refused to allow Robinson to join the Fort Riley baseball team, reportedly declared, "I'll break up the team before I'll have a nigger on it."[29]

Fortunately, another famous athlete was temporarily stationed at Fort Riley. Heavyweight boxing champion Joe Louis sought out Robinson, and the two began a lengthy friendship. Louis had captured boxing's most prestigious title in 1937. The following year, at Yankee Stadium, he avenged a lone loss in the ring to Germany's Max Schmeling. Many viewed the fight as a precursor to another possible world war, pitting Schmeling, a former world champion presented as the embodiment of German Nazism (although he hardly sympathized with the Nazis), against the Brown Bomber, viewed as representing American democracy. In 1942 Louis enrolled in the U.S. military. He admitted there were problems in America but condemned Adolf Hitler. Robinson soon informed Louis that he had not been allowed into OCS. The boxer responded by calling Truman Gibson, a black attorney who worked for Secretary of War Henry L. Stimson. Gibson flew to the base to meet with Louis, Robinson, and other black soldiers. Several blacks, including Robinson, were admitted to OCS shortly thereafter. Entering the program in November 1942, Robinson received his commission as a second lieutenant in the cavalry of the U.S. Army on January 28, 1943. He was granted leave in March and returned to California to propose to Rachel Isum, now a nursing student, but she remained unwilling to make such a commitment.

Back at Fort Riley, he served as morale officer for his company but continued to experience racial difficulties himself. That spring, he again hoped to play for the camp baseball team, which included major leaguers Dixie Walker and Pete Reiser, both stars with the Brooklyn Dodgers. Reiser recalled that a white officer informed Robinson, "You'll have to play with the colored team," although no such team existed. Robinson failed to respond but continued watching the players working out before finally departing. As Reiser remembered, "I didn't know who he was then, but that was the first time I saw Jackie Robinson. I can still remember him walking away by himself."[30] Responding to complaints from black soldiers about the racist treatment they were experiencing, Robinson called the provost marshal, Major Hafner, to complain about the abuse. At one point, Hafner, who did not know that the officer he was talking to was black, blurted out, "Lieutenant, let me put it to you this way. How would like to have your wife sitting next to a nigger?" Robinson exploded. "Pure rage took over" as he shouted into the telephone.[31]

The United States ironically experienced a series of deadly race riots in the very period when its soldiers battled with Axis forces that were determined to establish their own brand of racial supremacy. On June 3, 1943, the Zoot Suit Riots began in Los Angeles as sailors targeted Mexican American youth, tearing off their distinctive clothes, lopping off their hair, and pummeling them. Police arrested the victims rather than the perpetrators of the violence, who then went after blacks and Filipino Americans as well. Other racial disturbances soon followed in San Diego, Philadelphia, and Chicago. An actual race riot unfolded in Beaumont, Texas, on June 15 and June 16, after a black man was accused of raping a white woman. Beginning on June 20, the tinderbox that was Detroit also erupted in rage. Young blacks and white sailors fought. Talk of race war wafted through the air, with the police coming down heavily on blacks. Responding to requests from black leaders, Mayor Edward J. Jeffries had asked for federal troops to help quell the disturbances. An Axis radio broadcast charged that the riot had unveiled "the internal disorganization of a country torn by social injustice, race hatreds, regional disputes, the violence of an irritated proletariat, and the gangsterism of a capitalistic police." The local newspaper in Jackson, Mississippi, chastised the administration and particularly First Lady Eleanor Roosevelt. "You have been . . . proclaiming and practicing social equality. . . . In Detroit, a city noted for the growing impudence and insolence of its Negro population, an attempt was made to put your preachments into practice." Harlem exploded on August 1, leading to the deaths of five African Americans, the hospitalizations of several hundred more, the arrest of more than five hundred individuals, and five million dollars in property damage.

Meanwhile, conditions at Fort Riley hardly seemed to improve, although the battalion commander had intimated that he sympathized with Robinson, who no doubt received word of the racial conflicts flickering across the nation. During the fall of 1943, the coach of the camp's football squad attempted to convince Robinson to join the team while acknowledging that Jackie would not be allow to play in games against schools from the South or border states like Missouri. Robinson stated that he would not play under those conditions. The coach, a colonel, indicated that he could order him to do so. "You wouldn't want me playing on your team, knowing that my heart wasn't in it," Robinson responded.[32]

He was also concerned about his right ankle, which had been reinjured when he negotiated an obstacle course, and again during a softball game. Eventually, an x-ray revealed several bone chips in his ankle, and his medical record referred to his physical ailment as "arthritis, chronic, nonsuppurative, moderately severe, right ankle."[33] On January 5, 1944, he was admitted to Brooke General Hospital, located at Fort Sam Houston in San Antonio, Texas. The hospital board reported later that month that Robinson was "physically disqualified for general military service, but qualified for limited service." The board also stated, "He is not qualified for overseas duty at this time," and urged that he "not encounter calisthenics, marching, drilling, or other duties requiring strenuous use of the right ankle."[34] Robinson experienced another setback when his engagement to Rachel, who had finally agreed to marry him, was called off. She had chosen, against his wishes, to join the Cadet Nurse Corps, a student organization he disdained, fearing that soldiers preyed on its members. Robinson was treated for gonorrhea a short time afterward.

On April 13, 1944, Robinson and several other black officers from Fort Riley were transferred to Camp Hood, something of a vast wasteland holding 60,000 soldiers near Killeen, Texas. Jim Crow standards abounded both on and off the base. Robinson joined the all-black 761st Tank Battalion. Lt. David J. Williams, a white graduate of Yale University, remembered Robinson as "kind of aloof, very straight, dressed really sharp, didn't swear much, was religious. He was a really good person, but he was never close to anyone. . . . He was a very private person." Williams recalled the conditions on base: "gleaming white concrete buildings" and a dilapidated segregated area. Referring to the latter, Williams wrote about "this muddy open tract. . . . The only buildings there were a string of tents—old, ragged, World War One tents. There was one big circus-type tent—that turned out to be the place where they showed movies, it was the rec hall, where you went to socialize. That is where the black soldiers went to socialize." Williams continued, "It was unbelievable. The heat and mosquitoes, which you had no protection from, were unbearable. Sometime along the way, they got around to taking down the tents, and in their place they put up cardboard and tar-paper shacks. At least they had screens to keep out the mosquitoes. But that was it." Robinson put together a baseball team with Williams's assistance. The officers had a team of their own, and one recalled that "when Jackie came up, we just went back as far we could go. When he hit a ball, it didn't come at you round, it came at you like a disk."[35]

Robinson was under the command of Lt. Col. Paul L. Bates, a white native of California who had been an All-American football player at McDaniel College in Maryland. Aware that the War Department was planning to ship out the 761st to Europe, Bates, who greatly respected platoon leader Robinson, asked if he would join his battalion overseas as a morale officer. Jackie replied that his bad ankle would probably preclude his being sent abroad but expressed a belief that his men would succeed. Bates responded that he simply recognized that Robinson could induce the men to perform at their highest level. Bates then asked if Robinson would go to a nearby army hospital to sign a waiver absolving the military of any problems resulting from his physical condition that might arise during the regiment's assignment overseas. Jackie agreed to Bates's proposal.[36]

On June 26, 1944, Robinson underwent another examination by the Disposition Board at McCloskey General Hospital in Temple, Texas. Its members looked at the fracture in his right ankle first injured in 1937 and then reinjured during a professional football game four years later. The board proclaimed him fit for both "limited military service" and "overseas duty."[37] On July 6, Robinson left the hospital, boarding a bus at 5:30 p.m. He arrived at the black officer's club at Camp Hood two hours later. That evening, he got on another bus to return to the hospital where he was still a patient. He spotted Virginia Jones, the light-skinned wife of another lieutenant assigned to the 761st Tank Battalion, sitting in the middle of the bus. Robinson took up a seat next to her. A short time afterward, the bus driver, Milton N. Renegar, who must have thought that the black soldier was sitting with a white woman, demanded that Robinson move to the back of the bus. Buses in the area around Camp Hood adhered to segregation practices, but Robinson initially refused to even dignify Renegar's demand with a response. He was well aware that both Joe Louis and welterweight contender Ray Robinson had recently declined to follow such edicts in the American South. Robinson also knew that the army had banned racial discrimination on vehicles traveling through military bases in the United States. On discovering that Robinson had failed to move, Renegar came back, even angrier than before. Renegar shouted at Robinson and warned that he would get into "plenty of trouble."[38] Robinson defiantly retorted that he did not care what Renegar did and stated that he had been in trouble over and over again but knew what his rights were.

Renegar later accused Robinson of continually cursing and of warning one female passenger who demanded that his actions be reported, "You better quit fuckin' with me."[39] On hearing Bevlia B. Younger, the dispatcher for the Southwestern Bus Company, refer to him as "a nigger lieutenant," Robinson purportedly exclaimed, "No God-damned sorry son-of-a-bitch could call [me] a nigger and get away with it."[40] Puelor L. Wiggington, who insisted that Robinson's conduct toward superior officers was "very disrespectful," reported that the soldier warned him, "Captain, any Private, you, or any General, calls me a nigger, and I'll break him in two."[41]

When the bus arrived at its final stop on the base, Renegar leaped out, only to return shortly with a dispatcher and other drivers. Renegar exclaimed, "This nigger is making trouble."[42] Placing his finger in Renegar's face, Robinson hotly warned the dispatcher to leave him alone. As he headed to the bus with Virginia Jones, however, Robinson encountered two well-mannered military policemen who asked him to accompany them to see Capt. Gerald M. Bear, the military police commander. During the interrogation that followed, Robinson confronted a civilian woman who asked, "Don't you know you've got no right sitting up there in the white part of the bus?" and failed to await his response. Robinson finally demanded that she allow him to complete his answers without interruption. Bear snarled that Robinson "was apparently an uppity nigger" with "no right to speak to that lady in that manner." Jackie retorted, "She's asking the questions. I feel I have as much right to tell my story as she has to ask questions." Robinson's obvious refusal to defer to either the questioner or Bear further angered the MP commander. So did Jackie's own question: "Captain, tell me, where are you from anyway?" Bear insisted he was not prejudiced. He had, after all, several black employees in the laundry he owned back home. Robinson was reduced to laughter, further enraging the senior officer.[43]

Captain Bear later delivered a scathing report of the ensuing interrogation. He accused Robinson of repeatedly interrupting him and another officer, of offering "several sloppy salutes," and of behavior that "was disrespectful and impertinent to his superior officers, and very unbecoming to an officer in the presence of enlisted men."[44] Robinson charged that Bear treated him rudely and refused to accord him the respect he was entitled to as a fellow officer. A white private by the name of Mucklerath claimed that Robinson physically threatened him. Attempting to back up that charge, an MP declared, "Mucklerath came over to the pickup and asked me if I got that nigger lieutenant. Right then the lieutenant said, 'Look here, you son of a bitch, don't you call me no nigger. I'm an officer and God damn you, you better address me as one.'"[45]

Finally taken back to the hospital, Robinson encountered a white physician who urged him to submit to a blood alcohol test to refute accusations that he had been drunk during the incident. The test verified that Robinson, who abstained from alcohol, had not been drinking. He explained to Colonel Bates what had happened on the bus and during the interrogation, and Bates told him that Bear planned to initiate a court-martial. Bates then suggested that Robinson take a leave to visit San Francisco to spend some time with Rachel. After Bates refused to support a court-martial, Robinson got transferred to another battalion whose commander agreed to the prosecution. Robinson refused to go down without a fight. He contacted his friend Joe Louis, the black press, and Truman Gibson at the Department of War, determinedly skirting around military protocol. He also sent a letter to the NAACP asking for assistance. He declared, "I feel I am being unfairly punished because I wouldn't be pushed around by the driver of the bus." Robinson claimed that he had refused the bus driver's order because it violated an edict from the federal government preventing segregation on Army bases. The NAACP declined to provide immediate assistance to Robinson but promised to review the court-martial if he believed the sentence handed down to be unfair.[46] Sheridan Downey and Hiram W. Johnson, who represented California in the U.S. Senate, made inquiries of the Robinson case to the War Department. Maj. Gen. J. A. Ulio, the adjutant general, later fired off a telegram to the commanding officer at Camp Hood, expressing concern about Robinson, termed a

"Negro Football Star Alumnus of U of CLA of excellent family and reputation."[47] Col. Walter D. Buie, chief of staff at XXIII Corps, referred to the
Robinson case as "very serious, and . . . full of dynamite," demanding "very
delicate handling."[48]

Prior to the court-martial hearing, Robinson underwent another examination before the Army Retiring Board on July 21. Robinson acknowledged having injured his right ankle playing football several years earlier
but expressed no desire to leave military service. He also did not consider
his disability permanent. The report filed on Robinson noted bone frag-
ments in his right ankle and his complaints that the ankle swelled "after
walking over rough terrain." There also existed "some clicking or locking in
the ankle" but the examination revealed "no swelling or limitation of
motion." The board concluded that Robinson's incapacity was permanent.[49]

The court-martial proceeding began at 1:45 p.m. on August 2, 1944.
Robinson was charged with behaving disrespectfully toward a superior officer, Captain Bear, and with willfully disobeying him. The prosecution witnesses, including Bear himself, proved ineffective. Testifying on his own
behalf, Robinson denied having behaved disrespectfully toward any officer.
He recalled his grandmother, a former slave, explaining that a "nigger" was
"a low, uncouth person." Robinson now stated, "I don't consider that I am
low and uncouth," while acknowledging that he "objected to being called
a nigger . . . by anybody." Several witnesses spoke favorably about Robinson.
Colonel Bates affirmed, "Particularly with the enlisted men, he is held in
high regard." Bates attested to the fact that Robinson's overall reputation
was very positive and called him an excellent soldier performing excellent
work.[50] The four-hour trial concluded with a not guilty verdict. General
Ulio informed Senators Downey and Johnson that Robinson had been
absolved of all charges.

The Medical Corps assistants at Camp Hood agreed with the earlier
determination by the Army Retiring Board: Robinson was "incapacitated
for active service." The incapacity, Col. Arden Freer and Lt. Col. R. K.
Farnham agreed, was "*not* the result of an incident of service" but rather
due to the fracture of his ankle in a football game in Pasadena seven years

earlier. The officers recommended that Robinson "be retained in the military service in a limited duty capacity."[51]

Although returned to the 761st Tank Battalion, Robinson missed out on deployment overseas and service in Gen. George Patton's Third Army. Robinson was by now "pretty much fed up with the service."[52] Reassigned to the 659th Tank Destroyer Battalion, located at North Camp Hood, Robinson sought his release. He was ordered to join the 372nd Infantry Regiment at Camp Breckinridge in Kentucky, but in October 1944 he received his discharge from the U.S. Army. The order stated that Robinson was "honorably relieved from active duty . . . by reason of physical disqualification," which amounted to a discharge that provided for no veteran's benefits.[53]

Before his discharge became effective, Robinson evidently encountered a black soldier, Ted Alexander, who had played baseball with the Kansas City Monarchs of the Negro National League. The two spoke, and Alexander informed Robinson that a player could make "good money in black baseball" and indicated that the Monarchs were in the market for ballplayers. Another story has it that Negro league pitcher Hilton Smith urged Robinson to seek out a position with the Monarchs. Regardless of who first broached the idea, Robinson sent a letter to the Monarchs, who undoubtedly recognized his name because of his athletic career at UCLA and perhaps due to reports of the recent court-martial. The Monarchs invited Robinson to try out for a spot with the team during spring training.[54] Jackie saw a chance to get back into sports, something he had always excelled at, and this time at a professional level, albeit segregated. The Negro leagues had actually done pretty well during the war, with the annual All-Star contest in Chicago remaining a particular fan favorite. Helping out was the fact that blackball retained a number of its greatest stars, including Satchel Paige and Josh Gibson, in contrast to organized baseball, which lost several of its most illustrious performers, starting with Hank Greenberg and Bob Feller, due to military service. Jim Crow was one reason that black baseball was less affected by the war, as the Selective Service deliberately restricted the number of African Americans it drafted. A number of Negro leaguers entered the military or defense plants,

but attendance continued to increase, thanks to the availability of more dis-
cretionary income as the Depression ended. The Kansas City Monarchs particularly thrived during the war, as gate receipts increased and owner J. L.
Wilkinson continued to direct a well-run organization.

7

The Color Barrier Remains

A particularly telling turn of events involving the sport's possible integration either did or did not occur following the 1942 major league season, according to baseball historians. Bill Veeck Jr., son of the former Chicago Cubs president, later revealed an attempt to buy the Philadelphia Phillies, long a National League doormat. Veeck intended to offer tryouts before the next season, when he would welcome black players. Learning of Veeck's intentions, baseball officials led by Commissioner Landis refused to allow him to buy the Philadelphia franchise. Some baseball historians have pointed out that Veeck, who had bought the Milwaukee Brewers of the American Association the previous year, could have followed through with his plan at that level. They question the veracity of his account, which was not offered until several years after the attempted purchase supposedly took place. Veeck nevertheless might have decided to wait until he could change organized baseball at the highest level, reasoning that the impact of such a move would be considerably greater than even in the high minors.

Sam Lacy of the *Chicago Defender* met with Commissioner Landis on November 17, 1943, to discuss the issue of baseball's integration. Landis then agreed to a second meeting in which various black representatives would participate. The commissioner insisted, "This is the first time such a question has [been] brought into the open and I don't know what might come of it. I do know that the step is a healthy one and should clear the air for all concerned . . . in my position I listen . . . and let the men who own the teams state their case. I can't say where I stand—one way or the other— because the owners then could come to the meeting with minds made up for or against."[1] The meeting took place on December 3, 1943, with forty-four major league officials present, including National League president Ford Frick, American League president Will Harridge, and Commissioner Landis. The African American delegation was made up of black newspaper executives Ira F. Lewis, John Sengstacke, C. B. Powell, William O. Walker, Louis Martin, and Howard Murphy; sportswriters Dan Burley and Wendell Smith; and famed singer-actor Paul Robeson. Robeson had been an All-American football player at Rutgers in 1917 and 1918, a graduate of the law school at Columbia University, a celebrated Broadway performer, and a motion picture star. He was known as a man of the Left who had championed the Loyalists against fascist-backed opponents during the Spanish Civil War and viewed the Soviet Union through a rose-colored lens.

Landis opened the session by introducing Robeson: "Everybody knows him for what he has done as an athlete and an artist. I want to introduce him to you as a man of great common sense." Before letting Robeson speak, Landis also offered, "I want it clearly understood that there is no rule, nor to my knowledge, has there ever been, formal or informal, or any understanding, written or unwritten, subterranean or sub-anything, against the hiring of Negroes in the major leagues!"[2] Robeson then talked for several minutes, hearkening back to his own collegiate experiences as a black athlete and to his career in the theatre, where racial barriers were being obliterated. Sengstacke reminded those in attendance that "if any American organization establishes barriers . . . against any class of citizens, the security of all classes is placed in constant and potential jeopardy." Lewis expressed "the bitter pangs of sorrow and disappointment" experienced by black Americans about organized baseball's color barrier. He also called attention to the sea change in the attitude of those who attended sports events in the United States, as demonstrated at boxing matches. He noted that organized baseball could similarly profit. He went further, contesting the "tacit" or "gentleman's agreement" among owners that had established a "mean precedent" prohibiting the hiring of black players.[3] Nothing came of the meeting, to the bitter disappointment of those demanding that organized baseball be integrated.

As 1944 neared a close, Jackie Robinson departed from the ranks of the U.S. Army, once again in need of a job. Robinson now wrote to Thomas Y. Baird, a co-owner of the Kansas Monarchs. Baird soon offered Robinson $300 monthly, provided he made the team. Jackie suggested an additional $100 per month. Agreeing to Robinson's request, Baird told him to come to the Monarchs' spring training camp in Houston in April. Before spring training began, Robinson received an offer to teach physical education and coach basketball at Samuel Huston College in Austin, Texas, thanks to his old friend Karl Downs, now president of the small black school. Before heading for Texas, Robinson patched up his relationship with Rachel Isum, who accepted an engagement ring but still planned on moving to New York to work as a nurse. Robinson strove diligently in Austin to establish something of an athletic program at the college while looking forward to his tryout with the Monarchs. One student-athlete recalled Robinson as "a disciplinarian coach. He believed we should be students first and athletes second." Players simply had to attend class or face getting kicked off the team, in certain instances.[4] After leaving Sam Huston College, Robinson kept in touch with his students, encouraging them to continue their educations.

As 1945 began, the United States was in its fourth year as a belligerent in World War II. America itself remained beset by racial traumas. Black GIs were still treated as second-class citizens throughout the South. The nation still experienced lynchings. An editorial in the *Pittsburgh Courier* posed the question on January 6, 1945, "Will Our Military Policy Change?" referring to the Armed Forces' continued refusal to call on "the strength, bravery, intelligence and determination of ALL the people on our side and not simply the white people."[5] A *Courier* column also recognized that the recent decision of the U.S. Supreme Court in sanctioning the military internment of Japanese Americans, *Korematsu v. the United States*, struck close to home. A dissent issued by Justice Frank Murphy, former mayor of Detroit and governor of Michigan, warned that the court's exclusion of individuals of

Japanese ancestry "falls into the ugly abyss of racism" and decried "the legalization of racism." Murphy forcefully stated, "Racial discrimination in any form and in any degree has no justifiable part whatever in our democratic way of life."

One source of new opportunity, albeit of the segregated variety, promised to be the new United States League, with baseball clubs situated in Chicago, Philadelphia, Detroit, Pittsburgh, St. Louis, and Atlanta. Gus Greenlee, longtime owner of the Pittsburgh Crawfords and one-time head of the Negro National League, announced the league's formation. The *Courier's* sports columnist, Wendell Smith, applauded Greenlee's effort while reminding readers that the Crawfords boss had introduced the great pitcher Satchel Paige to the Negro leagues and brought black baseball to major league parks in New York City.

The newly convened 79th Congress grappled with the very issue that Swedish diplomat and author Gunnar Myrdal had highlighted in his recently published book, *An American Dilemma: The Negro Problem and Modern Democracy.* For the first time in over five decades, two African Americans—William L. Dawson and Adam Clayton Powell—now sat in Congress. Bills were offered, sponsored by Republicans and Democrats alike, to establish a permanent Fair Employment Practices Commission (FEPC), abolish the poll tax, and make lynching a federal crime. Republican representative Joseph C. Baldwin of New York asserted that in his estimation, the Atlantic Charter (a series of progressive war aims articulated by President Roosevelt and British Prime Minister Winston Churchill) "should begin at home. Surely we can't advocate the principles embodied therein abroad if we don't practice them here at home."

But the U.S. armed forces in fact remained segregated. Notwithstanding the presence of seven hundred thousand blacks in the American army, 60 percent of whom were stationed overseas, less than fifty thousand served in combat, and fewer than six thousand held commissions as officers. Black combat officers were not allowed to command white junior officers, few blacks became pilots, and the War Department appeared determined to maintain Jim Crow strictures. The NAACP fired off a letter to Assistant

Secretary of War John J. McCloy complaining about the humiliating, degrading treatment afforded black army nurses, who were forced to eat in a segregated dining room in the presence of German prisoners of war in Florence, Arizona.

Black newspapers and columnists like Wendell Smith, Sam Lacy of the *Baltimore Afro-American*, Joe Bostic of the *Harlem People's Voice*, and Fay Young of the *Chicago Defender*, along with Lesley Rodney of the *Daily Worker*, had long waged their own battle against segregation during World War II. They called for the eradication of the Jim Crow barrier in the national pastime, underscoring its corrosive effect on the morale of thirteen million African Americans. Brooklyn Dodgers manager Leo Durocher again expressed his willingness to add black players to his ball club.

As they experienced the loss of stars like Hank Greenberg, Bob Feller, Ted Williams, Joe DiMaggio, and now Stan Musial, as well as run-of-the mill players, the major leagues scrambled to fill rosters. Baseball magnates began looking more to Cuban ballplayers, at least those who were not obviously black. The precarious state of the game seemed to be exemplified by the readiness to turn to players right out of American Legion baseball or high school, and the St. Louis Browns' signing of Pete Gray, a one-armed outfielder, to a contract. All the while the Negro leagues continued to flourish with stellar, untapped talent. Columnist Smith charged that this indicated "once again that the big leagues will stop at only one point—where Negroes are concerned—to make money." Demanding the cessation of major league baseball for the duration of the war, the paper editorialized on January 21, 1945, "Organized Baseball, that leech that sucks Democracy's lifeblood, is one of the enemies the Negro soldier and Negro defense worker are fighting."[6]

A series of developments suggested that race relations were hardly improving. Many African Americans were enraged by the trial of the so-called Port Chicago 50, who demanded more stringent safety standards after 320 sailors, including 202 blacks, were killed as explosives were loaded on board two ships bound for the Pacific. The defendants were among 258 sailors who subsequently engaged in a work stoppage, with 208, after agreeing to return to work, nevertheless receiving summary court-martials and three-month prison sentences. The remaining fifty were tried and convicted of mutiny. First Lady Eleanor Roosevelt and the NAACP were among those who protested the convictions. Sixty black medical technicians assigned to the Women's Army Auxiliary Corps, fed up with being given only menial tasks, engaged in a sit-down strike at Fort Devens, Massachusetts, in March 1945. The hospital commander informed the disgruntled WAACs that "black girls" could perform only the lowliest type of work. Four refused orders to return to duty and were arrested. Court-martial proceedings later followed, leading to convictions, sentences of hard labor, and dishonorable discharges.

As spring training for the 1945 major league season opened, organized baseball continued to hew to its own rigidly drawn segregated path, to the chagrin of Wendell Smith and other critics. Smith pointed out in his column of March 10 that black ballplayers remained "conspicuous by their absence" as training camps started operations. Big league magnates sought the federal government's permission to initiate another season, contending that doing so buttressed the nation's morale. Smith called for a congressional investigation of the game's "rigid discriminatory policy" and a condemnation of "this un-American exclusion act" perpetuated by major league baseball annually.[7]

As stories were published of black soldiers eagerly heading into combat and veterans being beaten at the central railroad station in Jackson, Mississippi, by blackjack-packing police determined to enforce segregation ordinances, the Negro leagues readied for the start of their season. League stalwarts such as J. L. Wilkinson of the Kansas City Monarchs, Alex Pompez of the New York Cuban Stars, and Abe Manley of the Newark Eagles met in Chicago in early March. The Monarchs' personnel director, William "Dizzy" Dismukes, announced the signing of former UCLA football great Jackie Robinson as an infielder, which was viewed as a smart move because he was already well known to many African-Americans owing to his collegiate heroics and court-martial. The Monarchs had compiled a storied record, as befitting their greatest players over the years: Satchel Paige, Willard Brown, Bullet Joe Rogan, Hank Thompson, Hilton Smith, and

Cool Papa Bell. Longtime Kansas City second baseman Newt Allen delivered a report on Robinson for Monarch owner Wilkinson: "He's a very smart ball player, but he can't play shortstop—he can't throw from the hole. Try him at second base." Allen reported that Robinson "could run, and he could hit, and most of all he could think."[8] Dismukes agreed with Allen's assessment. He stated that Robinson "can make it at first base, second base, or third base, but he can't go to his right and make the long throw from the shortstop hole. We've got to convince him to play another position."[9] Robinson ended up playing shortstop for the Monarchs after starter Jesse Williams came up with a lame arm.

Shortly after Robinson signed with the Monarchs, President Roosevelt expressed a desire that organized baseball remain in operation. Wendell Smith deemed it unfortunate that Roosevelt, who had fathered the FEPC, had never addressed major league ball's segregation policy. This flew in the face of the president's insistence that employment not be based on race, creed, or color. Such a directive should apply to baseball, Smith contended. The sport was wholly dependent on government support for its very existence at this point. Smith considered it preposterous that baseball was depicted as "the grand old American pastime." It violated "the fundamental principles of Americanism by barring people because of their color and race." Major league baseball was maintaining the very evil American soldiers fought against overseas—racial discrimination and segregation—as "it still clings to the things which Hitler is trying to enforce upon the world." Smith again brought up the issue of one-armed Pete Gray's entrance into the majors while the Homestead Grays' great slugging catcher Josh Gibson was denied a similar opportunity.[10] The Council for Equal Participation in Organized Baseball petitioned FDR in late March 1945 to eradicate the game's racially discriminatory practices. The council insisted the continued exclusion of African American players was democracy's greatest stain.

While in Kansas City, Robinson stayed at the Street Hotel, one of the few in the area to welcome black patrons. He purchased shoes from Matlaw's, a fine clothing store located at 18th and Vine, at the center of Kansas City's black community. Along with New Orleans's Basin Street, Memphis's Beale

Street, New York's 52nd Street, and Los Angeles's Central Avenue, 18th and Vine was long one of the focal points for American jazz. Charlie "Bird" Parker, the brilliant jazz saxophonist, grew up in Kansas City, although he moved to New York City in 1939. Another Kansas City native and a rhythm and blues giant, Big Joe Turner, began his career as a singing bartender, crooning from 18th and Vine. Count Basie, Duke Ellington, Benny Goodman, and Louis Armstrong all floated through town. By the time Jackie arrived in Kansas City, the district's heyday had largely come and gone, along with the political machine headed by boss Tom Pendergast that tolerated alcohol, prostitution, and gambling. Robinson frequented the Ol' Kentuck' Bar-B-Q, a favorite dining spot.

On Sunday afternoon, March 3, he made his Negro league debut against a team of major and minor league all-stars in Houston, Texas. Less than two weeks later, reports circulated that the Boston Red Sox were offering tryouts to three or four top black players. This followed a phone call from Wendell Smith to Isadore Muchnick, a Boston councilman in the midst of a reelection bid in a largely black district. Smith suggested that Muchnick solidify his political base by nailing down tryouts for black players with the Red Sox and the Boston Braves. The *Courier* promised to pay the travel expenses of the ballplayers, several of whose names were being discussed. The paper indicated that tryouts might soon be forthcoming for Cleveland Buckeyes outfielder Sam Jethroe, Homestead Grays outfielder Dave Hoskins, Baltimore Elite Giants catcher Roy Campanella, and Monarchs shortstop Robinson, whose photograph in U.S. military attire was displayed on the *Courier's* front page. After Muchnick threatened to oppose the granting of a license to the Red Sox and the Braves to play Sunday baseball, the two teams agreed to tryouts. Robinson was being considered because his name was already well known to many due to his storied athletic career at UCLA, his brilliant performance in the College All-Star game against the NFL champion Chicago Bears, and his military background. In addition, he was articulate and had played both with and against whites in intercollegiate competition and semipro ball.

The Monarchs' owner, J. L. Wilkinson, was asked if he would allow Robinson to participate in the tryout at Fenway Park, home of the Boston

Red Sox. In relating the story, Smith referred to Robinson as a "sensational" collegiate star who was "being tabbed as the best young shortstop to appear on the Negro baseball scene in years." Wilkinson responded to the query regarding the workout: "I have no objections whatsoever. I wouldn't ever hold back a player if he had a chance to get in the majors." The Cleveland Buckeyes' owner and Negro American League vice president, Ernest Wright, agreed to allow Jethroe, the league's 1944 batting champion with a .353 average, to travel to Boston. "It is all right with me," he replied. "If Jethro(*sic*) has a chance—and I think he is definitely good enough—I'd be the last person to stand in his way. He has my permission to go." The Homestead Grays' business manager, Seward Posey, also indicated that Hoskins, another young Negro league star, could participate. Posey stated, "All I have to do is get an okay from the owners, Cum Posey and Rufus Jackson. I am sure they will not want to stand in Hoskins' way. You can count on his being in Boston."[11]

The Monarchs split an exhibition doubleheader with the Birmingham Black Barons on April 8, with Robinson experiencing a big day in the field and at bat in the opener as Kansas City romped in a shutout, 7–0. Robinson belted out a pair of hits, stole a base, scored a run, and played errorless ball in the field.[12] That same afternoon, two Negro league players—Terry McDuffie, a pitcher with the Newark Eagles, and Dave Thomas, a first baseman with the New York Cubans—participated in a tryout held at the U.S. Military Academy's field house. This followed negotiations involving Joe Bostic, sports editor of the *People's Voice*; Jimmy Smith, a correspondent with the *Courier*; and Branch Rickey, president of the Brooklyn Dodgers. Rickey stated that he would consider "a devil with a forked tail and horns" who might be able to play baseball but expressed displeasure at being forced to hold the tryout.[13] Wendell Smith applauded Bostic and Smith, claiming that they "achieved something no one else has been able to do before. It was, without a doubt, a great step forward, and one that will go down in history as a definite 'first.'" Smith also praised Rickey—soon reported to be interested in purchasing a Negro league franchise—"for being courageous enough to 'play the string out'" and allow the tryout to proceed. Smith contended that future tryouts needed to be lengthier than the one-hour session that had just taken place and that stronger, younger, and more skilled prospects chosen than the thirty-six-year-old McDuffie and the thirty-nine-year-old Thomas, whose best playing days were long past. This was essential because "the eyes of America—white and black will be on them," Smith warned.[14]

After several days passed, the Boston Red Sox reluctantly granted Jethroe, Philadelphia Stars second baseman Marvin Williams, and Robinson a tryout on Monday, April 15. While waiting for the actual tryout, Robinson angrily told Wendell Smith, "Listen, Smith, it burns me up to come fifteen hundred miles to have them give me the runaround." He stated, "We can consider ourselves pioneers. Even if they don't accept us, we are at least doing our part and, if possible, making the way easier for those who follow. Some day some Negro player or players will get a break. We want to help make that day a reality."[15] As he had promised, Monarch owner Wilkinson readily allowed Robinson to participate in the tryout. Along with Councilman Muchnick and Wendell Smith, the players arrived at 10:30 in the morning at Fenway Park, where they were met by Boston manager Joe Cronin and the team's general manager, Eddie Collins. The players worked out for almost two hours under the direction of Red Sox coaches Hugh Duffy and Larry Woodall. One story, offered years later by sportswriter Clif Keane of the *Boston Globe*, had one individual—reputedly either Red Sox owner Tom Yawkey, Cronin, or Collins—holler out, "Get those niggers off the field!" during the tryout.[16]

The *Courier* featured the tryouts, along with pictures of the funeral procession for President Roosevelt, on its front page, indicating that the paper "may break baseball ban." The *Courier* stated that African Americans would grieve FDR's death more than any other group, having benefited from New Deal programs, "the atmosphere of tolerance and goodwill" that the president fostered, and Roosevelt's unprecedented pattern "of inclusion and integration." FDR had failed to support legislation specially designed to safeguard the rights of blacks, including measures intended to make lynching a federal crime, eradicate the poll tax, and make the FEPC a permanent

organization. Still, as C. A. Franklin, editor of the *Kansas City Call*, articulated, many believed "the world has lost its first citizen" and blacks "the
best friend they ever had in the White House." The *Courier* editorialized
that Roosevelt was "The Man!" Many proved ready "to follow him through
the wilderness of war to the Promised Land of freedom."[17]

Wendell Smith wrote that Jethroe, Williams, and Robinson were descen-
dants of Crispus Attucks, the escaped slave who opposed British imperial
policy and became the first victim during the Boston Massacre. All three
men wanted to play in the big leagues, but like many others, they had been
denied the opportunity, owing to racial barriers. Smith likened the young
players to "confounded rebels" ready to contest "the divine right of baseball's
kings."[18] New York's Vito Marcantonio, among the most radical members of
the House of Representatives, broached the possibility of a full-scale inquiry
into organized baseball. Marcantonio declared, "The whole question of discrimination in what purports to be our national game has been discussed too
long behind closed doors." He promised to bring out "into the open" the fact
that major league baseball remained saddled with racially discriminatory
practices. The *Courier* maintained its decade-long campaign to convince big
league managers and owners to offer tryouts to black ballplayers. The editorial staff insisted that managers and players appeared willing to accept
African Americans on their teams. New York newspapers expressed unanimous support for ending baseball's Jim Crow practices. Only the owners
appeared reluctant to discard the sport's color barrier, but they now faced legislative efforts in states like New York to ensure fair employment practices.
The *Courier* worried that legal action would anger managers, players, and
fans alike, place inordinate pressures on black players, and permanently crip-
ple baseball. The paper hoped that big league moguls would "see the light
of reason and abolish the color bar." That would afford "all qualified players a real chance, irrespective of color or creed."[19]

As of late April, the three men who had received tryouts in Boston—
Sam Jethroe, Marvin Williams, and Jackie Robinson—still awaited a
report from Cronin, who was lying in a hospital room with a broken leg.
They did so anxiously, Wendell Smith wrote. Coach Duffy reportedly

declared that Jethroe, Williams, and Robinson were "fine fellows" who had performed "all right." He remained unable to determine whether they were suitable for the Red Sox franchise after the lone workout. Early indications suggested that Cronin, with his Red Sox off to a winless start in six games, had been particularly taken with Robinson and Williams. Joe Cashman of the *Boston Record* stated that Cronin had been "impressed by Robinson's fielding at shortstop. He's good and fast, fast as—well, Jack Robinson." Cronin filed information about Jethroe, Williams, and Robinson among his team's list of baseball prospects. The three players, Cashman indicated, "will be welcomed at some future date to test the sod and sight the targets at Yawkey's green pastures. Further observation may result in the Red Sox signing one of the trio and then schooling at one of the Sox farms." The *New York Post* delivered its own edict on Jim Crow ball as news about the tryouts continued to filter through the baseball world: "Baseball is not a monopoly of lily-whites or gray-greens. It belongs to all the people. It is the typical American game. And so it is part of the American melting pot. Into this sport have come men like Joe DiMaggio, an Italian; Hank Greenberg, a Jew; Alejandro Carrasquel, a Cuban; Lou Gehrig, a German; Sigmund Jacucki, a Pole, and others." The *Post* then pointedly stated, "There should be a place waiting in it for the ten per cent of Americans who are Negroes."[20]

The saga regarding Jethroe, Williams, and Robinson continued. The *Courier* expressed appreciation that the Red Sox, like the Dodgers under Branch Rickey, seemed to have given them a genuine tryout. This stood in sharp contrast to the Pittsburgh Pirates, whose owner, William Benswanger, had backtracked on a promise in 1942 to afford African American players a similar opportunity. Benswanger's excuse was that his plans had been "interfered with," without explaining what that meant. Rickey's name was also discussed in relation to the new United States League founded by Gus Greenlee and led by John G. Shackleford of Cleveland. Rickey's involvement, Smith suggested, might "result in a mild revolution" that could prove beneficial to both blackball and white baseball. In his column of April 28, 1945, Smith wrote that Rickey was clearly—albeit "in some vague" manner—interested in the Negro leagues and black players. Smith credited Rickey with being the first top figure in major league baseball to grant black players tryouts. Rickey also recently became the first big league magnate "to inject himself forcefully into the structure of so-called organized Negro baseball." Rickey's backing could enable the United States League to thrive, Smith believed. More important, speculation abounded regarding "what Branch Rickey intends to do about Negro candidates applying for positions with his Brooklyn Dodgers." Fans across the nation hoped that Rickey would "in the near future, employ at least one Negro player." No matter whether he did so or not, Rickey was owed "every possible kind of consideration, and above all, the benefit of doubt," Smith acknowledged. He was obviously sincere and had actually supervised the tryout conducted by the Dodgers.[21]

Smith and Rickey established a firmer relationship centered on the need to integrate organized baseball. At a meeting in Rickey's office in Brooklyn, Smith urged Rickey to sign Robinson to a contract. He told him that Jackie was "really good major league material" and suggested that Rickey make Robinson "Exhibit No. 1" in the quest to end segregated baseball.[22] The sportswriter and the famed baseball executive continued to discuss this very possibility over the next several months.[23]

Baseball owners named Senator Albert B. "Happy" Chandler, former governor of the state of Kentucky, as the new commissioner of organized baseball on April 24, 1945. The position had remained vacant following the death the previous November of Kenesaw Mountain Landis, who had been appointed to the job in November 1920 after news about the fixed 1919 World Series began to leak. Landis immediately acquired a reputation as a stern taskmaster, banishing eight members of the Chicago White Sox, including the peerless hitter, "Shoeless Joe" Jackson, implicated in a conspiracy to throw baseball's premier spectacle to the Cincinnati Reds. Ruling with an iron fist, Landis also achieved notoriety for refusing to end baseball's color barrier. Shortly after assuming the position of baseball commissioner, Landis attempted to prevent barnstorming ventures that pitted major and minor league players against Negro league performers. He rigidly maintained baseball's color barrier while insisting that no such edifice existed. Even during World War II, as the quality of major league baseball plummeted with stars and average players alike entering the U.S. Armed Forces, Landis refused to entertain the possibility of integrating the national pastime. On hearing that the Pittsburgh Pirates were thinking about signing Josh Gibson to a contract, Landis exclaimed, "The colored ballplayers have their own league. Let them stay in their own league." Landis's replacement by Chandler engendered hope among the editorialists at the *Courier*, who contended that the new commissioner could "immortalize himself and redeem the good name of baseball" by helping to remove the sport's "color bar." The paper now went further in stating, "Everybody knows that there are dozens of young Negro baseball players who are capable of playing on major league teams or on their farm teams." The *Courier* predicted that "their inclusion would add color and life to the game."[24] Rickey later revealed that during the meeting in which Chandler was elected commissioner, the owners voted 15–1 against integrating organized baseball. Several owners subsequently denied Rickey's charge, which came out three years later.[25]

Ric Roberts, assigned to the Washington Bureau by the *Courier*, conducted an interview with Chandler following the senator's selection as baseball commissioner. Chandler told them, "If it's discrimination you are afraid of, you have nothing to fear from me. Look at my record in Kentucky as Governor and you will discover that I have always tried to be fair with and considerate of colored people." He then stated, "Let's see now. Negroes are active in most of the major sports in this country, aren't they?" Affirming this, the reporters noted that baseball remained segregated. Chandler asked if they would allow him to devise policies favorable to African Americans. Admitting that he had "often been in error" in his political career, Chandler insisted "there never has been any question about my stand in any matter; when I feel that I am right there is no middle ground or compromise." Likening himself to Branch Rickey, Chandler stated, "My attitude toward Negro ball players is the same as toward any ball player. I am in there to win ball games and I like winning ball players, whatever their origin or race."

Chandler expressed no concerns about admitting black players into organized baseball. "Hell yes," he said. "If a black boy can make it on Guadalcanal, he can make it in baseball."[26]

The Negro American and National Leagues opened their latest season in early May, led by the defending champion Birmingham Black Barons and Washington Homestead Grays. The Grays had won the Negro National League each of the past eight years and were favored to prevail yet again with the return of catcher Josh Gibson and first baseman Buck Leonard. Despite the presence of the great Satchel Paige on the mound and the addition of one-time college star Jackie Robinson, the Kansas City Monarchs were predicted to finish near the bottom of the five-team Negro American League. Cum Posey, secretary of the Negro National League, discussed the beginning of the season and called for a Negro league commissioner, suggesting Judge W. C. Houston, former assistant to the postmaster general, as a possibility. Posey dismissed the recent visits by black players to the Dodgers training camp and Fenway Park. "To say these players got tryouts by major league clubs is a travesty." He charged, "It was the most humiliating experience Negro baseball has yet suffered from white organized baseball." The so-called tryouts involved only hitting and catching for a little while, except in the case of McDuffie, who tossed a few balls.[27]

Paige sent a letter to Wendell Smith regarding baseball's color barrier. The legendary pitcher insisted that tryouts would never work for big league managers and that owners would always discover "fault with our very best players." He insisted that the Negro leagues should instead organize a squad of All-Stars to go head-to-head with the finest major league team. Paige refuted the notion that the Negro leagues did not feature many good black players, pointing to Leonard and Gibson, among others.[28]

Following the surrender of Germany on May 7, 1945, the *Courier* recounted its role and that of black soldiers in World War II. Black troops "wrote glorious chapters in the names which are now legion," having fought in North Africa, Sicily, Italy, Normandy, Bastogne, the Ardennes, and on many other battlegrounds. Black soldiers "fought and toiled, bled and died, to wipe out the insult of Adolf Hitler and to purge the world of the Nazi philosophy of a 'superior race.'" Seven years earlier, the *Courier's* editor-publisher, the late Robert L. Vann, had gone to the White House to urge President Roosevelt to help eradicate Jim Crow in the U.S. military. Foreseeing another world war, the *Courier* had been "determined that Negro boys . . . not be subjected to the treatment they had received in the other world war."[29]

Commissioner Chandler agreed to discuss the fate of black players in organized baseball but refused to answer the question regarding their possible entry into the major leagues. Speaking with a reporter from the *Defender*, he said, "I am not sure the Negroes know whether they favor it or not. But this is a free country and everybody should have an equal opportunity. It does not follow, however, that by sitting two men down side by side that you're giving them equal opportunities." He continued, "I know nothing, from fact, of any discrimination against Negroes in the big leagues. There is a [*sic*] no rule against them. On the other hand, nobody can guarantee that they can make the grade. That's a matter of their own ability."[30] The president of the New York Yankees, Larry MacPhail, discussed a means to admit black players into organized baseball. Two Negro leagues could be permitted to play in big league ballparks with a certain number of players admitted into the major or minor leagues. "An all-Negro world series, and possibly an interracial series" would follow, MacPhail predicted.[31] The Kansas City Monarchs, meanwhile, won their home opener against the Chicago American Giants, 6–2, before a crowd estimated at 15,000. New shortstop Jackie Robinson helped turn a double play, smacked a double in four trips to the plate, stole a base, and scored a run.

The *Boston Globe* published an editorial lending support to the campaign to integrate organized baseball, declaring, "Negro men and women shine gloriously in all other athletic and professional fields—in science, law, medicine, music, the movies and the theatre. In baseball they surely might produce players comparable to Babe Ruth or Georgia's Ty Cobb." The *Globe* suggested "an intensive educational campaign" might help lessen the intolerance that kept blacks from competing on an even plane in baseball.[32] As organized baseball remained segregated in the United

States, black players like the stellar third baseman Ray Dandridge starred in the newly formed Mexican League. During the opening stages of the Negro leagues season, the Kansas City Monarchs stood atop the American League, while the perennial champion Washington Homestead Grays held the lead in the National League. With Satchel Paige, Hilton Smith, and rookie Jackie Robinson, the Monarchs proved a popular ball club, often selling out before the home crowd at Ruppert Stadium (which seated 17,000) and on the road.

Robinson became discontented with Negro league operations shortly after he joined the Monarchs. He found it strange that that the Monarchs never sent him a formal contract. He also disliked that spring training amounted to baseball contests rather than training exercises. Robinson's disillusionment only became more pronounced as the season began. Time away from the friendly confines of Kansas City frequently proved difficult at best for Jackie, as Negro league baseball tended to be inadequately financed, promoted, and managed. Travel schedules were "unbelievably hectic." Teams traveled throughout the Midwest, into the South, and back to the East. In his autobiography, Robinson reported, "For me, it turned out to be a pretty miserable way to make a buck. When I look back at what I had to go through in black baseball, I can only marvel at the many black players who stuck it out for years in the Jim Crow leagues because they had nowhere else to go." As he recalled,

Finding satisfactory or even passable eating places was almost a daily problem. There was no hotel in many of the places we played. Sometimes there was a hotel for blacks which had no eating facilities. No one even thought of trying to get accommodations at white hotels. Some of the crummy eating joints would not serve us at all. You could never sit down to a relaxed hot meal. You were lucky if they magnanimously permitted you to carry out some greasy hamburger in a paper bag with a container of coffee. You were really living when you were able to get a plate of cold cuts. You ate on board the team bus or on the road.[33]

Teammate Othello Renfroe recalled Robinson's becoming so angry on encountering segregated services stations in Mississippi that "we had to leave without our change."[34] Pitcher Hilton Smith, Robinson's roommate, told Buck O'Neil, a longtime Monarch player then stationed in the U.S. Navy, of an incident at a service station in Muskogee, Oklahoma. Players had purchased enough gas to fill up a pair of fifty-gallon tanks but were repeatedly denied use of the restroom. On one occasion, as the team bus rolled next to the gas pump so the store owner could begin filling the tank, Robinson headed for the restroom only to have the owner call out, "Hey, boy! You know you can't go in there." Robinson asked why not, and the owner replied, "Because we don't allow colored people in that restroom." Jackie calmly ordered the man, "Take the hose out of the tank." As the man hesitated Robinson repeated his demand and then told the other Monarchs, "Let's go. We don't want his gas." The owner was now concerned about losing a major purchase. He put the hose back into the tank and stated, "All right, you boys can use the restroom. But don't stay long."[35]

White ballplayers, Robinson recognized, possessed the opportunity to achieve "prominence or even stardom." But he wondered what black players could aspire to despite demands by black sportswriters and a small number of politicians that organized baseball be integrated. And yet as he later admitted, "I never expect the [Jim Crow] walls to come tumbling down in my lifetime." He instead reflected on other job prospects. He recognized that Rachel was becoming impatient. The two rarely saw one another because of his baseball schedule. Jackie "felt unhappy and trapped." If he abandoned baseball, then where would he go? Robinson wondered. "What could I do to earn enough money to help my mother and to marry Rachel?" he reflected.[36]

Meanwhile, Clark Griffith, owner of Washington's other baseball team, the Senators, indicated that Branch Rickey should stay out of black baseball. In his column of May 26, 1945, Wendell Smith defended Rickey while acknowledging that no one understood exactly why the Dodgers boss had suddenly demonstrated such an interest in blackball. Smith criticized Griffith as "one of the most bitter opponents" of those urging the integration of organized baseball. Griffith had refused to genuinely consider hiring two longtime Homestead Grays teammates, the peerless Buck Leonard and Josh Gibson. In contrast to Rickey, Griffith had failed to grant any tryouts to black ballplayers. He preferred to champion baseball's version of "white supremacy," Smith wrote. The columnist likened Griffith to Mississippi's John E. Rankin and Theodore G. Bilbo, who served in the House of Representatives and the U.S. Senate, respectively, and espoused rabidly racist beliefs. Griffith willingly brought in players from Cuba, Mexico, and Venezuela but drew the line when it came to African Americans. Smith charged that selfish economic reasons explained this to some extent, as the Washington owner rented out Griffith Stadium to the Homestead Grays. "Although he makes his money in the shadow of the Capitol of the United States, Griffith is in no way democratic on this issue of Negroes in the majors."[37] J. Cordell White of Kansas City, Kansas, subsequently fired off a letter to Griffith calling for a seven-game series between the Monarchs and the Senators, with the purchase of war bonds required for admission.[38]

At a still-early point in the Negro leagues campaign, the Monarchs headed for New Orleans, where they played the Birmingham Black Barons. Residents of New Orleans were said to be eagerly awaiting the game because of the anticipated appearance of Jackie Robinson. In an earlier game in New Orleans, Robinson had shone in the field, at the plate, and on the base paths. It increasingly appeared likely that Robinson and teammate Satchel Paige would be invited to participate in the top Negro league spectacle, the All-Star contest, which the Office of Defense Transportation was allowing to be held once again. That undoubtedly pleased Monarchs owner J. L. Wilkinson, the one white man in the upper ranks of the Negro leagues. Wendell Smith sang Wilkinson's praises, declaring that he "not only invested his money, but his very heart and soul" in his franchise for over twenty years. Wilkinson had helped Negro league founder Rube Foster establish organized black baseball in 1920, laying the foundation for the present Negro leagues. Significant too was the fact that Wilkinson was one of the few Negro league owners who "never pulled his punches on the issue of Negro players in the majors." Smith wrote, "While others have been blinded by their own selfish interests and would keep the Negro player in the bonds of slavery, [Wilkinson] has always said that a Negro player in the majors would help Negro baseball. He has never hemmed and hawed on this subject; has never compromised nor double-talked it."[39]

Jim Crow baseball continued throughout the summer of 1945 as veterans, including the Detroit Tigers' Hank Greenberg, slowly began to return to the minor and major leagues, and the Negro leagues' campaign proceeded. About a quarter into the season, the Homestead Grays, led by a hot-hitting Josh Gibson, held a comfortable lead in the Negro National League. The Cleveland Buckeyes, led by Sam Jethroe, had a one-and-a-half game advantage in the Negro American League. Jethroe was batting .381, ten points behind Jackie Robinson, who had belted out twenty-seven hits in sixty-nine at bats, along with scoring nineteen runs in twenty games. Six games later, the Monarchs had slid to third place in the Negro American League. Jethroe and Robinson had changed places in the race for the batting title, even though Jackie had cracked out seven straight hits in a doubleheader against the Homestead Grays, attended by more than twenty thousand fans.

The Kansas City Monarchs limped to the season's halfway mark, but Robinson continued to shine and was linked with Art Wilson of Birmingham and Jose Canizares of Cleveland as one of the "future greats of tomorrow." Having played twenty-eight games and compiled one hundred official at bats, Robinson had garnered thirty-five hits—including six doubles, four triples, and a pair of homers—for a .350 batting average. He had also scored twenty-five runs, batted in nineteen, and stolen seven bases. Wilson was already serving as captain of the Black Barons, while Canizares, a native of Cuba, and Robinson were seen as "the sparkplugs" of their respective infields. In his column of July 14, 1945, Wendell Smith again referred to Robinson's tryout with the Boston Red Sox and asserted that manager Joe Cronin had acknowledged that "Robinson had major league possibilities." All three of these outstanding young shortstops "should be given a chance to play in the major leagues," Smith wrote.[40] Black newspapers reported that interest in the fast-approaching Negro league All-Star game, where one or more of the three young shortstops was likely to play, was soaring, with a crowd of over 40,000 expected at Chicago's Comiskey Park. Meanwhile, New York assemblyman Philip J. Schupler fired off a letter to Branch Rickey, regarding talk that the Dodgers might rehire Babe Herman, who had not played in the majors since 1937. Proclaiming himself a stalwart Dodgers fan, Schupler suggested instead that Brooklyn hire black players to improve the team's performance and demonstrate belief in fair play.

Kansas City began the second half of the Negro league season in grand style by winning six in a row. Lineups for the Negro league All-Star game were announced and included most of the biggest names in black baseball. Willie Wells, Buck Leonard, Josh Gibson, Martín Dihigo, Roy Campanella, and Biz Mackey were on the favored East squad. The West roster contained players like Alex Radcliffe, Neil Robinson, Satchel Paige, and Jackie Robinson, now batting .333 for the year. Wendell Smith built up the event. He referred to it as "the most colorful, spectacular show in the whirling, dizzy sport world," where "the million dollar gems of the Negro National League match speed, brains and brawn with the sparkling jewels of the Negro American League."[41] The underdog West prevailed 9–6 in the game at Comiskey Park, although Robinson went hitless in five trips to the plate. No matter, since his appearance in Chicago, like his play in the Negro leagues, helped keep Robinson's name in the public limelight, where it remained for the rest of his life.

8

Greenberg Returns

During the 1944 off season, *Baseball Magazine* rendered an accounting of wartime service by major leaguers. Sportswriter Herbert Simons indicated that almost five hundred big leaguers had entered the U.S. Armed Forces. The *New York Times* reported in January 1945 that only four hundred of fifty-eight hundred professional ballplayers were not in the U.S. military. Scores of those athletes gave their lives for their country, including two former major leaguers in combat: Harry O'Neill, who had played in one contest as a Philadelphia Athletic, perished on Iwo Jima, and Elmer Gedeon, who had played in the outfield for the Washington Senators, was a bomber pilot shot down over France. White Sox pitcher Gene Stack died in a training camp. Both Philadelphia Athletics pitcher Phil Marchildon and Cincinnati hurler Millard Howell were POWs in Germany. Several players were wounded in action, including minor league pitcher Bert Shepard, who lost the lower portion of his right leg but later made an appearance in one major league contest for the Senators. Cecil Travis, a stellar shortstop with the Senators, suffered frostbite during the Battle of the Bulge. Dodgers outfielder Elmer "Red" Durrett experienced shell shock on Guadalcanal. St. Louis Cardinals outfielder Harry Walker earned a Purple Heart after suffering injuries in a clash with German forces. Cleveland Indians pitcher Lou Brissie received one following a shell explosion during the Italian campaign.

Hank Greenberg was the first major league star to enter the U.S. Armed Forces after Pearl Harbor and the one who lost the largest amount of playing time because of the war. He appeared in only nineteen games during the 1941 season due to military service, and then following his reenlistment in December of that year, missed the next three-and-a-half seasons. He entered the U.S. Army as a thirty-year-old superstar, just coming off a second MVP campaign in which he won his third home run and RBI titles while leading the Detroit Tigers to their third pennant in seven years. Arthur Daley offered a column on Greenberg that appeared in the February 14, 1945, edition of the *Times*. Daley declared, "He is a true credit to all sport."[1] Greenberg was decommissioned in June 1945, having earned four battle stars along with a Presidential Unit Citation. Finally returning to Tiger Stadium in July 1945, Greenberg was thirty-four years old, an age when many players had passed their peak or left the game altogether.

Other major league greats also lost years of their playing career due to service during World War II. Cleveland Indians fireballing right hander Bob Feller missed almost four full seasons, having just completed years in which he had won twenty-four, twenty-seven, and twenty-five games and had led the league in strikeouts four years running. "Rapid Bob" left the majors at the age of twenty-two, to return late in the 1945 season at the age of twenty-six with his fastball still intact. It would hold up for only another season or two. Boston outfielder Ted Williams, who also spent nearly two full years in the military as an aviator during the Korean War, entered the U.S. military following the 1942 season, not returning to the majors until 1946. The "Splendid Splinter" did so having hit .406 in 1941 and .356 the next year, when he turned twenty-four. Joe DiMaggio, the peerless center fielder known as the Yankee Clipper, spent the same amount of time as Williams in military attire during World War II, going in as a twenty-seven-year-old and coming out a thirty-one-year-old Army veteran. St. Louis Cardinals outfielder Stan Musial, "Stan the Man," missed out only on the 1945 campaign when he was twenty-four-years-old. The quality of major league ball suffered accordingly as many other players enlisted or were drafted. The long-basement-dwelling St. Louis Browns—who boasted more 4-F (not qualified for service) men than any other team—won their only American League pennant in 1944, although they fell to the crosstown

Cardinals in the World Series. With the quality of baseball obviously in question, talk of integration picked up once again.

Greenberg left the U.S. military in June 1945, having been out of baseball for the equivalent of four-and-a-half seasons. The *Detroit Free Press* excitedly indicated that the Tigers slugger was "back in town!" Greenberg posed for photographs after landing at the airport. He confirmed, "I'll be out at the ballpark early in the morning. There are a few things about a fast ball I'm anxious to find out. Chiefly, if I can still hit one." Tan and fit, Greenberg continued, "Fact is, I feel even better than I did then," referring to his departure from the major leagues in 1941. Greenberg revealed that he weighed about 210 pounds, five less than during his last stint with the Tigers. Asked when he might return to the lineup, Greenberg replied, "That is a very good question. Frankly, I don't know. I haven't swung at a baseball for a long long time. I haven't looked at a fly ball for just as long. But I feel like I can step back in there." He then suggested it would take a couple of weeks to get his timing down. Greenberg revealed that he had attempted to fly out of New York twenty-four hours earlier but had been bumped off the plane. "Right then I tell myself, 'Hank,' I says, 'you're a civilian again.'" Uncertain where he would play in the field, as Jimmy Outlaw had taken over in left field, Greenberg stated, "I just want to find out if I still can hit that ball. Where I play doesn't make a bit of difference. If I hit, I imagine I'll get in there someplace."[2]

Al Simmons, once one of baseball's greatest right-handed hitters, discussed Greenberg's impending return to major league baseball. Simmons stated, "This is the test for all ball players past thirty who have been away for more than a year." Refuting contentions long made by others, Simmons declared, "Hank has more equipment than the rest of 'em, more natural ability. He'll come back in good shape, because he's always kept himself in shape. And he'll be out there working at 8 o'clock every morning if necessary to get back on his stride." Then Simmons warned, "If he doesn't make it, the rest of 'em might as well not try. They better just take what pay they're entitled to and go home to the farm."[3] *The Sporting News* noted that no baseball player had sought reentry into the game after such an extended period of time. Writing for the Associated Press on June 22, Whitney Martin reported on Greenberg's return to the Tigers lineup. "No athlete ever had more horseshoes or other good luck tokens draped around his neck than the genial giant from the Bronx," Martin offered. "There isn't a fan or a rival player who doesn't wish for Big Hank anything but the best of luck." As for the fans, they "wish him well because he always was a gentleman and a credit to the game, and because they admire him for his army record." The players too "are pulling for him because, in addition to being a fine fellow, he is more than just a baseball player trying to resume an interrupted career." Greenberg "will be watched as a symbol of hope to all the other ballplayers in the service who fear their absence from the game might impair their effectiveness and money-earning capacity. He is in the nature of a test case; the answer to the question: Can the Major League stars in the service come back?" Greenberg was after all "the first of the really outstanding stars to try a comeback after a prolonged service in which he and baseball were strangers." Greenberg was now "34 years old, an age at which making a sports comeback after a long absence comes under the heading of almost super-human tasks. But he's the fellow [who] could do it if anyone could," Martin offered. Greenberg possessed "tenacity of purpose," as he had displayed during both his military service and playing career. "You can bet he won't let his buddies down by failing to make the grade," Martin predicted.[4]

Greenberg's anticipated return to the majors was important for another reason. He was the greatest Jewish star in America's favorite sport, hardly an insignificant matter, particularly given recent revelations that suggested the enormity of Nazi perfidy. During the spring of 1945, the war in Europe ended as Allied soldiers entered the death camps, where Hitler's henchmen had worked overtime to bring about the führer's Final Solution. It took time to unveil the approximate number of Jews slaughtered in Europe's killing fields. Those included villages, towns, large cities, and concentration camps alike, along with actual extermination centers at Auschwitz, Treblinka, Chelmno, Sobibór, Majdanek, and Belzec. The butchery evidenced by piles of bones and bodies and by the haunted, gaunt visages and emaciated bodies of the displaced persons was all too obvious as British,

Soviet, and American troops entered the inhumane abattoirs designed to annihilate European Jewry altogether. Jews in particular, but certainly others as well, consequently attained satisfaction from watching or reading about the exploits of their brethren who excelled in the military and in civilian life.

As the *Free Press* sports columnist Lyall Smith noted, Hank Greenberg's Tigers teammates readied for the return of his "big bat" to the Tiger lineup.[5] Smith reported on Hank's reappearance at Briggs Stadium. Wearing his uniform with the famous number 5 displayed, Greenberg was warmly greeted by teammates. Serving as batting pitcher, manager Steve O'Neill asked, "Ready, Hank?" when Greenberg strode up to the plate. With photographers recording his actions, Greenberg ripped at the first pitch. He drove it back hard at O'Neill, who was sheltered by a screen. Swinging at the next offering, Greenberg displayed "the same effortless grace" he had before his military service, the ball flying out to left field where it landed inches from the stands. Infielder Eddie Mayo exclaimed, "How about that? That guy is ready to get in there right now. He really can swing." Greenberg departed from home plate after a few more strokes, with one more ball driven deep to left. Fans scattered throughout the park applauded. Greenberg next headed for left field. Smith reported, "If he has been gone from baseball since 1941, his actions didn't show it." In Smith's estimation, Greenberg "still moves with loping ease." While clearly not pushing his throwing arm, "he still was pegging the ball easily and accurately." He also easily participated in infield drills at first base. Greenberg blurted out afterward, "Whew," with sweat dripping from his face. "Feels pretty good. It feels pretty good." Smith indicated that the Tigers had just hired "a small boy to sit out in the left field stands and throw back the balls Hank hits in there."[6] The *Free Press* displayed a cartoon image of Greenberg two days later with the heading, "Hank Can Provide an Answer." The newspaper suggested that DiMaggio, Williams, and New York Giants slugger Johnny Mize would track Greenberg's progress.[7]

Smith indicated on Sunday, June 26, 1945, that Greenberg was returning to the Tiger lineup for that day's doubleheader against the Philadelphia

Athletics. Detroit general manager Jack Zeller stated, "Hank says he's ready to play. All that has been bothering him are his hands. He has been growing a pretty heavy set of blisters, but he thinks he'll be all right." Smith noted that Greenberg had been hitting well in batting practice against Bill Crouch, who was acting "as his private pitcher." Still, he was returning to the majors after the equivalent of "only 10 days of spring training." But he had worked hard and had left the army in such good shape that he appeared to be making the transition easily.[8]

The June 30, 1945, edition of the *Free Press* contained a picture of Greenberg with his bat cocked, apparently staring intently at the pitcher. The headline read, "Welcome Back, Hank Greenberg," with the subheading, "A Great Soldier, A Great Ball Player." The paid advertisement by the J. L. Hudson Company stated, "All Detroit is Rooting for You and the Tigers—Hit 'em Hank!" It read:

> You served your country well for more than four years. In the Army your indomitable will to succeed helped you go to the ladder steadily from private to captain. Wherever your duties placed you, whatever your assignment, you carried it out zealously and with characteristic thoroughness.
>
> And now you are back home again. May your return to civilian action be signalized by the crashing zing of base hits. And may your success serve as concrete encouragement to the millions of your comrades who some day soon will be picking up the old-time ties.[9]

Now thirty-four years old but quickly demonstrating that he still possessed a quick bat, Greenberg appeared in his first game back on July 1 before almost 48,000 cheering fans at Briggs Stadium in Detroit. The Tigers were in the midst of a heated pennant race. Greenberg again rose to the occasion, belting a homer—the 250th in his career and his 1,300th hit altogether—off Charlie Gassaway in the 8th inning to help the Tigers defeat the Athletics 9–5. Spectators enveloped Hank as he crossed home plate. Detroit now led New York by 3½ games.

Sportswriter Herbert Simons in *Baseball Magazine* later asserted that Greenberg's return to the majors "was the first of the major post-Service debuts after V-E day." Simons emphasized, "Its significance was far broader than the personal future of the tall, handsome slugger or the success it indicated for the Tigers." For "each blow broadcast to all players all over the world as they awaited V-J day and separation from the armed forces that they could come back successfully in their chosen profession, despite the inroads of war and the millions of pessimistic words authored during the conflict on the improbability of baseball comebacks." Yet to be determined "was how their legs would stand up." Batting eyes and pitching arms appeared to be in good shape, if Greenberg's performance and that of forty-year-old hurler Red Ruffing were any indication.[10]

On August 19, Yankees outfielder Charlie Keller came back to the big leagues after 20 months in maritime service. He belted a homer his third game back, at Comiskey Park. On August 24, Bob Feller returned to the majors, appearing before 46,477 spectators in Cleveland Stadium. Feller had served for 44 months in the U.S. Navy, much of that time aboard the USS *Alabama*, having won 5 campaign ribbons and 8 battle stars. In his first game back, only two days after being deactivated from military service, Feller bested Tiger ace Hal Newhouser, striking out 12 in a 4–2 victory. Detroit's Tommy Bridges, now thirty-eight years old, returned from nearly twenty-four months in the Navy, beating the Chicago White Sox 6–5 on Labor Day, with 53,953 fans present at Briggs Stadium during the thick of the pennant race.

American Jews delighted not only in Greenberg's baseball heroics but in the announcement on September 8 that Bess Myerson, a dark-haired beauty from the Bronx, had become the first Jew to win the Miss America competition. Myerson, like Greenberg, declined to downplay her Jewish ancestry, dismissing exhortations by Miss America officials that she change her name. Myerson actually came from far less comfortable environs than Greenberg. She grew up in a Jewish immigrant family in New York City that was working class and associated with the socialist movement. A graduate of Hunter College, Myerson entered the beauty contest, hoping to win the $5,000 top prize that might enable her to pursue graduate studies in music.

The journalist Andrew Kopkind explained three-and-a-half decades later how the exploits of Greenberg and Myerson affected him in 1945, when he was only ten years old. Kopkind admitted, "I can think of no public personages in all the succeeding years whom I've followed with such fawning." The baseball slugger and the beauty queen seemed as if "secular saints," who were "symbols of a sudden legitimacy which my family and friends seemed to sense in a nation under reconstruction." Both Greenberg and Myerson "were winners," in the fashion of the Yankee Clipper Joe DiMaggio and movie star Betty Grable, whose pinup had been revered by American GIs during the war. But Kopkind considered Greenberg and Myerson even "smarter." They appeared "as American as apple pie and the Fourth of July—and as Jewish as knishes and Yom Kippur." For a generation of American Jews, who had experienced anti-Semitism even in their native country and now were becoming more fully cognizant of the Holocaust in Europe, Greenberg and Myerson represented something special. They "belonged to a race of victors, not victims," transcending the stereotyping experienced by other well-known Jews. "For the first time, the Jews had successfully crossed over from ethnic favorites to national heroes without being isolated or absorbed." In addition, both Greenberg and Myerson's ancestors were Russian, Kopkind mistakenly asserted, and the success of the two stars demonstrated how American Jews with Eastern European roots were matching the accomplishments of their German American Jewish brethren.[11]

On September 30, the Tigers, having clinched a tie for the pennant, battled against the defending American League champion St. Louis Browns in a hard-fought contest. The Browns captured the lead, 3–2, in the bottom of the 8th inning. In the top of the 9th, Hub Walker pinch hit for pitcher Hal Newhouser, who was soon named American League MVP once again. Walker managed a single. Attempting to bunt Walker over to second, Skeeter Webb tapped the ball to first base, but the attempted force out of Walker left all hands safe. A sacrifice bunt moved Walker to third and Webb to second. Browns manager Luke Sewell ordered pitcher Nelson Potter to intentionally walk Doc Cramer, thereby loading the bases. Suffering from "a charley horse, blistered hands, a sore arm and a sprained ankle," Greenberg stepped to the plate. With the count even at one ball and one strike, Potter delivered the pitch. Greenberg hit it cleanly—he recognized that a screwball was coming—driving it well into the left field bleachers for a grand slam that effectively clinched the pennant for the Tigers. The *New York Times* asserted, "Never was a title won in more dramatic fashion." The paper reported that Greenberg's teammates cheered him at the plate after he rounded the bases and then again in the locker room as the celebration of the Tigers' seventh American League crown began.[12] Greenberg later heard that members of the second-place Washington Senators complained, "Goddamn that dirty Jew bastard, he beat us again."[13]

The front page of the *Free Press* on October 1, 1945, exulted, "Hank's Bat Wins Flag." Lyall Smith saluted Greenberg as "a champion of champions!" Smith cheered, "Call him the hero of Bengaltown!" and praised Greenberg as the man who delivered the winning blow to enable the Tigers to capture the pennant. "Drama . . . thrills . . . nerve-wracking realization of a frustrated dream of 1944. They all were there," Smith wrote. The reporter talked about the outcome of the game falling "on the shoulders of Big Hank. . . . the man who came back from four years in the service of his country to play baseball."[14] The *Free Press*'s sports section contained a picture of joyous teammates greeting Hank as he crossed home plate. Iffy the Dopester recalled the moment "when Homer Hank, the Big Greenberg Boy, came out of the Army after four years of service" and went to bat for the first time in a clutch situation. Tigers pitcher Tommy Bridges had said, "Iffy, I would give everything but my pitchin' arm to see the Big Feller smash one." Greenberg proceeded to do exactly that. Iffy applauded Greenberg's latest dramatic home run and the comeback occurring "at his age, after four years away from the plate." It "took the ultimate in courage and dogged determination" to regain "the old rhythm. Hank's hands were bleeding and raw and looked like hunks of beefsteak," but he simply refused to quit. "And that's why he moves today into the hall of immortals," Iffy wrote.[15]

Playing in 78 regular season games, Greenberg rapped out 20 doubles and 13 home runs, compiled 60 RBIs, and batted .311, while the Tigers drew 400,000 more fans than the previous season. He then starred in the World Series against the Chicago Cubs. Greenberg smashed a three-run homer to provide the winning margin in a 4–1 game two victory and helped Detroit prevail in seven games, delivering a pair of homers and driving in seven runs. The Tigers received a record share $8,000 apiece for capturing the World Series. Asked about his plans following the season, Greenberg replied, "Collapse!"[16] The *Free Press* saluted the Tigers for having accomplished on the playing field what the city had contributed in the way of war production. In early December, the Newspaper Guild of New York gave out "Page One Awards" to several distinguished individuals, including the late war correspondent Ernie Pyle, Gen. Dwight David Eisenhower, Eleanor Roosevelt, cartoonist Bill Mauldin, actor-singer Bing Crosby, Hollywood director Frank Capra, and Greenberg.

The ability of Hank Greenberg to return to the majors and perform nearly at the level he had before the war, when he was arguably the game's greatest slugger, was a stunning testament to both his devotion to the game and work ethic. The accomplishments particularly resonated with American Jews, who by the end of the 1945 season were more fully aware of the enormity of the Holocaust that had decimated European Jewry. Greenberg's stardom, like Bess Myerson's triumph, must have represented hope and the possibility that a brighter day might be forthcoming.

9

The Signing of Jackie Robinson

Discussion regarding segregation in organized baseball gathered momentum by August 1945 during the heat of the major league pennant races, following a series of "behind closed door" sessions and the picketing of major league ballparks. New York mayor Fiorello H. LaGuardia set up a biracial committee headed by Charles Evans Hughes Jr., the former U.S. solicitor general, to examine the issue. Yankees president Larry MacPhail represented the American League, and Dodgers president and general manager Branch Rickey, the National League, while former judges, educators, a minister, and *New York Times* sportswriter Arthur Daley also sat on the committee. The mayor referred to baseball as America's national game and noted that many ballplayers were themselves the children of immigrants. Committee member MacPhail admitted that if the Negro leagues collapsed, the Yankees would lose income from black teams playing at Yankee Stadium and in top minor league parks in Newark, Kansas City, and Norfolk.

A report circulated in mid-August that Kansas City Monarchs shortstop Jackie Robinson had agreed to coach football at Samuel Huston College in Austin, Texas. Robinson denied the report. He indicated instead that he might play for the Pacific Coast Professional Football League, a rival of the National Football League, which maintained Jim Crow standards of its own. Founded in 1940, the PCPFL featured Kenny Washington, who, playing alongside Robinson in the backfield, had been an All-American halfback at UCLA. Robinson had played for the semipro Los Angeles Bulldogs in 1941. But as *Pittsburgh Courier* columnist Wendell Smith continued his campaign to integrate organized baseball, Robinson received a call from Brooklyn Dodgers scout Clyde Sukeforth, who indicated that Branch Rickey wanted to meet with him. A strong sense of morality evidently drove Rickey, who had been a longtime baseball executive with the St. Louis Cardinals and the Dodgers. Rickey often spoke of his experience over forty years earlier when a black catcher on his Ohio Wesleyan University team had not been allowed to enter a hotel in South Bend, Indiana. Rickey encountered the young man crying and tearing at his hands that evening. "It's my skin, Mr. Rickey," the player said. "If I could pull it off, I'd be just like everybody else."[1] By all accounts, Rickey never forgot that incident. While a young manager with the St. Louis Browns, he had been quoted in a 1915 article, "Rickey Claims Base Ball Is Moral Guide"; there, he extolled baseball as "the great American sport."[2]

Back in 1943, Rickey had broached the subject of hiring black players with George V. McLaughlin, president of the Brooklyn Trust Company, which held a mortgage on the Dodgers. After McLaughlin expressed his approval, Rickey next went to the Dodgers board of directors, who unanimously agreed to his plan and promised to remain mum about it. Talk of Rickey's involvement with the segregated United States League was always a subterfuge, albeit one unknown to Gus Greenlee and other league founders. Rickey recognized the obstacles confronting him, such as the discriminatory practices still afflicting St. Louis's Sportsman's Park. He recognized the need for "a superlative man, a man who had to be an outstanding player on the field, and a thorough gentleman off it." The search for the best candidate to break baseball's color barrier eventually led to Jackie Robinson, who was handsome, articulate, well educated, and a teetotaler, in addition to being a world-class athlete. Attractive too was Robinson's temperament. Jackie was proud and determined to withstand racial onslaughts. More worrisome were his fiery makeup and sometimes explosive nature. The twenty-six-year-old Robinson became the top choice, selected ahead of Baltimore Elite Giants catcher Roy Campanella, four years younger than Jackie;

Newark Eagles pitcher Don Newcombe, who was only nineteen years old; Homestead Grays catcher Josh Gibson, the greatest Negro league slugger; and Piper Davis, a smooth infielder for the Birmingham Black Barons. The Dodgers had received "glowing reports" about Robinson from several of their top baseball analysts, including Tom Greenwade and George Sisler.[3]

Sukeforth realized that the proposed meeting was "the real thing" and that Rickey did not want to talk to Robinson about joining the Negro league Brooklyn Brown Dodgers. Rickey had sent the scout to watch Robinson play against the Lincoln Giants in Chicago. He told Sukeforth, "I want you to pay particular attention to a shortstop named Robinson. I want you to identify yourself and tell him I sent you. If you like this fellow's arm, bring him in." Robinson was not in the lineup that night because of a shoulder injury, but Sukeforth reasoned that it did not matter if Jackie had a strong enough arm to play shortstop. He could always handle second base or left field. Sukeforth revealed that he had been sent by Rickey to check Jackie out and particularly his throwing arm. The scout reported that there was little doubt regarding Robinson's overall ability as he could obviously run and hit. When the two men met at the Stevens Hotel where the Monarchs were staying, Sukeforth asked about Robinson's departure from the U.S. Army. Robinson revealed that "an old football ankle" had led to his discharge, but the injury no longer bothered him. Sukeforth followed Rickey's order not to inform the press about his visit to Chicago.[4]

Robinson believed that Rickey might want to talk about the United States League, as the Dodgers president was still thought to be interested in setting up a team in Brooklyn for the new circuit. Robinson agreed to the meeting after first speaking with Sukeforth in New York City. The two men arrived at Rickey's office on August 28, 1945. During the session, Robinson discovered to his astonishment that Rickey, who did not consider Jackie the best Negro league player, was interested in signing him to a contract with the Dodgers franchise. Rickey asked at the opening of the three-hour session, "You got a girl?" After Robinson mentioned Rachel, Rickey offered, "You know, you *have* a girl. When we get through today you may want to call her up because there are times when a man needs a woman by his side."

Robinson became more excited, wondering why Rickey had wanted to meet with him. Rickey then informed Robinson that he was not being scouted for the Brooklyn Brown Dodgers. "I think you can play in the major leagues. How do you feel about it?" Rickey asked. The Brooklyn magnate pressed the temporarily speechless ballplayer. "You think you can play for Montreal?" Rickey asked, referring to the Dodgers' top minor league squad. Robinson managed an affirmative response. Rickey and Sukeforth then discussed Robinson's merits. The scout asserted, "He is the Dodgers' kind of player."[5]

Rickey then turned to Robinson and said, "I know you're a good ballplayer. What I don't know is whether you have the guts." Robinson was unable to respond before Rickey revealed that he had conducted an extensive search for a black player to challenge baseball's color barrier. Rickey then stated, "I've investigated you thoroughly, Robinson." He mentioned that some had viewed Jackie as a "racial agitator" when he attended UCLA. Rickey knew that Jackie's fierce competitiveness would be appreciated if he were white, but "we can't fight our way through this, Robinson." The older gentleman then admitted that he had no army, few backers, no sympathetic owners, and only a small number of sportswriters "on our side." Rickey bluntly offered, "We can win only if we can convince the world that I'm doing this because you're a great ballplayer and a fine gentleman. . . . If you're a good enough man, we can make this a start in the right direction. But let me tell you, it's going to take an awful lot of courage. . . . Have you got the guts to play the game no matter what happens?" Robinson responded, "I think I can play the game." Rickey warned that beanballs and verbal brickbats would be hurled at Jackie. He would also be attacked physically but had to restrain himself. Robinson asked, "Mr. Rickey, are you looking for a Negro who is afraid to fight back?" An angry Rickey retorted, "Robinson, I'm looking for a ballplayer with guts enough not to fight back" and indicated that Jackie's opponents would "taunt and goad" him. "They'll do anything to make you react. They'll try to provoke a race riot in the ball park." Resorting to role-playing, Rickey acted like a white player who had torn into Robinson before tossing out racial epithets.

Finally, Rickey offered Robinson a contract with the Montreal Royals that would pay $600 a month along with a $3,500 signing bonus. Rickey also informed Jackie that he could tell only Mallie Robinson and Rachel about the agreement.[6]

As information about the meeting between Rickey and Robinson remained under wraps, Wendell Smith continued his relentless quest to support the integration of organized baseball. In his column on September 1, 1945, Smith refuted a statement attributed to Rickey in which the Dodgers president declared that the large black population in St. Louis had not "got into the habit of supporting major league baseball." Rickey wondered, "What is to be done about St. Louis?" but Smith had a question of his own for Rickey: "What the hell is so complicated about St. Louis?" The sportswriter then stated that if organized baseball wanted to help out the Browns and Cardinals franchises, black players should be placed on the rosters. That would terminate the present "vicious discriminatory policy" practiced by all major league squads. St. Louis teams had discriminated against black players and fans, with the latter compelled "to sit in a special jim-crow section" until recently. Only St. Louis' Sportsman's Park, where both the Browns and Cardinals played, segregated black fans in such a manner. Smith reminded his readers that such a policy was maintained throughout much of Rickey's sixteen-year-long supervision of the Cardinals. Referring to the tryout the Dodgers gave McDuffie and Thomas, Smith expressed belief that Rickey was "sincerely interested in the fate of the Negro player." That was why Rickey's recent discussion about St. Louis dumbfounded him. Smith declared the answer was "obvious. . . . Hire Negro ball players! And that goes for Brooklyn too, Mr. Rickey!"[7] A few days after the column appeared, the Birmingham Black Barons and the Indianapolis Clowns played before 21,000 fans at Sportsmen's Park. Smith declared that St. Louis' big league clubs were "'killing' themselves by continuing their vicious policy of discrimination against Negro players. They would rather sink financially than hire Negro players."[8]

The September 8, 1945, edition of the *Courier* contained an article by Smith about the recent meeting between Branch Rickey and Jackie

Robinson, whom he referred to as "a sensational shortstop." The meeting remained "shrouded in mystery," with no statement forthcoming from the ballplayer. Somehow, Smith had received word about the session, but not concerning its full implication. Or possibly Rickey or Robinson apprised Smith of the encounter, while swearing him to secrecy regarding particular details. Responding to an inquiry from the *Courier*, Rickey said he had talked to Robinson about the Negro baseball situation in order to "get some ideas from him." Rickey fibbed, "We did not discuss the possibility of Robinson becoming a member of the Brooklyn Dodgers organization. That problem was not touched." He went on to say, "I wanted to talk with Robinson about the organization of Negro baseball. At the present time, the Negro leagues are not in the true sense of the word organized. I would like to see them established on a firm basis. And that was the nature of our discussions." Questioning Rickey's explanation, Smith declared it illogical for a rookie to be consulted about black baseball's future. During the interview with the *Courier*, Rickey also expressed continued interest in purchasing or supporting a black team. As for the young man he had spoken with in his Brooklyn office, Rickey stated, "Robinson is a real gentleman and a great athlete. I would like to have him on a Negro team if I invest in one."[9] Helping maintain the pretense, Robinson told Smith that Rickey asked if he "would like to manage the Brooklyn black ballclub."[10]

Early in September, Robinson departed from the Monarchs as the 1945 Negro leagues season neared a close. At season end, the Cleveland Buckeyes had easily won the Negro American League. The Kansas City Monarchs with their 32–30 record finished in fourth place. The Washington Homestead Grays won the Negro National League. The Grays then dropped four straight games in the Negro World Series, with Josh Gibson, Buck Leonard, and Cool Papa Bell all hitting poorly. Sam Jethroe repeated as Negro American League batting champion, Jackie Robinson came in second to Chicago's Alec Radcliffe in the home run race, and Cleveland's Willie Jefferson was the top pitcher. Robinson also belted out 10 doubles, smacked 4 triples, and batted .345 in Negro leagues games, tops on the Monarchs, and .387 overall. In the Negro National League, Ed Stone of the Philadelphia Stars was the batting titlist, although some accounts place Gibson as both the batting champ and home run leader. Washington's Roy Welmaker was the circuit's finest pitcher.

Investigating Jim Crow baseball, the LaGuardia committee remained in operation. Committee member and Yankee executive Larry MacPhail admitted in September 1945 that he had no thoughts about hiring a black player. As MacPhail saw it, there were "few, if any, Negro players who could qualify." Major league teams garnered too much money from the Negro leagues through leasing stadiums to desire a change in relationships, and the Negro leagues remained largely unorganized. Black baseball therefore needed to "put its own house in order and establish itself on a sound and ethical operations basis," Wendell Smith paraphrased MacPhail as stating. Smith bemoaned the absurdity of MacPhail's analysis and the fact that major league teams drew $500,000 annually from the Negro leagues.[11]

Jackie Robinson rejoined the Royals for Winter League exhibitions, which the *Courier* highlighted. After a game against the Service All-Stars in early October, the *Courier* headlined, "Robinson Sparkling on the Coast." It began the article by referring to "the peerless all-around play of short-stop Jackie Robinson." Robinson smacked a pair of doubles and an inside-the-park home run, scored four runs, "was a riot on the paths," ran "the opposition daffy on the bases," and "fielded brilliantly."[12] Following a doubleheader against Vince DiMaggio's Major League All-Stars, sportswriter Herman Hill reported that Robinson notched the lone run in the opener as he "beat out a perfect bunt," advanced to second on a fielder's choice, then scored on a hit to left. In the second game, Jackie enthused the crowd of 8,000 by offering "thrills aplenty" after being hit by a pitch, then frustrating the pitcher into tossing away the ball, allowing him to advance two bases. Robinson was hardly finished. Hill wrote, "Prancing up and down the third base line and making fake dashes for home, Jackie upset the pitcher's poise." The pitcher finally hurled an errant toss over Pittsburgh catcher Billy Salkeld, enabling Robinson to score standing up.[13]

Branch Rickey quietly continued orchestrating Robinson's entry into organized baseball. He sent a letter to Arthur Mann on October 7, 1945,

Hank Greenberg as a high school basketball player at James Monroe High School, 1929. *Photo courtesy the National Baseball Hall of Fame Library (Cooperstown, NY).*

Jackie Robinson as a long jumper for UCLA. *Photo courtesy the National Baseball Hall of Fame Library (Cooperstown, NY).*

A full-length shot of Hank Greenberg. *Photo courtesy the National Baseball Hall of Fame Library (Cooperstown, NY).*

The Detroit Tigers' Hank Greenberg batting in a game, September 23, 1935. *Photo courtesy the National Baseball Hall of Fame Library (Cooperstown, NY).*

The New York Yankees'
Lou Gehrig with the Detroit
Tigers' Hank Greenberg.
*Photo courtesy the National
Baseball Hall of Fame Library
(Cooperstown, NY).*

Satchel Paige with
Jackie Robinson.
*Photo courtesy the
National Baseball Hall
of Fame Library
(Cooperstown, NY).*

The legendary
Satchel Paige
with his teammate
Jackie Robinson,
Kansas City Monarchs,
1945.

Fort Riley, Kansas
in 1943
with Roscoe Devoe.

The Detroit Tigers' 1934 infield: 1B Hank Greenberg, 2B Charlie Gehringer, SS Billy Rogell, 3B Marv Owen. *Photo courtesy the National Baseball Hall of Fame Library (Cooperstown, NY).*

Group in front of the dugout, August 14, 1934, Yankee Stadium. From left to right: Hank Greenberg, Babe Ruth, Charlie Gehringer, and Lou Gehrig. *Photo courtesy the National Baseball Hall of Fame Library (Cooperstown, NY).*

Throughout his career, Hank Greenberg was one of the most powerful sluggers in major league baseball, falling just short in 1938 in his bid to equal Babe Ruth's single-season home-run record. *Photo courtesy the National Baseball Hall of Fame Library (Cooperstown, NY).*

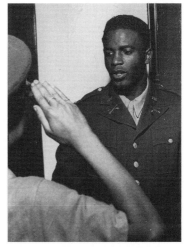

Hank Greenberg served in the U.S. Army from 1941 to 1945, losing four-and-a-half years of his playing career, more than any other major league star. *Photo courtesy the National Baseball Hall of Fame Library (Cooperstown, NY).*

Jackie Robinson being sworn into service. *Photo courtesy the National Baseball Hall of Fame Library (Cooperstown, NY).*

Hank Greenberg departing the train, February 27, 1941. *Photo courtesy the National Baseball Hall of Fame Library (Cooperstown, NY).*

Jackie Robinson attended officer candidate school, and received a commission as second lieutenant in the U.S. Army. *Photo courtesy the National Baseball Hall of Fame Library (Cooperstown, NY).*

Jackie Robinson with his family, *Look* magazine shoot, 1945. *Photo courtesy the National Baseball Hall of Fame Library (Cooperstown, NY).*

Cartoon depicting Jackie Robinson's breaking of the color barrier in baseball. *Photo courtesy the National Baseball Hall of Fame Library (Cooperstown, NY).*

Hank Greenberg
after hitting a
home run to clinch
the 1945 pennant.
*Photo courtesy the
National Baseball
Hall of Fame Library
(Cooperstown, NY).*

One of the largest baseball players of his
era, Greenberg had a presence along the
Detroit dugout, in the batter's box, and at
home plate that was undoubtedly an
unwelcome sight for opposing pitchers.
*Photo courtesy the National Baseball Hall of
Fame Library (Cooperstown, NY).*

Following the 1946 season, Hank
Greenberg was traded to the Pittsburgh
Pirates, where he played one more year,
helping to mentor National League
home run king Ralph Kiner. *Photo
courtesy the National Baseball Hall of
Fame Library (Cooperstown, NY).*

ABOVE:
Jackie Robinson and
Rachel Isum getting
married, February 10,
1946. *Photo courtesy
the National Baseball
Hall of Fame Library
(Cooperstown, NY).*

RIGHT:
Hank Greenberg with
his wife, Caral Gimbel
Greenberg, and her
horse, My Bell, in
1947. *Photo courtesy
the National Baseball
Hall of Fame Library
(Cooperstown, NY).*

Jackie Robinson
and Pee Wee
Reese. *Photo
courtesy the
National Baseball
Hall of Fame Library
(Cooperstown, NY).*

Brooklyn Dodger group (left to right): Spider Jorgensen, Pee Wee Reese, Eddie
Stanky, and Jackie Robinson, 1947. *Photo courtesy the National Baseball Hall of Fame
Library (Cooperstown, NY).*

Jackie Robinson and
Branch Rickey signing
a contract in 1950.
*Photo courtesy the
National Baseball Hall
of Fame Library
(Cooperstown, NY).*

Jackie Robinson after a first-inning home run. *Photo courtesy the National Baseball Hall of Fame Library (Cooperstown, NY).*

Jackie and Rachel Isum Robinson. *Photo courtesy the National Baseball Hall of Fame Library (Cooperstown, NY).*

Hank Greenberg, GM and part owner of the Chicago White Sox, in his office. *Photo courtesy the National Baseball Hall of Fame Library (Cooperstown, NY).*

Joe Cronin and Hank Greenberg at their induction into the National Baseball Hall of Fame in 1956. *Photo courtesy the National Baseball Hall of Fame Library (Cooperstown, NY).*

Jackie Robinson during his 1962 induction into the National Baseball Hall of Fame. *Photo courtesy the National Baseball Hall of Fame Library (Cooperstown, NY).*

Hank Greenberg and Whitey Ford at the Mets' Old Timers game, June 28, 1975.
Photo courtesy the National Baseball Hall of Fame Library (Cooperstown, NY).

Gov. Nelson Rockefeller with Jackie Robinson at Robinson's home in Connecticut in 1968.
Photo courtesy the National Baseball Hall of Fame Library (Cooperstown, NY).

telling the sportswriter to hold off on an article involving the termination of Jim Crow baseball. Rickey wrote, "The thing isn't dead, not at all. It is more alive than ever and that is the reason that we can't go with any publicity at this time." He continued, "There is more involved in the situation than I had contemplated." Rickey noted that other black players were involved, but he was unable to line them up for two or three months. He acknowledged no desire to be a crusader. Rather he wanted to be fair to all parties concerned but hoped "to win baseball games."[14]

Branch Rickey then stunned the nation by announcing on October 23, 1945, that he had signed Robinson to a minor league contract with the Montreal Royals. Wendell Smith, who had crusaded for this day to happen, lauded Rickey for having "defied a baseball world he knew would be rebellious because he was exploding its most sacred and vicious policy—the unwritten ban against Negro players." Smith credited Rickey with being determined to do "the right thing." Despite confronting the wrath of "some of his most prejudiced colleagues," Rickey believed Robinson was "a great prospect," and the Dodgers general manager proved determined to break baseball's color barrier. Rickey recognized that the prohibition against black players was "un-Christian" and violated his own religious beliefs. He insisted that "a boy should be permitted to use his talents without being penalized because of race or religion." Robinson was "a fine young man," Rickey said. "He is modest, intelligent and has ability. At least five different scouts reported to me and told me he was a fine prospect and a gentleman." Looking ahead Rickey declared, "If Jackie is good enough, I won't hesitate to place him with the Dodgers. He can go as far as he is capable of going." Denying being motivated by the antidiscrimination measure that New York had recently enacted, Rickey indicated the decision to sign Robinson was the byproduct of a three-year quest. The Dodgers executive expressed no concerns about opposition from other baseball leaders or from Southern ballplayers, including Brooklyn's own Dixie Walker, who expressed displeasure with the latest turn of events. "I am not worried about what anyone says," Rickey stated. "We pay those players to play ball. The job of picking players is my job. I'll sign any player I think is good enough."

Rickey dismissed talk about possible obligations to Negro league teams, stating, "I don't care what they say about contracts, suspensions and fines. They don't have a league. They're simply a booking agent's paradise . . . and have no right to expect organized baseball to respect them." Black baseball organizations needed to "clean house." At present "they have the semblance of a racket and operated for the best interests of certain individuals," Rickey charged.[15]

Columnist Tommy Holmes of the *Brooklyn Eagle* suggested that Robinson's entry into organized baseball might be blocked "by members of his own race," including representatives of the Kansas City Monarchs. Should baseball commissioner Happy Chandler uphold a protest from the Monarchs signifying that the Dodgers had raided Robinson, it might "be years before another opportunity opens up for a Negro in Organized Baseball again," Holmes warned. He called Robinson "an able prospect of much greater all-around accomplishment" than the typical baseball recruit and referred to Robinson's "great all-around athletic record at UCLA" and performance in the Negro leagues. Robinson "represents for his race an ideal candidate," Holmes wrote, "to crash through the inevitable color line." His placement in Montreal also appeared opportune, as "less race prejudice" existed in Canada. The International League—where the Montreal team was situated—was largely northern, with the striking exception of Baltimore. Holmes predicted that in spite of that fact, "It won't be easy for Robinson. It wouldn't be easy if he had all that talent plus Paul Robeson's baritone voice." Holmes pointed to spring training in Daytona Beach, Florida, where Robinson would have to find places to sleep and eat. He would be compelled to travel through "deepest Dixie." Holmes then presciently wondered how Robinson would be treated in cities like St. Louis and Cincinnati if promoted to the Dodgers.[16]

Writing in the *Brooklyn Eagle* on October 26, 1945, sportswriter Harold C. Burr reported that no one, white or brown, appeared ready to prevent Robinson from entering organized baseball. Minor league boss William G. Bramham revealed that "no baseball law" existed to preclude Robinson from joining the Montreal Royals. He nevertheless seemed to imply that Rickey's tactics could be likened to those of a carpetbagger, the much-despised Northerner who went down South after the Civil War to help usher in Reconstruction. Bramham revealed his belief "that if the Negro is let alone and aided by his own unselfish friends of the white race, he will work out his own salvation in all lines of endeavor." Dismissing Bramham's concerns, Rickey stated, "It all leaves me pretty cool, considering the source." Burr provided his own analysis while predicting that the rank and file of ballplayers would accept Robinson, no matter how a few hotheads responded.[17]

Hall of Famer Rogers Hornsby warned that the black player would have more difficulty adapting to the major leagues than white players would have in accepting him. He bluntly stated, "Rickey is wrong. The idea won't work out."[18] Hornsby went on to predict that a considerable amount of racial strife would ensue. Holmes indicated on October 31, 1945, that Hornsby's "honest and forthright" opinion was hardly unique. The sports columnist suggested that only the public could overcome Jim Crow. "The experiment will fail" if Robinson's entry into the big leagues triggered racial strife among ballplayers and that spread to the grandstands. If he played and played well, no racial conflict resulted, and the public applauded, then other blacks would enter organized baseball. Holmes hoped the experiment would succeed but admitted he had no idea if it would. "And don't kid yourself—neither does any one else," he wrote.[19] Holmes neatly underscored the tenuous nature of what came to be known as baseball's great experiment. The integration of the national pastime required a confluence of events: the willingness, no matter how reluctant, of white players to compete against blacks; management that failed to put up insurmountable roadblocks; the acquiescence, at a minimum, of fans; and, of course, the ability of Robinson to perform at a high level while walking something of a tightrope.

Robinson offered his own perspective in an article, complete with his byline, that also showed up on the front page of the November 3, 1945, edition of the *Courier*, where Smith's article had appeared. He had wanted to play organized baseball ever since he first took up the game back in Pasadena, California. "Just like all kids on the sandlots in every city in the country, I dreamed of being on a big league team. I used to picture myself in a big league uniform, socking that old ball all over the lot and being thrilled to the roar of the crowd." He still had those dreams despite recognizing that he might never prove to be a good enough ballplayer for the majors. But at least he was being afforded the opportunity. Robinson applauded the courage of both Rickey and Hector Racine, president of the Montreal Royals, for having broken baseball's color barrier. He well recognized how momentous this development was. He affirmed, "I am representing a whole race of people who are pulling for me." He promised to "try not to do a single thing other than that which will be creditable." Robinson referred to the "social implications of this situation" but expressed no worries. He declared himself able to get along with people and make friends. He had played against Southern boys on a series of Texas teams during his collegiate years and came to view them as "fine fellows" who were happy to have competed against him. He recognized that "tongue beatings" would ensue but insisted, "I can take that. At least, I think I can." He predicted "a terrible riding from the bench jockeys" in the International League but would attempt to follow the dignified lead of his friend, heavyweight boxing champion Joe Louis. In closing, Robinson thanked the black press, especially the *Courier*, for having campaigned for organized baseball's integration.[20]

Other members of the black press, along with Negro league representatives and players, responded to the Robinson signing with surprise, trepidation, and delight. Monarch owner J. L. Wilkinson declared, "Although I feel that the Brooklyn club or the Montreal club owes us some kind of consideration for Robinson, we will not protest to Commissioner Chandler." Wilkinson continued, "I am very glad to see Jackie get this chance, and I'm sure he'll make good. He's a wonderful ballplayer. If and when he gets into the major leagues he will have a wonderful career." Monarch co-owner Tom Y. Baird reacted more angrily in blurting out, "We won't take this lying down."[21] Baird soon claimed he had been misquoted and assured that "we would not do anything in any way to impede the advancement of any Negro ball player [into] of the major leagues."[22] He continued to believe, as did many other Negro League executives and supporters, that "something should be done to prevent white organized baseball from just stepping in and taking our players without giving us some kind of consideration."[23] Negro American League president J. B. Martin fired off a letter to Rickey, expressing "great pleasure in congratulating you for your moral courage in making the initial step which will give Negro ball players a chance to participate in the major leagues in this, our great democracy."[24] The *Michigan Chronicle*, an African American newspaper published in Detroit, also quoted Martin as declaring, "Mr. Rickey said the Negro Leagues were a racket, but we have never gone out and signed players without giving the owners some consideration" and suggested that the Brooklyn general manager was "too big not to compensate the Monarchs for Jackie Robinson."[25] The *Courier* stated that it did not wish "to jeopardize the best interests of Negro organized baseball in any way." It disapproved "of raiding or other unfair practices." However the Robinson signing "transcended anything else at this particular time." The solution to the conundrum was for the Negro leagues to petition to enter organized baseball, the *Courier* offered.[26] Commissioner Happy Chandler did not respond to a letter sent by Negro league representatives protesting the failure to compensate the teams that developed black ballplayers.

In his column in the *Michigan Chronicle*, Russ J. Cowans referred to Bob Higgins, George Stovey, and George Walker, African Americans who had played in organized baseball during the latter part of the nineteenth century. He also mentioned Charlie Grant, the black second baseman John McGraw had tried to pass off as a Native American. Then Cowans explored Robinson's "chances of making good," regardless of how fine an athlete he was. "It will take more than physical ability to hurdle the obstacles which will be placed in his path," Cowans warned, before reminding his readers about the tough treatment Paul Robeson received when he tried out for the Rutgers football squad. During spring training, "Robinson will be on the hot spot," Cowans continued. "Only his ability to take an insult and continue the fight will enable him to make the grade." If Robinson proved to be "made of the same fibre as Robeson," he would play for the Montreal Royals. "If he's the kind of a fellow who cannot take an insult, a dig in the shins with a pair of spikes, and come up smiling, you can tear up his contract now." All major league teams included at least one bench jockey, and those "jockeys will begin to ride Robinson as soon as he enters the game," Cowans warned. Then the columnist stated, "I believe Jackie comes from the same pattern that made Robeson an All-American end." If promoted to the big leagues, Robinson would confront "some more obstacles," including fierce competition to play shortstop for the Brooklyn Dodgers. Cowans predicted that no matter how things turned out, "Robinson, by his deportment on and off the field, will reflect credit to all sport loving fans."[27]

The *New York Amsterdam News* referred to the signing as "just the drop of water in the drought that keeps faith alive in American institutions." World War II had to be waged to eradicate "vicious racial theories, racial and religious discrimination and segregation," the newspaper exclaimed. "Yet the fact that Jackie Robinson, a young Negro who is intellectually, culturally and physically superior to most white baseball players, has signed a contract to play in a minor league has caused a national sensation." By contrast, Roy Wilkins's column in the *Michigan Chronicle* insisted that the announcement underscored "in a new and dramatic fashion the fact that the Negro is a citizen with talents and rights." The millions of baseball fans did not likely attend "lectures on race relations" and probably knew nothing about the great black scientist George Washington Carver. "But Jackie Robinson, if he makes the grade, will be doing a missionary work with these people that Carver could never do. He will be saying to them that his people should have their rights, should have jobs, decent homes and education, freedom from insult, and equality of opportunity to achieve."[28] In a page one article in the *Amsterdam News*, Dan Burley indicated that Robinson had been a greater star in football, track, and basketball, where his feats while at UCLA "were prodigious." Accompanying photographs contained captions referring to him as "the terror of the gridiron," "one of the greatest of all" basketball players, and a broad jumper who could have been a world champion.[29] Writing in *The Crisis*, Burley asked, "What's Ahead for Robinson?" and referred to Rickey as the crusading "John Brown of baseball." Robinson was the "symbol of hope of millions of colored people in this country and elsewhere," he stated. If that were not burden enough, Robinson also carried "the hopes of millions of fair-minded whites who want to see every American get a chance regardless of race, creed, or color."[30]

Informed of the signing of Jackie Robinson, Satchel Paige reflected, "I hadn't thought it would ever happen." If it did occur, "somehow I always figured it'd be me. . . . It was my right. I got those white boys thinking about having Negroes in the majors, but when they got one, it wasn't me."[31] Buck Leonard recalled thinking that Robinson "was a hustler, but other than that he wasn't a top shortstop. We said, 'We don't see how he can make it.'" Moreover Leonard believed "we had other ballplayers who were better players than he. We thought maybe they were going to get there, but we didn't think he would." Addressing the seriousness of Rickey's experiment, Leonard also worried that if Robinson "doesn't make it, they're going to be through with us for the next five or ten years. But if he does make it, maybe they are going to keep him in the minors for a long time."[32] Jimmy Crutchfield saw things differently. He believed that many of the finest players in the Negro Leagues "were over the hill." Robinson, on the other hand, was "a cinch" to make the majors within two years "and lead the league in everything."[33] Monarchs teammate Othello Renfroe declared, "They picked him for his intelligence. But we had a lot of better ballplayers."[34]

White executives, sportswriters, and players also reacted to the Robinson signing in a variety of ways. Pacific Coast Baseball League executives expressed a wait-and-see attitude, with some proving more supportive than others. Dick McCann of the *Washington Times-Herald* wrote, "We don't agree with those who think that other major league ballplayers will resent Jackie Robinson and others of his race, if and when they make the grade. Your American athlete is, essentially, a good sport . . . far fairer than even the American fan." Jimmy Powers of the *New York Daily News*, who had long pushed for the integration of organized baseball, nevertheless now warned that with all the young talent and the return of veterans, Robinson was only "a 1,000–1 shot to make the grade." Dan Parker of the *New York Daily Mirror* found it difficult to understand why black athletes were not welcomed in organized baseball, as they were in basketball, boxing, and college football. John P. Carmichael of the *Chicago Daily News* noted that Robinson was "a well known athlete of pronounced ability [whose] own personality will go a long way toward easing his progress."[35] Lee Dunbar of the *Oakland Tribune* deemed it "fitting that the end of baseball's Jim Crow law should follow the conclusion of a great war fought to preserve liberty, equality, and decency." By contrast, Larry MacPhail and even Branch Rickey supposedly did not believe there existed "a single Negro player with major league possibilities for 1946," or so *The Sporting News* contended. Satchel Paige was too old and made too much money to agree to a contract with organized baseball. Robinson would have a chance as a prospect if he were several years younger and being sent to a Class B team. Hundreds of veterans, after all, were returning to the minor and major leagues. *The Sporting News* questioned building the story of Robinson's signing "out of proportion to the actual vitality of the story" but at the same time covered it extensively. The sports publication predicted that Robinson might "discover that as a 26-year-old shortstop just off the sandlots, the waters of competition in the International League will flow far above his head." Rickey explained that Robinson—who was quoted as saying "Guess I'm just a guinea pig in this noble experiment"—was "not Dodger quality. Not yet."[36]

The Sporting News reported that Rickey had evidently signed another black player, Roy Campanella, to a contract with the Montreal farm club. Reporter Harold C. Burr suggested this would be a smart move by the Dodger organization or otherwise "Robinson would be a lonely boy without a member of his own race around. He would be homesick by himself." Robinson "is really on the spot and has a hard, uphill fight to overcome prejudice."[37] Wendell Smith soon wrote to Rickey, suggesting that he consider hiring another black player, Kenny Washington, Robinson's teammate at UCLA. Washington was "a much better ball player than Robinson," Smith declared.[38]

The star Cleveland Indian pitcher Bob Feller "just couldn't foresee any future for Robinson in big league baseball" although he admitted that Jackie was a good fielder, "was fast as blazes and a great athlete." Robinson, as a former football player, "was tied up in the shoulders and couldn't hit an inside pitch to save his neck," Feller contended. "If he were a white man I doubt if they'd even consider him as big league material." Other than Satchel Paige and Josh Gibson, Feller was hard pressed to name black players ready to enter the big leagues.[39] In a letter to Wendell Smith, Robinson refuted Feller's analysis, indicating that he had little doubt he could hit in the big leagues. He expressed perplexity regarding Feller's statement that he had "football shoulders." Robinson thanked Smith and the *Courier* for supporting him and promised to do the best he could. No matter what Feller stated, "it's still all up to Jack Roosevelt Robinson, who is quite a ball player in my little black book," Smith wrote.[40]

Robinson seemed to bear out Smith's analysis as he wrapped up play in the California Winter Baseball League, having been named to the All-Star team. He then traveled to Venezuela to join a Negro league squad. Buck Leonard led the team in hitting with a .425 batting average, and Sam Jethroe hit .333, while Robinson compiled a .281 mark and Roy Campanella batted only .211. Smith deemed the signing of Robinson the biggest sports event of the year. The "bronze-colored" Robinson, Smith wrote, "has the hopes, aspirations and ambitions of thirteen million black Americans heaped upon his broad, sturdy shoulders," because of baseball's stature. "Whatever happens to him in 1946 will be historically significant," Smith predicted.[41]

As 1945 neared a close, months after the end of World War II, America continued to grapple with the issue of race, as it had throughout the war. Many, both at home and abroad, viewed the war as having pitted democracy against right-wing totalitarianism but also as having given lie to the notion of white supremacy. Racial problems continued to beset the United States. Leading black businessmen, professionals, and actresses, including Horace Clark, who owned the Clark Hotel; band leader Noble Sissle; and actresses Hattie McDaniel and Louise Beavers confronted efforts to remove them from their homes in Los Angeles' affluent Blueberry Hill district. Legal action had been undertaken to exclude them from the area in keeping with a racial covenant that prevented residence by individuals "not entirely of the white blood." Various branches of the U.S. military remained segregated, although a bill had been proposed in Congress allowing for more black officers. The NAACP complained about actions by the commanding officer at Fort Benning, Georgia, that resulted in black soldiers being forced out of the camp cafeteria, restricted from using the air-conditioned theater, and denied the right to use a whites-only bus system. Black veterans—some disabled—asserted that they had been roughed up and arrested by Atlanta police after being charged with vagrancy and loitering. Interstate transportation in the American South remained segregated, leading to wholesale indignities, as when black passengers had to stand during long trips. The Ku Klux Klan initiated another hate campaign, this time targeting blacks, Jews, and communists. Klan members in Knoxville, Tennessee, urged white veterans just back from military service "to do something about the niggers who got all the good jobs while you were in uniform."[42]

10

A Year of Transition and Hope

On February 15, 1946, World Series hero Hank Greenberg, having turned down an offer of at least $100,000 to join the Mexican League, signed a contract for $65,000 for the upcoming season. Four days later, "baseball's outstanding bachelor" and top-paid player eloped with Caral Lasker Gimbel, a raven-haired thirty-year-old department store heiress worth millions with whom he would have two sons and a daughter. Caral's father, Bernard, was a sports fan who was best friends with former heavyweight boxing champion Gene Tunney. Caral knew next to nothing about baseball. She and Hank had met at her family estate in Greenwich when Louis Marx, the Gimbel toy manufacturer, brought the ballplayer over. Caral was immediately attracted to him. She recalled, "I just thought Hank was fabulous looking and a giant of a man. . . . I thought he was the most gorgeous, handsome, virile man I had ever met, and he had a divine sense of humor. He also had this mar-velous modesty."[1] Like Hank, Caral was a nonpracticing Jew, so their wed-ding took place in the living room of county ordinary judge Edwin W. Dart, who married the couple in Brunswick, Georgia. Gimbel was dressed "in a dark blue suit, pearl necklace, pearl earrings and orchids," while Greenberg wore "a pepper and salt business suit." Following the ceremony, Hank and Caral headed to the Darts' residence in St. Augustine, Florida.[2] As Caral later recalled, "I entered the world of baseball." Through Hank, she met some of his best friends in the game, including fellow stars Ted Williams, Joe

DiMaggio, and Bob Feller.[3] She also had to contend with Greenberg's mood swings, which largely depended on how things were going on the baseball diamond.

Despite homering in the opening game played before a home crowd of over 52,000, in which the Tigers nipped the St. Louis Browns 2–1, Greenberg struggled throughout the first months of the season as he switched back to first base, and reports of his impending retirement surfaced. He even had difficulty with fastballs, which he had always easily handled. Fans began booing Greenberg, as he indicated to a New York sportswriter. "They sure are giving it to me this year. The other day, during infield practice, I let one get by and they gave me a blast that almost carried me out of the ballpark." Greenberg denied that the razzing bothered him and said, "It's all part of the game."[4] Discussing the rumor of Greenberg's impending retirement in his column in the *New York Herald Tribune*, Red Smith stated that "if this is so then baseball is about to lose one of the greatest players of our time, one of the most unselfish team men, one of the finest gentlemen." He had only been a credit to himself since coming up to the majors for good in 1933. Smith recalled Al Simmons's observations about Greenberg as Hank readied to return to the majors. Simmons suggested that if Greenberg were unable to do it, then no one could. The columnist also remembered Greenberg's first game back, when he smashed a homer to the "unrestrained joy of the crowd" and, more important, "the undisguised pleasure that the other players on both teams displayed." That demonstrated the esteem in which Greenberg was held and explained why no other player appeared to begrudge his status as the sport's highest paid player since Babe Ruth. Teammates and opponents alike clearly respected how he had worked diligently to become the game's top first baseman and then performed even more strenuously to convert himself into an outfielder when the Tigers asked. Although he entered the U.S. military at the height of his career, he displayed no regrets for the sacrifices he made; rather, as Smith suggested, Greenberg "has a sense of dignity that always has become him." On his return from military service, Greenberg continued to perform heroically on the playing field, helping carry the Tigers to the 1945 American League pennant and World Series title. Now, even though he was slumping, Greenberg would return for "one more good year," Smith hoped.[5] Greenberg had admitted to a reporter from Boston, "Playing baseball isn't fun anymore. It's hard work."[6] Nevertheless, the thirty-five-year-old ballplayer denied reports that he intended to quit the game, indicating, "I wish they'd ask me. The way I figure it, if I'm so bad I ought to quit." Still, he believed there were "a lot of other guys around in the league in the same category," referring to other aging veterans.[7] He recognized that age was catching up to him. His legs lacked their usual power, necessary for a slugger to drive the ball. Pitchers he had always been able to handle easily were getting him out now, while his return to first base had not proceeded smoothly.

Greenberg soon went on a tear, beginning in late August, to end up as the American League leader in both homers (44) and RBIs (127), beating out Ted Williams in each category. Before that surge he continued to experience boos from his home crowd and apparently twice offered to retire, but Tigers management turned him down. On September 17, the *Detroit Free Press*'s Lyall Smith mentioned both Greenberg's resurgence and continued talk that he was over the hill. After noting that Greenberg was then only a single homer behind Williams in the home run race, Smith wrote, "In recent weeks, I have been thinking that Hank Greenberg is a remarkable person, and he is. He is held together with tape and piano wire. He spends most of his time on a rubbing table. He is an old man in the mountains, in a baseball sense. But old as he is and leg-weary as he is and patched up as he is, he's fighting everybody for the leadership in hitting homers and runs batted in." When the season ended, Greenberg finished runner-up to Williams in slugging percentage with a .604 mark and 316 total bases. The *New York Sun*'s Grantland Rice wrote, "In my opinion Greenberg's surge is one of baseball's greatest achievements, when you consider all the angles involved—the four years away from action, Greenberg's age, the handicap he faced in moving after such a power hitter as Williams has become."[8] He did wind up with a .277 batting average (the first time in his major league career that he had finished below .300 for a full season) but ended up eighth in the balloting for American League MVP, won for the first time by

Williams. The Tigers, with a 92–62 record, finished second behind the Boston Red Sox, twelve games back.

While few sportswriters remarked that baseball's greatest Jewish player had returned for his first full season since 1940, they avidly followed the story of another baseball pioneer in 1946. On January 31, *The Sporting News* offered an editorial titled, "Chandler and the Negro Baseball Problem." The commissioner, the publication offered, was "honestly and sincerely . . . sympathetic to the Negro's major league aspirations." *The Sporting News* reported that the Mayor's Committee of New York, which was carefully investigating "the Negro baseball problem," underscored the fact that the Negro leagues needed to get their own houses in order. They required greater organization, from the ground floor up, and they needed to boot out the "gamblers." After doing so, they could then go to Commissioner Chandler to bring about "an alliance between Organized Ball and the Negro leagues."[9]

In an article that initially appeared in *Yank, The Army Weekly* and was later reprinted in a condensed version in *Baseball Digest*, Sgt. Bob Stone declared that Robinson, "the sensational backfield star" at UCLA, was "about to shoulder one of the toughest and most responsible post-war jobs." Consequently "the eyes not only of the sports world but of everybody concerned with the destruction of racial prejudices in America will be upon him." Looking forward, Robinson admitted, "Maybe I should buy a lot of cotton to stuff in my ears." He good-naturedly indicated, "I don't think I'll have to take anything I didn't have to take before but maybe there'll be more people ready to give it to me." Regarding worries that white Southerners would not accept the integration of baseball, Robinson noted, "I played football against Southern Methodist, Texas Christian and Texas A & M. Those boys played hard football and they really gave me a smacking at times. But I can say with perfect honesty that I never saw any of those things that would indicate they were giving me the business because I was a Negro. The white boys were getting smacked just as hard as I was."[10]

In his column in the *Pittsburgh Courier*, Wendell Smith continued to push for the integration of organized baseball. Smith contended that many sportswriters exuded a liberal and fair attitude about black athletes, with Joe Louis, Henry Armstrong, Satchel Paige, and Josh Gibson among those garnering good press. He nevertheless viewed baseball writers in another light, charging that most possessed "a passive attitude" about ending Jim Crow baseball. He decried a recent banquet put on by the New York chapter of the baseball writers' organization where Robinson was portrayed as a butler, humbly offering a series of "massas."[11]

On a happier note, Jackie and Rachel were married on February 10, by his old friend, Rev. Karl Downs. Nora Holt, writing in the *New York Amsterdam News*, subsequently referred to the couple as "typical of the clean, decent American family. Brought up to respect parents and hold allegiance to the home."[12] They soon readied for spring training camp, which Rickey insisted that Rachel attend. The Robinsons' journey to the camp was arduous and resulted in their being bumped from an early morning flight out of New Orleans due to military priorities. Robinson later referred to this as "another typical black experience." The airport coffee shop denied them service, and a nearby restaurant would sell take-out sandwiches but not allow them to eat there. Tired and hungry, they "decided to skip food until we reached a place where we could be treated as human beings," Robinson later wrote. Jackie and Rachel went to get some rest at a dilapidated hotel, as their promised brief delay amounted to twelve hours. On arriving in Pensacola, they were again bumped from their scheduled flight with no reason given this time as a white couple took their seats.[13]

Forced to spend the night in town, Jackie and Rachel stayed in a private house before undertaking a sixteen-hour bus trip to Jacksonville, during which they were compelled to sit in straight-backed seats at the very back of the bus. As Rachel recalled, "I buried my head behind the seat in front of me and started to cry. I finally began to realize that where we were going with Mr. Rickey's plan, none of us had ever been before. We were setting out on something we really didn't understand. And right in front of me, it was changing my life, changing who I was, or changing who I thought I was." Rachel later remembered having seen Jackie adopt the posture of "the white South's 'boy,' in order to keep us safe." Yet Rachel also believed that she and Jackie possessed "the survivor's most crucial traits—resilience and indestructible hope."[14] Robinson wanted to return home because Rachel was so miserable. When they finally reached the bus station in Daytona, journalists Wendell Smith and Billy Rowe greeted them. Rachel was exhausted and depressed from the trip. The white players resided at a hotel, while Jackie and Rachel stayed at the home of a local African American politician.

Rachel Robinson later explained the role she undertook, which developed gradually and became more important with the passage of time as her husband became more involved with the campaign to integrate organized baseball: "My most profound instinct as Jack's wife was to protect him— an impossible task. I could, however, be a consistent presence to witness and validate the realities, love him without reservation, share his thoughts and miseries, discover with him the humor in the ridiculous behavior against us, and, most of all, help maintain our fighting spirit. I knew our only chance to survive was to be ourselves."[15]

The March 2, 1946, issue of *Collier's* magazine contained a feature article about Robinson by Arthur Mann, who compared him to Jim Thorpe as an all-around athlete. Like the great Native American star, Robinson was "least brilliant in baseball." Still, several Dodgers scouts agreed that "he was the very best Negro player in the country." Robinson neither smoked nor drank, in contrast to Thorpe. Reminded of Bob Feller's criticisms, Robinson stated, "Anybody who says I can't make it doesn't know what I've gone through, and what I'm prepared to go through to stay up."[16]

As the Royals opened spring training camp in Sanford, Florida, Rickey urged that Robinson and former Negro league pitcher John Wright (he had not been officially signed yet), who arrived on March 4, be treated fairly. Rickey also denied having signing the Negro league players because of political pressure. "We signed 'em because of our desire to have a winning team in Brooklyn. I would have signed an elephant as quickly if the elephant could have played center field." Time spent at the ballpark proved tense, with the white minor leaguers intently watching them. White residents informed the Royals during the second day at Sanford that white and black ballplayers would not be allowed on the field together. Outside the park, people, some sporting sticks, bats, or rocks, hurled "vile epithets," Sam Lacy reported. Robinson and Wright could not check into the lakefront hotel, staying instead at private residences in a segregated section of Sanford. The Royals soon relocated to Daytona Beach, but the black players could only play in that city's Island Park. Robinson also had to contend with prejudice on his own team. During one preseason practice session, Rickey and Montreals manager Clay Hopper watched Robinson make an incredible play at second base. Hopper asked, "Mr. Rickey, do you really think a nigger's a human being?" but the Brooklyn baseball executive declined to answer.[17]

Corresponding with a friend, Ralph P. Norton, on March 12, 1946, Robinson declared that he and Wright had received supportive letters and argued, "It is going to be tough keeping us off the club." He indicated that up to that point, "it has been a real pleasure playing here with the fellows. Everyone has been so nice and they have given us help all along." Although he had not anticipated any trouble, he had also not expected to be treated as well as he had been. Robinson reasoned "that if we make the club it will be on our own merit," and "if not it will be due to the fact that the many ball players Montreal has are better than we are." Hopper had proven to be "very helpful" in affording his new black players "every chance possible."[18] Jackie struggled mightily at first, undoubtedly due to the inordinate amount of pressure he was experiencing.

Robinson practiced at first base, second, and shortstop. As Royals teammate Al Campanis later remembered, "He had the greatest aptitude of any player I've ever seen. In one half hour he learned to make the double play pivot correctly." Despite "some limitations" involving his arm strength and ability to range leftward, Robinson "overcame both deficiencies because he was such a great athlete and applied himself to the game with such intensity."[19] Various white players helped him, including second baseman Lou Rochelli.

As Robinson and Wright participated in spring training, Smith also decried the biased articles that appeared in the *New York Daily News* and the *New York Daily Mirror*. Indeed, Smith charged that sportswriters Jimmy

Powers and Dan Parker were delivering "vicious, putrid and violently prejudiced stories" about Robinson and Wright while also slamming Rickey, apparently for opening organized baseball to black ballplayers. Powers and Parker blasted Rickey for purportedly attempting "to pass himself off as 'another Abraham Lincoln.'" All of this was particularly disconcerting to Smith, as the two New York writers had earlier presented themselves as champions of baseball integration. They had done so, he reasoned, to appeal to the vast array of readers in Harlem. Powers now extolled the South for paying black garbage collectors $5.50 daily, and Parker spoke of the vague unhappiness Robinson and Wright were experiencing. Parker continued, "They certainly aren't having as much fun as they would with their rollicking teammates in Negro baseball who play the game as if they were having the time of their lives." This was perplexing to Smith, who pointed out that Parker had not even attended the Montreal training camp.[20]

On April 2, 1946, Robinson, who had been battling a sore shoulder, got his first hit, in an exhibition game against the Brooklyn Dodgers, a sharp single into right field, and a near-certain steal of second, which was only prevented by the catcher throwing out another runner at third base with two outs. *The Sporting News* reported, "That one incident was enough to show that Robinson, if he can get on base, could give the enemy a fit. He can really fly over the ground." Referring to the fact that Robinson seemed to be pressing at the plate, Hall of Famer, Brooklyn special instructor, and scout George Sisler responded, "That's understandable enough. When you come to think of it, he's facing a pretty tough assignment." After watching Robinson at the plate and in the field, Branch Rickey observed, "He'll make the Montreal team this year. And he definitely is a big league prospect."[21] By the time the 1946 baseball season opened, Branch Rickey had signed four more Negro league players to minor league contracts: pitcher Wright, catcher Roy Campanella, pitcher Don Newcombe, and pitcher Roy Partlow. Wright and Partlow would be assigned to the Montreal Royals, with Campanella and Newcombe going to play for Nashua in the Class B New England League. The St. Louis Cardinals signed Negro leaguer Vincent "Manny" McIntyre to a contract with their Class C team in Sherbrooke, Quebec.

Playing before more than twenty-five thousand fans at Jersey City on April 18, 1946, Robinson proved an immediate sensation in leading the Royals to a 14–1 victory. In five trips to the plate, he smacked four hits, including a three-run homer, scored four runs, batted in four runs, and drove pitchers to distraction while pilfering a pair of bases and inducing a balk that enabled him to cross the plate. He also helped turn a double play, but he did commit an error. A week later, the infamous "black cat" affair occurred, although baseball historians continue to debate its existence. After Robinson grounded out in an away game against the Syracuse Chiefs, someone supposedly threw a black cat onto the field. Robinson responded by tripling with the bases loaded. Rachel Robinson stated years later that the incident did indeed take place. "It was another one of those taunting things that somebody decided to do."[22]

By the time Montreal completed its initial home stand on May 26, Robinson appeared to have convinced Hopper that he could play for a team that had a sizable lead in the pennant race. Acknowledging that Robinson had endured "terrific pressure," Hopper stated that there was no better second baseman in the International League. Robinson had made only two errors in twenty home games and was batting .340 in the team's first thirty-six games. In an article in *The Sporting News* titled "Robinson Rivets Royal Keystone Job on Hitting, Fielding and Base-Stealing," Lloyd McGowan acknowledged that "the road is long and tough" and reminded his readers that Robinson was undertaking his first season in organized baseball. For now, "the grandstand chant for him is: 'Glad to have you with us.'"[23] Jersey City manager Bruno Betzel claimed that Robinson was "a better bunter than Ty Cobb," while Hank DeBerry, a scout for the New York Giants, declared, "Robinson is the greatest player in the game today. Whoever is playing the position he wants at Brooklyn had better move over, because Robinson is on his way."[24]

On May 16, 1946, Jackie received a letter from his friend Ralph P. Norton, congratulating him on his early success with the Royals. Norton stated that by "religiously" following the box scores of Montreal's games in *The Sporting News* or the *Toronto Globe and Mail*, he could tell Robinson had "certainly shown the doleful doubters that you mean business in your bid for a professional baseball career." Like many sports fans, his friends "predicted dourly that high spikes, bean balls, bench jockeying and like troubles . . . would make life in organized ball intolerable for you." Now, Norton felt more comfortable in saying, "I told you so." He also wondered if the Pasquel brothers, who sought to raid players from organized ball and the Negro leagues for the Mexican circuit, had attempted to attract Robinson or John Wright. Norton asked if Robinson had difficulty obtaining accommodations in hotels or restaurants during his travels with the Royals.[25] Robinson's former troopmate at Fort Riley, Ed English, later expressed pleasure that Jackie was doing so well. "They couldn't have picked a better more deserving man for the honor which is yours," English wrote.[26]

The pressure on Robinson throughout the season proved unrelenting. Fans in Baltimore, "the Southernmost city" in the International League, repeatedly hurled invectives at him, which Rachel considered "the worst kind of name-calling." At one point, she broke down in tears, worrying about his safety, and considered that he might end "baseball's great experiment."[27] Like John Wright, Robinson was forced to stay with friends in Baltimore rather than register at the hotel where the other Royals players stayed. Declining to protest, Robinson indicated that he respected the city's customs. In other International League cities, Robinson was allowed a room in the hotels where his teammates were, but he was instructed by Royals officials to keep away from the lobby. The stress he endured led Robinson to inform general manager Mel Jones on a number of occasions, "Nobody knows what I'm going through this season." And "yet, never once did he mention quitting."[28]

Writing in the *Daily Mirror*, sportswriter Dan Parker effectively charged that, encouraged by Rickey, Robinson had violated his contract with the Monarchs. On July 13, 1946, Robinson wrote to Rickey, stating that he never had a contract with the Negro league team. He simply "received an offer in a letter" from Kansas City and consequently reported to the ballclub. Robinson recalled Monarch co-owner J. L. Wilkinson's acknowledgment that he had no contract with the Monarchs. And he remembered that

moment during his initial encounter with Rickey when the Dodger president asked him directly, "Are you under any obligation of any sort whatever
as to your future services in baseball?" Robinson replied, "None whatever,"
and agreed to indicate as much in writing.[29] In August Robinson received
a letter from his former coach at UCLA, Wilbur Johns, who applauded his
performance on the playing field. Johns referred to a recent note from
Robinson indicating that he was confronting some difficulties that "demand
your self control." The coach reminded Jackie, "You and I have discussed
this often and I know you will take care of any situation in the manner
becoming a gentleman. Just remember that you won't lower yourself to the
level of any of the 'baiters.'"[30]

On August 3, 1946, Red Smith wrote about Robinson in his column
that appeared in the next day's edition of *New York Herald Tribune*. Smith
referred to Robinson as "the model Negro infielder" who was playing on
"the Dodgers' model Montreal farm." Notwithstanding various injuries,
Robinson at the time was batting .352, the second best mark in the
International League, and was second in stolen bases with thirty-one. He
also helped to make up the circuit's top double-play unit, proving to be a
major attraction at the box office. The Royals expected to draw over five
hundred thousand fans, which would quadruple the previous year's total.
Hopper said about Robinson, who had recently jammed his ankle, "Yes, I
think he's a major leaguer. He goes hard all the time and he has great hands
for an infielder." But Robinson did appear "a little frail," Hopper suggested.
"Maybe because he goes so hard." Chuckling at the notion that he was
somewhat "frail," the heavily muscled Robinson stated, "I'm not brittle.
Football never hurt me. Anybody hitting the bag the way I did the other
night would have hurt his ankle." Robinson also denied that he had experienced any trouble. He indicated, "I haven't heard anything worse than
you hear in college football." As for the fight against Jim Crow, Robinson
said, "I think it's won, for now. But it could easily start all over if something
should happen." When asked to compare the International League with
the Negro National League, Robinson referred to "the organization of
teams, accommodations, parks and such." He also pointed to the fact that

"the baseball here is better than down the line. That is, there are more good players." Robinson enjoyed playing before large crowds, actually seeming "to rise to those occasions," Smith noted.[31]

Through mid-August, Robinson continued tearing up the International League. Robinson raised his batting average to a league best .371 after a 10-game stretch in which he rapped out 22 hits in 39 trips to the plate. In addition, during the first 110 games, he had committed only 7 errors, having gone two-and-a-half months at one point without a miscue. Jones foresaw Robinson's entry onto the big stage the following season. "He can run faster than 75 percent of the players in the majors today. He can bunt better than 90 percent of them. He has good hands, a trigger quick baseball mind and an accurate and ample arm. And what makes him look like a big timer is that he never makes any play around second base look hard, not even the difficult ones." Jones cuttingly asked, "What can't he do except eat in the dining room at the Waldorf Astoria?"[32] Betzel declared, "I'd like to have nine Robinsons. If I had one Jackie, I'd room with him myself and put him to bed nights to make sure nothing happened to him." Regarding whether Robinson was tough enough to endure the inevitable beanballs that would be thrown at him in the majors, former Dodgers pitcher Curt Davis, now a member of the Royals, reported, "He's been thrown at more than any batter in the league. . . . Jackie can take it. He brushes himself off and comes back as if nothing happened. I haven't heard him make one single complaint this season, and he's had to take plenty." When asked about being brushed back, Robinson denied having been thrown at more than any other hot hitter. "It doesn't bother me. I expected that, for it's part of the game."[33]

Both *Time* and *Newsweek*, in their August 26, 1946, issues, reported on Robinson's early success in organized baseball. *Time* indicated that the previous year, Branch Rickey had "tossed a bomb into baseball and stuck his fingers in his ear" in signing Robinson to a baseball contract. This enabled the first African American athlete to play in the high minors without being "passed off as a Cuban, a Mexican, or an Indian." Defying the skeptics, the "rangy, graceful" Robinson was a star in the International League. He had "already accomplished his mission" while compelling other major league owners to seek out promising black players.[34] *Newsweek* quoted Hopper, who stated that Jackie was "a player who must go to the majors. He's a big-league ballplayer, a good team hustler, and a real gentleman." Robinson informed *Newsweek*, "I've had great luck and great treatment. This is the greatest thing that has ever happened to me."[35]

On August 27, 1946, major league owners gathered in Chicago, where they received copies of a report produced by a six-member steering committee that had examined various issues confronting organized baseball, including the "race question." Recipients were asked to destroy their copies, and word of the report's existence did not leak for some time. As the committee saw matters, African Americans were among the staunchest supporters of professional baseball. The American people were most concerned about sports performance, not "the color, race or creed of the performer." Black stars had shone in a variety of sports, including football, boxing, and track and field. Fifty-four Negro league players had served in the U.S. military during World War II. One had been killed and several wounded. The report stated bluntly, "Baseball will jeopardize its leadership in professional sport if it fails to give full appreciation to the fact that the Negro fan and the Negro player are part and parcel of the game." However, "pressure campaigns," conducted by those seeking publicity, were being undertaken to compel organized baseball's integration. The report then dismissed the notion that "a Jim Crow flag" or racial discrimination prevented blacks from entering the big leagues. It instead pointed to the fact that professional baseball was "a private business enterprise" that demanded profit to survive. Jackie Robinson's tremendous gate appeal was alluded to, but that was seen as a troublesome sign. At various games, blacks exceeded 50 percent of those in attendance in both Newark and Baltimore. The committee worried that a similar scenario might unfold in New York City and Chicago, thereby endangering the economic worth of the Yankees, Giants, and White Sox franchises.[36]

"The thousands of Negro boys of ability" who sought to play professional ball should be afforded "a better opportunity," the committee acknowledged. Indeed, all American boys, regardless of race, color, or creed, "should have a fair chance in baseball." However, the signing of a small number of black players by major league teams "would contribute little or nothing towards a solution of the real problem." A major leaguer required more than "great natural ability," the committee offered. He needed "the technique, the co-ordination, the competitive aptitude, and the discipline" that usually resulted only after extensive minor league training, which amounted to seven years on average. "The young Negro player never has had a good chance in baseball," and consequently "few good young Negro players are being developed." The report quoted from Sam Lacy of the *Baltimore Afro-American*, who had reluctantly admitted "that we haven't a single man in the ranks of colored baseball who could step into the major league uniform and disport [*sic*] himself after the fashion of a big leaguer." Some might excel at various aspects of the game, but those who did so in multiple phases "are few and far between—perhaps nil." Lacy's perspective, the report insisted, was shared by almost all blacks and whites who were "competent" to examine the situation. The report next referred to the fact that Negro baseball was itself "a $2,000,000 business" and pointed out that the Negro leagues required good players to continue attracting fans. Indeed, for the leagues to survive, their standard of play had to improve. If organized baseball raided the black teams, taking their finest players, those circuits "will eventually fold," wiping out the investments of club owners and costing a lot of black players their jobs. Such a development would also damage major and minor league clubs, which rented their ballparks to the Negro leagues. The report continued, arguing that organized baseball could not sign players who were under contract to black teams. "This is not racial discrimination. It's simply respecting the contractual relationship between the Negro Leagues and their players."[37]

The committee concluded its analysis with an observation, clearly directed at Branch Rickey and the Dodgers. "The individual action of any one Club may exert tremendous pressure upon the whole structure of Professional Baseball, and could conceivably result in the lessening of the value of several Major League franchises." The committee felt compelled to follow that declaration with a statement that it did not seek "to question the motives of any organization or individual" who was "sincerely opposed to segregation" or believed that "such a policy is detrimental to the best interests of Professional Baseball." The committee closed by stating that this was "an overall problem which vitally affects each and everyone of us" and called for "a fair and just solution" that would prove "compatible with good business judgment and the principles of good sportsmanship."[38]

It was during this same time period that Rickey spoke to a largely affluent black audience made up of members of the Carlton Branch of the Brooklyn chapter of the YMCA. Referring to Robinson, he warned, "The biggest threat to his success is the Negro people themselves." Rickey worried that blacks "will go and form parades and welcoming committees . . . strut . . . wear badges . . . hold Jackie Robinson Days and Jackie Robinson night . . . get drunk . . . fight . . . [and] be arrested." He predicted that "if any individual, group, or segment of Negro society" responded to baseball integration "as a symbol of a social 'ism' or schism, a triumph of race over race," then he would ensure that the game "is never so abused and misrepresented again."[39]

Robinson for his part refused to complain about how he had been treated. He stated in early September, "The sports fans of this country are fair, and have been very fine to me. I have no complaints." Robinson was well aware, J. G. Taylor Spink of *The Sporting News* indicated, "that he was the guinea pig in the Rickey Emancipation plan." As Robinson acknowledged, "It wasn't a question of the players getting along with me. I was on the spot to see if I could get along with them." Many of his teammates were Southerners, and Robinson "had to win their respect, first," as he recognized. As the International League entered its final week, Robinson continued to avoid arguments on the baseball diamond. It was increasingly clear that his teammates were ready to defend Robinson if a close play went against him. He had to keep out of the way because he remained "a marked man" who could not afford to anger either umpires or fans. "Mr. Rickey foresaw all the situations I would encounter, and I have tried to follow his advice," Robinson revealed. Spink reported that the Brooklyn president recognized that "he has a drawing card for the National League who may rival Bob Feller and Ted Williams in the American League." Robinson had helped Montreal pull in more than eight hundred thousand fans, and his manager applauded him for "playing his best ball before the largest crowds; the bigger the turnouts, the more sensational he has been." No player since Dizzy Dean possessed "as much crowd appeal as the soft-voiced, dynamic Negro lad from California," Spink suggested.[40]

By season's end, Robinson's hair was already turning gray, and he experienced constant stomach problems. At one point, he had gone to a doctor, who affirmed that Jackie was undergoing a great amount of stress and instructed him to stay away from the game for a full week. Rachel believed the problem arose from Jackie's inability to strike back. Despite all the pressure, which wore away at some of the other recently signed Negro league players, Robinson thrived on the baseball diamond. He hit .349 to win the International League batting crown, led the circuit in runs scored with 113, drove in 66 runs, stole 40 bases to finish second in the league, fielded at a league leading .985 clip, was named the Most Valuable Player, and helped carry Montreal to the Little World Series, during which he batted .400. When Montreal prevailed in the final game against the Louisville Colonels, elated Royals fans carried Robinson on their shoulders to the team locker room. The *Courier*'s Sam Maltin reported that "thousands of baseball fans . . . waited to bid goodbye to the most popular" Royals player.[41] Hopper shook hands with Jackie and declared, "You're a real ballplayer and a gentleman. It's been wonderful having you on the team."[42]

After watching Robinson play in an early postseason exhibition contest, Wendell Smith reported that Brooklyn manager Leo Durocher considered Jackie "good enough to stick with the Dodgers in 1947." Durocher stated, "What amazes me about Robinson is his arm. It is 100 per cent stronger than when I saw him last spring at Daytona Beach. He can make that quick throw now and put something on it. He should be quite a help. I don't know where he'll play, but he'll help." The Dodgers manager's attitude scarcely surprised Smith, who recalled that during the just-concluded season's pennant race, Durocher was asked if he would use Robinson, should the front office sign him. "Would I use him?" Durocher responded. "Hell yes. I'd sleep with him and watch him like a mother watches her newborn baby." Smith now predicted that Robinson would make the Dodger squad in 1947, provided "he is good enough."[43]

Robinson next participated in a barnstorming tour that left him holding $3,500 worth of checks, most of which bounced. Needing the money, he played basketball with a semipro team, the Los Angeles Red Devils, earning $50 a game. After playing well in a number of games, Robinson had a tough outing against the Chicago American Gears, led by center George Mikan, the greatest professional basketball star of the era. Jackie possibly hurt his back golfing, and Branch Rickey, meeting with Robinson in Los Angeles, apparently convinced him to abandon the basketball court. Months after his spectacular debut in organized baseball, Robinson still awaited word from Rickey on whether he would be promoted to the Dodgers for the 1947 major league season. The Dodgers boss continued to plot how to bring about the integration of the majors, something he was now truly committed to pulling off as soon as possible. Rickey evidently thought this was the right thing to do. At the same time, he had already tapped into the wealth of talent that the Negro leagues offered, and he hoped to thereby strengthen Brooklyn into a National League powerhouse.

11

Greenberg's Final Season and Baseball's Great Experiment

A salary dispute with Tiger management led to the home run and RBI king's being waived out of the league. Hank Greenberg heard about the news on the radio rather than from club personnel. "It's a blow to learn that you're not worth $10,000 to any club in the American League," Greenberg admitted. Stunned by Detroit's move to dump him and not wanting to uproot his wife and infant son, he appeared ready to leave baseball. In reality, the Yankees, among other teams, would undoubtedly have picked up Greenberg if the Tigers were not determined to drive him out of the league altogether.[1] New York manager Bucky Harris spoke to Detroit general manager Billy Evans about this. "Billy, I want you to give me a frank and honest reply. Could we have had Hank if we had declined to send in waivers on him, and informed you that in no circumstances would we change our attitude?" Evans responded, "Bucky, in no circumstances would the Yankees have got Greenberg if they had refused to waive on him. As a matter of fact, we had decided not to let him go to any team in the American League. Had you refused to waive, Greenberg would have remained with the Tigers."[2] It was subsequently announced that the Pittsburgh Pirates of the National League had acquired the rights to Greenberg, purportedly for $50,000. Greenberg received word through a telegram that read, "THIS IS TO INFORM YOU THAT YOUR CONTRACT HAS BEEN ASSIGNED TO THE PITTSBURGH CLUB OF THE NATIONAL LEAGUE."[3]

The release of a four-year-old photograph of Greenberg attired in a Yankee uniform evidently helped convince the Tigers to dump him. That photograph had been taken in August 1943, when Greenberg was stationed at the Army Air Force base in Fort Worth, Texas. He had been ordered to fly to New York to participate in an All-Star war bond contest but made the trip without any baseball equipment. He borrowed a New York Yankee uniform for a workout at Yankee Stadium. A photographer subsequently captured Greenberg sporting the attire of the Tigers' hated foe. Following the 1946 season, when the photograph appeared in print, Detroit newspapers slammed "the Babe Ruth of the Bengals," Dan Daniel of the *New York World-Telegram* reported. The Tigers turned down repeated attempts by the Yankees to acquire Greenberg while making one counteroffer involving infielders Snuffy Stirnweiss and Aaron Robinson that New York was certain to refuse.[4] The Yankees were willing to spend as much as $75,000 to purchase the rights to Greenberg, who envisioned ending his playing career in his home city, but the Tigers refused to consider that option. The Yankees then decided they would rather have Greenberg waived out of the league.

Writing in *Baseball Magazine*, Daniel expressed shock that a player of Greenberg's caliber would be so unceremoniously disposed. Daniel called Greenberg's transfer to the Pirates unprecedented in the annals of major league history. Sluggers Babe Ruth, Bob Meusel, and Hack Wilson had all been dropped by their home clubs, but that was only when their careers had nosedived. Daniel believed this was the first time a still-great hitter had been dumped. Moreover, Greenberg was in shape, battled diligently for his team, and continued to produce at a high level. *New York Times* columnist Arthur Daley indicated that his fellow sportswriters "will resent bitterly the way Greenberg presumably is getting pushed around in this latest switch in clubs. Big Hank has no firmer supporters than among the typewriter pounders. He always had been gracious and nice to everyone of them; talks intelligently and interestingly on every occasion; has always been overpoweringly friendly and has been a colorful personality down through the years—well, they're all in his corner to the very last man."[5]

Reluctant to move over to the National League, Greenberg spoke over the telephone with John Galbreath, who, along with Frank McKinney and Bing Crosby, had just purchased the Pittsburgh franchise. Hank stated, "Mr. Galbreath, I'm not going to play anymore. I've announced my retirement and I mean it." Galbreath responded, "I don't want to talk you into playing. I just want to have lunch with you." When they met, Galbreath said, "Tell me what your objections are to playing with Pittsburgh." Greenberg replied, "I don't have my heart in it. I've played all my career with Detroit and that's home to me. Not to mention things like the fences in your ball park. Pittsburgh has a big ball park. I'm used to a park that's 340 feet down the left-field line. Yours is 380 feet. I don't want to disappoint everybody." The Pirate co-owner countered, "Don't worry about that. How far is it in Detroit? 340? Well, we'll make Pittsburgh 340, too. We'll bring the fences in so it'll be 340." Greenberg then indicated, "That's not so important. There a lot of things. For instance, I can't ride those trains anymore. The berths are too small. Every time I go in them I get a crick in my back." After Galbreath indicated that Greenberg could travel by plane, Hank indicated he did not want to have to contend with a roommate. Galbreath agreed to that condition as well. Greenberg said, "Well, if I ever did play for anybody, they'd have to give me my outright release at the end of the season. I never want to hear on the radio again that I've been traded or sold." Once more Galbreath accepted Greenberg's condition, and then the two men talked about salary. When told that Hank had received a hefty salary the previous season, Galbreath asked what he wanted for the upcoming year. Greenberg declared, "I'd say $100,000," and Galbreath said, "Fine, you got it."[6]

The Pirates signed Greenberg to the then most lucrative contract in major league history. The deal made him the senior circuit's first $100,000 player but might have paid as much as $45,000 more. McKinney, Galbreath, and Crosby also agreed to allow Greenberg to become a free agent at season's end. The Pirates placed a bullpen in front of the left field wall at Forbes Field, which became an area fans referred to as Greenberg Gardens and provided a target for both Greenberg and young slugger Ralph

Kiner, whom he mentored. Greenberg visited an ailing Babe Ruth at the legendary ballplayer's apartment in Manhattan prior to the start of the season. Bob Considine wrote about the meeting in *The Sporting News*, indicating that "Greenberg was like a boy sitting at the feet of the stricken master." Ruth at one point said that he was going to tell Greenberg something he had revealed only to Lou Gehrig: how to belt home runs. Ruth also advised, "Don't quit until every base is uphill."[7] Word of Greenberg's signing enabled the Pirates to sell several hundred thousands dollars of advance tickets, far more than they had previously. The sales increase was especially noteworthy, as Pittsburgh had finished near the bottom of the National League the previous year.

In August 1947, during the midst of another trying season, the Pittsburgh Pirates held Hank Greenberg Day. "I've never wanted a 'day' in a ball park," he told the crowd, which included several of his high school teammates. "The only day I ever desired was one with a chance to hit in the winning runs, and fortunately I've had a few of those in my time." Greenberg explained that he had agreed to this special occasion provided all contributions benefited the Rehabilitation Institute, which helped out those who were physically handicapped. After he was finished, one individual in the press box stated, "You can safely say that's the longest speech ever made by a ball player at home plate." Another one responded, "And the most intelligent."[8]

In his final year as a big league player, Greenberg hit only .249 but belted 25 homers, the eighth highest total in the National League, and led the league in walks with 104. Tutored by Greenberg, Kiner, in his sophomore year, tied the Giants' Johnny Mize for the home run title with 51, the most hit in the National League since 1930. Indeed, Kiner, who had long idolized Greenberg, later acknowledged, "Hank was the biggest influence in my life." Greenberg taught Kiner how important hard work was, with the two taking extra batting practice even after road games. Kiner fondly recalled, "No one except Hank taught me anything." It was Greenberg who told him to move closer to the plate and work at pulling the ball. The two spoke constantly about various pitchers. Kiner often signaled Greenberg as to what pitch was coming next. Greenberg demonstrated how important it was to sometimes deliberately look off stride in an early at bat, to entice the pitcher to throw the same pitch at a crucial moment later in the same contest. Kiner remembered too how Greenberg helped him pick out nicer clothes to wear away from the ballpark. Caral and Hank took him out to dinner, and the older ballplayer introduced him to the famed Copacabana nightclub in Manhattan.[9]

Although he thoroughly enjoyed mentoring Kiner, Greenberg recognized that he could no longer play at the level he was accustomed to, and he was frustrated by the Pirates' poor performance. They tied the Phillies for the league's worst record, a full thirty-two games behind the pennant-winning Brooklyn Dodgers. The lackadaisical play of several of the Pirate players and the apparent inability of manager Billy Herman to control his team hardly helped either. This was certainly difficult for a player like Greenberg, who had starred on four pennant-winning and two World Series championship teams with the Detroit Tigers. And even when the Tigers had failed to end up in first place, they almost always finished in the first division. When the 1947 season ended, Galbreath wrote appreciatively to Greenberg, who had helped Pittsburgh draw a record attendance of almost 1.3 million, over 400,000 better than the team's previous best mark.

> I want to say, Hank, that you fulfilled every promise you made. No one could have tried any harder or given any more time and effort to try to earnestly carry out every letter of a contract than you did. . . . I could not let the season pass without saying for the record that you did everything that was expected of you—and more. You did something for the Club and for the owners that scarcely anyone could have done and I am proud to have had a part in bringing you to us. The sentiment I have expressed also represents the thinking of the other owners of the Pirates.[10]

Greenberg's major league playing career was meteoric but abbreviated because of injuries and military service. He effectively played only 9½ seasons but scored 1,051 runs; belted 379 doubles, 71 triples, and 331 homers, including 11 grand slams; drove in 1,276 runs; walked 852 times; batted .313; and compiled an on-base percentage of .412 and a slugging average of .605. At the time he retired, his regular season home run total was the fifth highest in major league history, surpassed only by Ruth, Foxx, Ott, and Gehrig. He ended up with four home run and four RBI titles and was twice named American League MVP, while helping make the Detroit Tigers a perennial contender. In four World Series, he batted .318, with 5 homers and 22 RBIs.

And yet Greenberg's record, as impressive as it was, could have been still more remarkable. Perhaps only Sandy Koufax—ironically the only man to compete with Greenberg for the title of the game's greatest Jewish ballplayer—had such a brilliant career over such a short span of time. Greenberg effectively lost 5½ seasons, during which his career totals would undoubtedly have been among the sport's most historic. Only Ted Williams—who lost almost five years of his playing time due to service in World War II and the Korean War—suffered as much from a baseball vantage point. Two other great players of the era, Bob Feller and Joe DiMaggio, also had their career totals decidedly altered due to at least three years of wartime service. Willie Mays later experienced something of the same fate, with a pair of seasons virtually extinguished because he was drafted into the army during the Korean conflict.

At the same time, Greenberg will be remembered as the first great ballplayer to enter the U.S. military during World War II, a gesture of great symbolic importance because of his Jewish heritage. At the end of the war, he returned to the baseball diamond, again performing heroics. Because of all this, other Jewish players, including Indians third baseman Al Rosen, considered Greenberg a role model. Rosen, who twice led the American League in homers and RBIs and received an MVP award, viewed Hank as "a pathfinder," much like Jackie Robinson. In Rosen's words, Greenberg "paved the way for people like me." The great Cuban outfielder Minnie Miñoso who hit over .300 eight times in the majors and won four Gold Gloves, named Greenberg and the legendary Cuban star Martín

Dihigo, admitted to baseball Halls of Fame in five different countries, as his favorite ballplayers.

The final year of Greenberg's playing career was Jackie Robinson's first in the major leagues. In his initial column appearing in 1947, the *Pittsburgh Courier*'s Wendell Smith discussed the previous year as a breakthrough for professional black athletes. Heading the list was Jackie Robinson, the "Athlete of the Year," who seemed ready to join the Brooklyn Dodgers. If Robinson were added to the major league squad, "it will climax a long and unceasing fight for Negroes in the majors," Smith continued. Professional football had also opened its doors to black players for the first time in several years, as the new All-American Conference featured Cleveland's Marion Motley and Bill Willis, along with Los Angeles's Kenny Washington and Woody Strode, two former UCLA teammates of Robinson's.[11]

The January 1947 issue of *Sport* magazine contained an article by Tom Meany, titled "What Chance Has Jackie Robinson?" Robinson had hit well with the Royals, displaying little home run power but an occasional ability to drive fastballs for extra bases. Meany referred to Robinson's "amazing defensive record" with the Royals and indicated that during the course of the previous season, Jackie "mastered the art of pivoting, stepping across the bag and throwing across his chest, getting rid of the ball quickly." The sportswriter stated, "There is no doubting Robinson's speed. He can get down to first base faster than any other right-handed hitter in baseball, major or minor." He was a superb base runner, driving pitchers to distraction and helping players with pitch counts because of the numerous times opposing catchers called for pitch-outs or fastballs.[12]

Branch Rickey prepared to promote Robinson, who would be paid the league minimum of $5,000, to the major league team in 1947, believing the Dodgers would recognize that he "could mean a pennant, and ball players are not averse to cashing World Series checks." As Brooklyn readied for spring training in 1947, the Dodgers brass decided to relocate from Daytona Beach, Florida, to Havana, to avoid racial incidents in other towns and cities in the Sunshine State. Robinson hoped to be treated like "just another ballplayer," stating that "it upsets me when members of my own race make a big demonstration for me in the stands over some perfectly ordinary plays I've made. It could cause trouble and I wish they wouldn't do it. I just want to be judged on my merits as a ballplayer."[13] Rickey scheduled seven games for the Dodgers against the Montreal Royals, beginning in mid-March, telling Jackie, "I want you to be a whirling demon against the Dodgers in this series. I want you to concentrate, to hit that ball, to get on base *by any means necessary*. I want you to run wild, to steal the pants off them, to be the most conspicuous player on the field—but conspicuous only because of the kind of baseball you're playing." Such a performance, Rickey was convinced, would impress Robinson's teammates and lead New York sportswriters to help foster a demand by fans that Jackie be promoted to the big leagues. The *Brooklyn Eagle* predicted that African Americans would "storm the gates to play homage to the first member of their race to play professional ball" in the 20th century.[14] Robinson proceeded to hit .625 and steal seven bases, but several Dodgers were determined to prevent his promotion to the team.

Outfielder Dixie Walker, coming off a season in which he batted .319 and drove in 116 runs, passed around a petition opposing Robinson's joining the Dodgers, soliciting signatures from his teammates, many of whom came from the South. Walker also sent a letter to Rickey, asking to be traded as soon as possible, indicating, "For reasons I don't care to go into I feel my decision is best for all concerned."[15] Shortstop Pee Wee Reese, a Kentuckian, refused to support the petition, stating, "If he can take my job, he's entitled to it." On being informed of the petition, Dodgers manager Leo Durocher exploded. In a late-night meeting that he called, Durocher informed Walker and other protestors, "I don't care if the guy is yellow or black, or if he has stripes like a zebra. I'm the manager of this team and I say he plays. What's more, I say he can make us all rich. . . . An' if any of you can't use the money, I'll see that you're traded." In a column in the *Brooklyn Eagle*, Durocher contended that "a Robinson base hit or two" might alter players' minds about the black player. He continued, "If this fellow proves to be a winning player in the next three weeks, they will want Robby as much as I do."[16]

Tracking the Jackie Robinson story perhaps more diligently than any observer beside Branch Rickey, Wendell Smith praised the ballplayer in mid-March for enduring "the greatest test last year any baseball player has experienced in the history of the game." Robinson had to perform on the playing field and to remain "'the perfect model" at the same time. He was compelled to hold back when ridiculed or harassed. He was forced to reflect, "Although I want to rise up and fight back and challenge my tormentors, I can't. Even if I am right, someone will try to prove that I am wrong. There are no less than 14 million Negroes involved in this thing. I am their representative and I can't afford to let them down. I'll just have to stick it out and do the very best I can." Robinson proceeded to shine brightly in International League play and was now "worth $50,000 to any big league club," Smith suggested. The sportswriter then disclosed that Robinson had succeeded at risk to his own well-being. "Just before the season ended he was almost a physical wreck." The stress compelled him to visit a physician in Montreal, who warned, "You are on the verge of a nervous breakdown. You must have complete rest and stay away from the ball club." After taking three days off, Robinson had returned to help lead the Royals to the playoffs.[17] Like Arthur Daley of the *New York Times*, Smith had apparently been informed by Rickey that Robinson would soon join the Dodgers. For the time being, the two sportswriters were sworn to secrecy.

Writing to his friend Ralph P. Norton on March 24, 1947, Robinson acknowledged being "a bit bored with the headlines" but promised to keep attempting to earn them. Jackie was still hitting over .600 in games against the Dodgers, Cuban All-Stars, and Panamanian teams in Havana, Cuba. His early success convinced him that he could hold his own against major league pitchers. He was also handling the assignment at first base—rather than second, where more collisions would likely occur—so easily that "the fellows don't believe this is my first crack at that position." Robinson admitted that newspaper reports had been favorable but he had "been careful not to say anything out of the way."[18] Ambition, determination, and sheer talent were driving Robinson, as some began to quickly acknowledge. Dodgers pitcher Clyde King, eventually a major league manager, later reflected, "In all my 53 years in baseball, Jackie was the best base runner I've ever seen. I'm not talking about base *stealing* or *speed* on the bases but *instinct*. It was there that first spring training. I'll never forget how he would be on first base, and there would be a base hit to left field, and he'd take a big turn around second, and the left fielder would throw behind him into second. He'd keep going and trot into third. It took time around the league before the leftfielders realized that Jackie was suckering them. We'd sit on the bench and just laugh."[19] Undoubtedly to alleviate pressure on Robinson, Rickey accomodated Dixie Walker's desire to be traded, sending the star outfielder to the Pittsburgh Pirates.

In his column on March 31, 1947, Tommy Holmes responded, "He is a terrific natural player." Although Robinson had made mistakes at first base, those were the kinds any player would commit on playing an unfamiliar position. Holmes remained uncertain if Rickey would promote Robinson to the Dodgers or send him back to Montreal. "I've given up trying to read Branch Rickey's mind," Holmes admitted.[20] On April 9, Holmes wrote, "It is doubtful that any ball player at any time ever went through a set of circumstances calculated to construct a mental ordeal as Jackie did this Spring." Rickey too appeared to be "on the spot," having to decide where to play Robinson. If Rickey sent him back to the Royals, he would basically be admitting that "his entire program of breaking down the color line in baseball has failed."[21]

On April 10, Rickey announced that Robinson would be playing first base for the Dodgers. Robinson received a Brooklyn uniform with the number 42 and signed a contract for the major-league minimum salary of $5,000. Baseball's "noble experiment" continued, as the Robinsons took up residence in a five-room, second-floor flat located on McDonough Street in a black district in Brooklyn. When not playing or practicing, Robinson generally remained at home, often taking care of his infant son Jackie Jr. or reading newspapers. Wendell Smith discussed what the stakes were in his column in the *Courier*. "No player in history has tried harder to become a big leaguer. And no owner in history has tried harder to make a player a big leaguer. If Robinson fails to make the grade, it will be many years before a Negro makes the grade. This is IT! If Jackie Robinson is turned down this week, then you can look for another period of years before the question ever arises officially again."[22] *PM* columnist Tom Meany predicted that

Jackie "will have a rough time in the National League" because of bigots who would "make it unpleasant" for him.[23] Referring to his former star, Royals manager Clay Hopper pointed out, "I had him at first one day and back at second the next. And he had to go and get sick and was badly shaken up in that collision with Bruce Edwards at first base in Havana." Hopper continued, "Why, last year he had never played second before but when I threw him in there he turned out to be the best! He's a good ball player!"[24] After Robinson played in an exhibition contest against the New York Yankees, coach Clyde Sukeforth, who had temporarily taken over the Dodgers following a year-long suspension of Leo Durocher for consorting with gamblers, declared that Jackie was "going to be alright. He's a great ball player and will prove it as soon as he gets adjusted. He can hit, run and field. He's a great all-around athlete and can't miss."[25]

One factor operating in Robinson's favor was the borough of Brooklyn. As baseball owner Bill Veeck Sr. indicated, "If Jackie Robinson was the ideal man to break the color line, Brooklyn was the ideal place."[26] Brooklyn boasted around 200,000 African Americans and one million Jews among its 2.7 million residents. Brooklyn revered the Dodgers, who played at cozy Ebbets Field. At the same time, intercity rivalries with the Giants and the Yankees remained fierce, particularly during pennant races and crosstown World Series. Remarkably, between 1947 and 1956, at least one New York team made it to the World Series every year except in 1948, and only in that year and 1954 did two New York squads fail to do so.

ESPN television reported fifty years later that a conspiracy existed to prevent Robinson from ever playing in a major league game. Former Pirates player Al Gionfriddo stated, "I think every team in the league voted," while Cubs pitcher Hank Wyse recalled that his teammates "voted 25–0 or 24–1 to strike." Chicago catcher Dewey Williams remembered waiting for a phone call that was to trigger the strike: it was to come from one of the Dodgers players, Dixie Walker. The call never arrived and the season opened as scheduled.[27]

Robinson went hitless during his major league debut against the Boston Braves on April 15, 1947. Over 26,000 fans, more than half of whom were black, showed up at Ebbets Field to watch the historic occasion, but Robinson was unable to figure out pitcher Johnny Sain. He indicated in his autobiography, "I did a miserable job. If they expected any miracles . . . they were sadly disappointed." He did reach base on a throwing error and scored the winning run in a tight ballgame, crossing the plate after a double by outfielder Pete Reiser. Robinson "was mobbed by youthful autograph hunters" after the contest, compelling him to "literally . . . fight his way through the press of admirers."[28] Tommy Holmes wrote that the reactions to Robinson during Opening Day indicated that "the heavens are not going to fall because a Negro baseball player is in the major leagues." Also "Jackie's bearing and intelligence as well as his athletic ability impresses people."[29] In his fourth game in the big leagues, Robinson smacked a double and a pair of singles, thrilling "his big Harlem following" despite the Dodgers' falling to the Giants, 4–3.[30]

African American publications celebrated Robinson's first game, with the *Boston Chronicle* ringing out, "TRIUMPH OF WHOLE RACE SEEN IN JACKIE'S DEBUT IN MAJOR-LEAGUE BALL." The Boston newspaper deemed the appearance of the "very colored" young ballplayer at Ebbets Field "one of the most dramatic stories in the whole saga of American democracy." It "climaxed" a struggle over the span of more than a decade to compel the major leagues to terminate "their discrimination against colored players." Still more important, the *Boston Chronicle* continued, "it marked the breakdown of segregation in the nation's largest and most popular sport, and presaged their inclusion in the others which still bar them." The *Boston Chronicle* credited the *Daily Worker* for initiating "the crusade" and applauded *PM* for backing the campaign almost as soon as that left-wing New York newspaper began operations in 1940.[31]

The *Atlanta Daily World* editorialized, "Achievement is not a matter of race and color. It is a matter of environment and opportunity," then indicated that "American prejudice charges it up to race" when blacks performed and behaved badly. "That is why Negro American may take pardonable pride in the worthwhile achievements of their people, whether in the field or sports; in the arts and sciences; in business or the professions.

They have got to make the grade, or else it is going to be written off as a racial and color weakness." As exemplified by his performance in a recent exhibition game, Robinson had "achieved notably, not alone for himself but for his race, although he has expressed the hope that he be judged only as an individual." The editorial praised Branch Rickey's "bold stroke" and suggested that the nation could learn "another important lesson" from Robinson's entrance into major league baseball. "That the names of Jackie Robinson, Joe Louis, George Washington Carver and hundreds upon hundreds of others, didn't just happen; that in spite of the barriers of race and color, distinguished achievement, industry and manliness are traits which must eventually be recognized under any skin."[32]

By contrast, the *New York Amsterdam News* declared that despite Robinson's deserved promotion, "democracy still marches at a snail's pace. For in the year 1946 A.D. the fact that a qualified ball player who happened to be colored was signed by a major league baseball club (at a notoriously low salary) was looked upon as earth shaking." The *Amsterdam News* denied that the United States "has become of age and is accepting the colored man or woman on merit. Unfortunately, Jackie Robinson is still a Negro ball player first and a big leaguer second." Moreover, "the few Negroes employed in positions rarely held by other members of that race only emphasizes how deep rooted is discrimination in this country."[33]

The *Michigan Chronicle* featured a front page article on Robinson's "auspicious debut"; an editoral titled "Another Hero"; a cartoon of the physically sculpted player, stating that "Jackie Robinson Fans" could be found in the right field grandstands, with a caption reading "Who Said We Can't Get To First Base?"; a photograph of Robinson at the plate; an article on favorable press coverage; another one on his stardom at UCLA; and a sports column on him. The editorial opened with the statement, "Last week the great day came for Jackie Robinson and a new page in the history of our national sport and in the history of our people was written." The editorial affirmed, "Jackie Robinson is qualified by training, background and experience to open the door of our national sport to Negroes and we have no question in our minds about his success. He will make good because he is just that kind of a guy and because he has the opportunity to do so." The newspaper declared, "This is a great victory for us and it is also a big victory for our own country," terminating a longstanding "symbol of intolerance and of bigotry which put us to shame all over the world." The article discussed his collegiate days and closed with the observation that Robinson had succeeded in the sports realm due to "superior athletic ability, a well-rounded personality, and a basic intelligence which directed him when to make the right moves at the right time." In his column, Russ J. Cowans offered that Robinson augured "a new era in baseball," bringing back speed to the game and attracting African American fans from across the country. Given Robinson's early performance in the major leagues, *Michigan Chronicle* sports editor Bill Matney offered, "He will likely remain there for some time to come." By this point, even Dixie Walker was insisting he had been "misquoted" regarding his supposed opposition to Robinson. Matney wrote, "Evidently Branch Rickey's ultimatum was directed and carried enough steam to get it across to the boys that he meant business."[34] Following his second big league game, in which he garnered his first hit (a bunt single), Robinson had a new manager, Burt Shotton, who had taken over as Dodgers acting manager after Sukeforth declined to fill the position for the rest of the season.

Robinson soon suffered through a game on April 22 that "brought me nearer to cracking up than I had ever been," he later recalled. Members of the Philadelphia Phillies, bellowing out from their dugout, called him "nigger" and "black boy" and told him to "go back to the cotton fields," "the jungles," or "the bushes." The Phillies asked their opponent, "Hey, snowflake, which one of you white boy's wives are you dating tonight?"[35] All of this was almost too much for Robinson, who "for one wild and rage-crazed moment" was prepared to say "to hell with Mr. Rickey's 'noble experiment' . . . to hell with the image of patient black freak." Instead, he singled and scored the game's only run. And the abuse pouring forth from Philly manager and Southerner Ben Chapman "did more than anybody to unite the Dodgers," Rickey later revealed. During one game with the Phillies, Dodgers infielder Eddie Stanky finally blurted out, "Why don't you guys go to work on somebody who can fight back? There isn't one of you has the guts of a louse!" Both the *New York Daily Mirror* and the black press laid into Chapman as they condemned the Phillies' "guttersnipe language" while praising Robinson's "admirable restraint." Commissioner Chandler chastised Chapman and instructed him to pose for photographs with the black player. Philadelphia pitcher Freddy Schmidt later reported that after the photographers departed, Chapman told Robinson, "Jackie, you know, you're a good ballplayer, but you're still a nigger to me."[36] While at the time he indicated that Chapman "impressed me as a nice fellow," in his autobiography Robinson admitted, "Having my picture taken with this man was one of the most difficult things I had to make myself do." In a column titled "Jackie Robinson Says" that appeared in the *Courier*, the newest Dodger wrote, "The things the Phillies shouted at me from their bench have been shouted at me from other benches and I am not worried about it. They sound just the same in the big leagues as they did in the minor league."[37] The Dodgers next traveled to play the Cincinnati Reds, who cried out at Robinson, "You nigger sonofabitch, you shoeshine boy." They also taunted shortstop Pee Wee Reese: "How can you play with this nigger bastard?"[38]

Performing erratically in his first several weeks in the National League, and little helped by an ailing right shoulder, Robinson went 0 for 20 during the last part of April. Critics called for his benching, and teammates like pitcher Rex Barney could tell that he was struggling. He took early morning batting practice to pull out of the slump. Robinson began to take off in early May as he compiled a 14-game hitting streak. Team captain Reese recognized, as did many on the team, that the talented and gutsy Robinson was going to make it.

As the Dodgers readied to play the Phillies again in Philadelphia, Rickey received a call from Herb Pennock, the former great pitcher who was serving as the Phillies general manager. Pennock said, "[You] just can't bring the nigger here with the rest of your team, Branch. We're not ready for that sort of thing yet. We won't be able to take the field against your Brooklyn team if that boy Robinson is in uniform."[39] After getting to Philadelphia, the manager at the Ben Franklin Hotel told road secretary Harold Parrott not to bring the Dodgers back as long as the team had black players. Parrott proceeded to book the team into the Ben Franklin while Robinson stayed at the Attucks, an all-black hotel. Over the course of the 1947 season, the Phillies, led by manager Chapman, proved the most abusive in their treatment of Robinson.

On the morning of May 9, Stanley Woodward of the *New York Herald Tribune* reported that National League president Ford Frick had felt compelled to quash another potential players strike intended to drive Robinson from organized ball. The players were members of the world champion St. Louis Cardinals but did not include the team's great star and reigning league MVP, Stan Musial. Woodward paraphrased the National League executive as stating,

I do not care if half the league strikes. Those who do it will encounter quick retribution. All will be suspended and I don't care if it wrecks the National League for five years. This is the United States of America, and one citizen has as much right to play as another. The National League will go down the line with Robinson whatever the consequences. You will find that if you go through with this . . . that you have been guilty of complete madness.[40]

The NAACP congratulated President Frick: "Your statement has been applauded by all lovers of fair play and especially by Negro citizens and sports fans. The consensus of opinion is that it is the most pointed and unequivocal pronouncement on fair play in sports, so far as racial minority participation is concerned, that has ever been made."[41] Later accounts questioned the veracity of Woodward's story, indicating that the Cardinals had simply been tossing out idle threats and that no concerted plan existed for a walkout. Even the sportswriter's quoting of Frick was called into question, with Woodward supposedly admitting that the commissioner had not been interviewed.[42]

Robinson reacted to the purported controversy by having his best game yet in the major leagues, the *New York World-Telegram's* Bill Roeder suggested. In a losing effort, Robinson singled, doubled, scored two runs, and played brilliantly in the field. Rickey informed the press the same day that police were investigating threats on Jackie's life. He also shipped off Brooklyn's second-string first baseman, Howie Schultz, to the Phillies and announced that earlier efforts to purchase New York Giants slugger Johnny Mize were at an end. Rickey proclaimed, "We'll be all right. I don't have the slightest doubt of Robinson's ability. He is finding his way around first base and hitting with more confidence." Jimmy Cannon of the *New York Post* felt compelled to ask that Jackie "be judged by the scorer's ledger and not by the prejudices of indecent men" while claiming that Robinson was a major leaguer possessing only "ordinary ability." Cannon went on to reveal something of how trying Robinson's first few months with the Dodgers were proving to be. "In the clubhouse Robinson is a stranger. The Dodgers are polite and courteous with him, but it is obvious he is isolated by those with whom he plays. I have never heard remarks made against him or detected any rudeness where he was concerned. But the silence is loud and Robinson never is part of the jovial and aimless banter of the locker room. He is the loneliest man I have ever seen in sports."[43]

Others later disputed Cannon's characterization of Robinson, and Jackie himself expressed appreciation for "the courage and decency" displayed by Dodgers shortstop Reese. During one game, as the Boston Braves heckled Robinson, they began directing some of it at the Kentuckian Reese for playing alongside a black man. Without a word or a look in the direction of the taunting Braves players, Reese walked over to Jackie, placed a hand on his shoulder and spoke with him. Robinson considered this a "gesture of comradeship and support." The taunting dissipated.[44]

On May 19, 1947, Rodney Fisher of Richmond, Virginia, sent a note to Robinson to congratulate him on "doing a swell job out there." Fisher wrote, "I happen to be a white Southerner. But I just wanted you to know that not all us Southerners are S.O.B.'s. Here's one that is rooting for you to make good—and, to tell the truth, I imagine there's a lot more of us that feel the same way." Fisher commended Robinson for withstanding "the tremendous pressure put on you" while performing at a level equal to Booker

T. Washington, George Washington Carver, or Marian Anderson. He declared, "I should also say that you're doing a darned fine job for all Americans."[45] G. Gilbert Smith from Jersey City, New Jersey, wrote to Robinson on June 1, 1947, sharing his experiences of having served as the first African American machinist in a shop of about four hundred men during World War II. "They did all the little dirty underhanded things to me that they must be doing to you," he wrote. Smith developed a "thick skin," knowing he "couldn't fight back because my side would never have been considered in a showdown." He was writing to assure Jackie "that there are plenty of people, black and white, who are rooting for you," because he recognized "how much guts" were required to "play the kind of ball you're playing under so much pressure."[46] Later that season, Bernice Franklin wrote to Jackie, mentioning that she resided in "a small all negro town" in Arkansas. For residents of her community, "there is no greater thrill than a broadcast of the Dodgers' ball game." Franklin informed Robinson, "We are so proud of you, and want you to know we southerners think you are tops."[47]

One player who clearly empathized with Robinson was Pittsburgh Pirates first baseman Hank Greenberg. Hank followed Robinson's progress as the 1947 season continued. Obviously relating to the tribulations Robinson endured, Greenberg predicted, "The more they ride him the more they will spur him on. It threw me a lot when I first came up. I know how he feels. . . . They will keep needling Jackie, and he will react by forcing himself to play over his head. I'll be awfully surprised if I hear that Robinson fails to hit and hold his job." In May in the first of a three-game series in Pittsburgh, the two men literally collided during a game, when Jackie, razzed by Greenberg's teammates as a "dumb black son of a bitch," bunted and raced for the base covered by Hank.[48] The throw from pitcher Ed Bahr pulled Greenberg off the bag and resulted in a collision with Robinson. Falling down, Robinson managed to get up and scampered over to second base. Greenberg later told Robinson, "Hope I didn't hurt you, Jackie. I was trying to get that wild throw. When I stretched out to get the ball you crossed the bag at the same time. I tried to keep out of your way but it was impossible." Robinson replied, "No, Hank, I didn't get hurt. I was just knocked off balance and couldn't stay on my feet." Greenberg then asked, "How are things going, Jackie?" Robinson answered, "Pretty good, but it's plenty rough up here in the big leagues." Greenberg told the Dodger, "Listen, I know it's plenty tough. You're a good ball player, however, and you'll do all right. Just stay in there and fight back, and always remember to keep your head up."[49] As Robinson later reflected, he believed that the Jewish player was "sincere because I heard he had experienced some racial trouble when he came up. I felt sure that he understood my problems."[50] Following the game, Robinson spoke to reporters about Greenberg. "He sure is a swell guy. He helped me a lot by saying the things he did. I found out that not all the guys on the other teams are bad heels. I think Greenberg, for instance, is pulling for me to make good."[51]

Other Pirate players continued to hurl abusive language, including "nigger," at Robinson. Pittsburgh third baseman Frank Gustine later recalled, "The language was brutal. But he held up." During that same series with the Pirates, Dodgers teammates expressed support for Robinson after he was hit by pitcher Fritz Ostermueller. Led by Eddie Stanky, the Dodgers warned their opponents, "Don't forget, you guys have to come to bat, too." Another Dodger snarled, "We'll get even with you, and we'll keep you guys in the dirt."[52] That level of support led Wendell Smith to dispute Jimmy Cannon's observation that Robinson was "the loneliest man in sports." Smith contended that instead "harmony and unity" existed on the Brooklyn squad. Robinson seemed well liked. He had become "an important cog in the lineup."[53]

In its June 1947 issue, *Baseball Magazine* referred to Robinson's entry into the majors and the breaking of the sport's color barrier as the "most significant" development in the current baseball season. The publication acknowledged that "no highly publicized rookie has ever broken into the majors under as much pressure." He had entered the big leagues at the age of twenty-eight, following a lone season in organized minor-league baseball. "Robinson is traveling a rough road," the magazine concluded.[54] But after a four-hit game on June 1 that included a double and a triple against the Cincinnati Reds, Robinson's batting average shot above .300, for the first time in the majors. He batted nearly .400 during the month of June.

His twenty-one-game hitting streak ended on July 4, a mere game short of the major league mark for rookies, but he soon initiated another one that lasted nearly as long. In July, Cleveland Indians owner Bill Veeck brought up Negro league outfielder Larry Doby, while Bill and Charlie DeWitt, the brothers who ran the St. Louis Browns, inked Negro leaguers Henry Thompson and Willard Brown to contracts. The headline of Tommy Holmes's column in the *Brooklyn Eagle* read, "Jackie Robinson Is No Longer Unique." One unnamed major league manager criticized the latest signings. "Robinson has been successful," he contended, "and more power to him. But Rickey brought him up in the right way. He not only proved his ability in the International League but conditioned himself at Montreal for the circumstances he'd have to face in the National League. In other words, he was trained in every respect for a tough assignment." The major league skipper then warned, "These other Negroes lack that background. They may or may not have the necessary ability but they are not as well prepared as Robinson was."[55]

On August 25, Rickey added Negro league pitcher Dan Bankhead to the Dodgers and also assigned black pitchers Al Preston and Fred Shepherd to minor league teams. That was also the month when the Cardinals' Enos Slaughter, supposedly one of the leaders of the aborted strike earlier in the season, appeared to deliberately attempt to park his spikes on Robinson's leg at first base. The next inning, Robinson singled and, according to Dodgers pitcher Rex Barney, told Cardinals first baseman Stan Musial, "I don't care what happens, but when I get to second base, I'm gonna kill somebody. I'm gonna knock him into center field. I don't care what kind of play it is, he's going down." When Musial replied, "I don't blame you. You have ever right to do it," Robinson then decided not to retaliate.[56] Following the game, some of his teammates urged him, "If they give you the works, give it back to them—and the team will be behind you 100%."[57] Thus as Robinson saw it, the Slaughter incident "unified the Dodger team."[58] In mid-September, when the Cardinals again met the Dodgers, whom they trailed by 4½ games, Robinson was spiked once more, this time by catcher Joe Garagiola. During the next inning when Robinson went to the plate, he got into a heated argument with Gargiola that ended only when the umpire intervened. It appeared that Robinson had made a statement that he would not allow himself to be treated as he had been throughout much of the season.

In September, the young singer and Brooklyn resident Lena Horne told *PM*, "I'll never forget how frightened I was for Jackie Robinson, how we were frightened because we knew that if he made the normal mistakes that any ballplayer made it would be a reflection on his race. We felt, oh God, he must perform magnificently or those white players will scorn him."[59] The September 22, 1947, cover of *Time* magazine featured a likeness of a smiling Jackie Robinson, along with a caption, "He and the boss took a chance." The lengthy article called his first season "the toughest" ever faced by a ballplayer. "He had made good as a major leaguer, and proved himself as a man," and had captured the initial Rookie of the Year honor selected by *The Sporting News. Time* praised Robinson as "one of the great all-around athletes of his day," likening him to football star Glenn Davis and track-and-field champion turned golfing great Babe Didrikson Zaharias. The magazine said the "jackrabbit fast" Robinson was "one thought and two steps ahead of every base-runner in the business." Robinson possessed "intelligence, patience and willingness" and was "a natural athlete," something Branch Rickey, "the smartest man in baseball," had recognized, the article indicated. Rickey called Robinson "the best batter in the game with two strikes on him." When asked who taught the ballplayer how to run the bases so brilliantly, Rickey answered, "Primarily God."[60]

In proclaiming Robinson the Rookie of the Year, *The Sporting News*'s editor J. G. Taylor Spink declared,

That Jack Roosevelt Robinson might have had more obstacles than his first-year competitors, and that he perhaps had a harder fight to gain even major league recognition, was no concern of this publication. The sociological experiment that Robinson represented, the trail-blazing that he did, the barriers he broke down, did not enter into the decision. He was rated and examined solely as a freshman player in the big leagues—on the basis of his hitting, his running, his defensive lay, his team value.

Spink quoted Dixie Walker, who admitted, "No other ball player on this club, with the possible exception of Bruce Edwards, has done more to put the Dodgers up in the race than Robinson. He is everything Branch Rickey said he was when he came up from Montreal." Spink deemed Robinson, who had stolen home three times, "a National League eye-popper" who "has run the bases like an Ebony Ty Cobb." Noteworthy too was the fact that "when he bunts, Jackie is likely to light a fire under the best pitchers in the game." Spink concluded, "Jackie Robinson has done it all, in his first year as a major leaguer. What more could anyone ask?"[61]

Late in the season, the Dodgers held Jackie Robinson Day at Ebbets Field. Over 26,000 fans showed up to watch Robinson receive a bevy of gifts, including a television set, a radio, an electric broiler, and a car, valued altogether at $10,000. He had started the baseball campaign "as a lonely man, often feeling like a black Don Quixote tilting at a lot of white windmills." He concluded his first year in the majors "feeling like a member of a solid team." He had acquired a large degree of self-control and had managed to earn his teammates' respect. They in turn now recognized "that it's not skin color but talent and ability that counts."[62] Robinson completed his rookie major league season with a .297 batting average, 12 home runs, and a league-high 29 stolen bases as he helped lead the Dodgers to the National League pennant. He came in fifth in the balloting for league MVP, an award won by Boston third baseman Bob Elliott. The Dodgers flourished at the gates, establishing a regular season attendance record of 1,807,526 fans. During the World Series, the end-of-the-season spectacle in which Robinson proudly became the first black man to play, huge crowds turned out at Yankee Stadium and Ebbets Field to watch the crosstown teams compete. The Yankees won the title, defeating the Dodgers 5–2 in the seventh game. Robinson batted .259 in the series, collecting 7 hits, including 2 doubles, while scoring and driving in 3 runs each. He also swiped a pair of bases, but the Dodgers lost for the third time in three World Series appearances. More end-of-the-season or World Series heartbreaks would be in store for the Brooklyn Dodgers, later referred to as the Boys of Summer.

Robinson's feats on the baseball diamond during the 1947 season were remarkable enough for any ballplayer, but far more so considering the magnitude of the experiment that he and Branch Rickey had undertaken in integrating the national pastime. The journalist David Halberstam, an astute chronicler of the postwar scene, later called Robinson "history's man. Nothing less." Robinson's role in integrating organized baseball was monumentally important. He helped contest stereotypes about what African Americans were or were not capable of while challenging barriers that restricted them, thereby violating "elemental fairness," as Halberstam put it. The fact that Robinson's breakthrough occurred when it did was still more noteworthy. The nation had just participated in a crusade to defeat the Axis powers, including Nazi Germany, with its ghastly glorification of a supposed Master Race and systematic program to annihilate Europe's Jews and gypsies and enslave millions throughout Central and Eastern Europe. Now one white man and one black man were engaged in their own quests to shatter discriminatory practices at home. No major leaguer was more respected than Hank Greenberg, now at the end of his career. And it was clear by the end of 1947 that Rickey had made a wise choice in selecting Jackie Robinson as an American racial pioneer. Robinson was, as Halberstam records, more than a gifted athlete. He was also "a gifted human being, proud, strong, disciplined, courageous," serving as an exemplar for many others far beyond America's athletic domain.[63]

12

A Tiger's Horizons Expand

While attending the 1947 World Series between the Brooklyn Dodgers, led by Jackie Robinson, and the New York Yankees, still spearheaded by Joe DiMaggio, Hank Greenberg ran into the maverick owner and president of the Cleveland Indians, Bill Veeck. The two had dinner at Toots Shor's Restaurant, located at 51 West 51st Street in Manhattan. As Veeck later reported, "I didn't know exactly what he could do for us, but I did know that baseball couldn't afford to let a guy like Hank Greenberg get away." Veeck told Greenberg that "he was too good a baseball man, we'll find something for you."[1]

American popular culture began presenting Jews more favorably than in the past. RKO Radio Pictures released *Crossfire* on July 22, 1947, starring Robert Young, Robert Ryan, Robert Mitchum, Gloria Grahame, and Sam Levene, and directed by Edward Dmytryk. Ryan played the part of an anti-Semitic soldier who murdered a war hero because he was a Jew. *Crossfire* received an Oscar nomination for best picture of the year. Twentieth Century Fox premiered *Gentlemen's Agreement* on November 11, 1947, an adaptation of the bestselling book by Laura Z. Hobson, with Gregory Peck and Dorothy McGuire in the lead roles. Peck took on the part of Philip Schuyler Green, an investigative journalist who pretended to be Jewish so he could write about anti-Semitism. The film, directed by Elia Kazan, received three Oscars, including the Academy Awards for Best Picture and

Best Director. Other works, including a series of well-received novels, portrayed Jews, albeit frequently secularized ones, as in Saul Bellow's *The Victim*, more favorably than had often been the case. Norman Mailer's *The Naked and the Dead* and Irwin Shaw's *The Young Lions*, each released in 1948, helped establish the literary reputations of those young Jewish authors. Arthur Miller's play *Death of a Salesman* garnered the 1949 Pulitzer Prize for Drama, and the Tony Award for Best Play on Broadway.

Meanwhile, Veeck attempted to convince Greenberg, who had $300,000 saved in Treasury bonds, to become a minority owner of the Indians. Greenberg agreed to the proposition, meeting Veeck in Tucson during spring training. Veeck wanted Greenberg to put on a uniform again, but after working out with the team, Hank declined. While the original idea of purchasing a minority share of the Indians also fell through, Greenberg became Veeck's assistant at a salary of $15,000. The Indians were involved in a tight pennant race during the 1948 season. Former Negro league outfielder Larry Doby batted .301 in his first full season with Cleveland, and the great Satchel Paige, now reportedly forty-two years old, joined the Indians in mid-season, compiling a 6–1 win-loss record with 2 shutouts and a 2.47 earned run average. Veeck sought to persuade Greenberg to replace star shortstop Lou Boudreau, whose mother was Jewish although he was raised a Christian, as Cleveland's manager. Greenberg declined, and the thirty-year-old Boudreau completed a dream season, batting .355 and leading the Tribe to a playoff victory over the Red Sox to capture the American League pennant. He then guided the Indians to a World Series triumph over the Boston Braves.

Following the season, Greenberg told Veeck that he wanted to return to New York to seek other opportunities. Veeck then placed Greenberg in charge of the minor league operations and the eighteen farm clubs of the Cleveland Indians. Veeck sold his interest in the team in 1949, and Greenberg became general manager. He almost immediately encountered anti-Semitism. American League executives planned to stay at a large hotel in Phoenix to hold winter meetings. An employee of the hotel let it be known that Greenberg would not be allowed to stay there because the former slugger was

Jewish. The American League representatives then moved over to the Arizona Biltmore, owned by the Wrigleys, who also owned the Chicago Cubs. Greenberg "was shocked, and angry" when informed about the incident.[2]

In his column of December 3, 1949, Wendell Smith extolled the hiring of Hank Greenberg as the Cleveland Indians general manager. "It is good for the Tribe, it is good for Cleveland and it is good for baseball." Smith continued, "It is particularly good for those advocating the continued advancement of the Negro ball player." Greenberg needed to be applauded because he had earned the promotion and also "because he has maintained an attitude with respect to race, color and creed throughout his career that has been consistent." Smith recalled how Greenberg was one of the first ballplayers to acknowledge Jackie Robinson's presence in the majors. "Greenberg went out of his way to let Robinson know that all the big stars in the game did not resent his presence." Greenberg would be as happy as Jackie that Robinson had become such a great ball player, thereby fulfilling a prediction of Hank's, Smith suspected. Greenberg's empathy resulted from the fact that he had experienced similar prejudice on entering the big leagues. Players "taunted him, chastised him and made life miserable." Bench jockeys on the other teams "rode him every day, every inning." Greenberg proved resilient and became an even better, more determined competitor. Smith declared, "That's why he was so conscious of Robinson's position when Jackie came up. That's why he went out of his way to encourage him. He never forgot the road he traveled and knew that Jackie's was going to be even tougher." In Smith's estimation, "Greenberg's words of encouragement went a long way towards helping Robinson make the grade." Robinson had repeatedly acknowledged "that Greenberg's 'little talk' helped him tremendously." Robinson particularly appreciated Greenberg's offer to have dinner with him and Rachel.[3]

The March 1950 issue of *Baseball Magazine* featured an extended article titled "Henry B. Greenberg, Executive." Author Ed Rumill acknowledged that "life in baseball has never been a bowl of big red cherries for Hank." From the outset "it has been a rugged, uphill struggle," demanding "courage and determination" to enable Greenberg to accomplish what he had. As a player he exuded a never-say-die attitude and was likely to become the same kind of executive, Rumill believed. Greenberg appeared well suited for his current post as the Cleveland GM, possessing "a sound knowledge of the game, the energy and determination of a player, and the personality of a gentleman." The writer emphasized that Greenberg "was always a gentleman," no matter what he endured. At the same time, this "giant of a man" was "as gentle and gracious as the servant of a royal family," ever exuding polish and class.[4]

Sportswriter Ed Fitzgerald published a full-length article, "Hank Greenberg: A Study in Success," which appeared in the March 1951 issue of *Sport* magazine. Fitzgerald asked Greenberg if his own career helped him to better understand what players experienced. Greenberg replied, "I think it helps, of course. I'm fair with the ballplayers because I am naturally sympathetic to them. On the other hand, I'm difficult in that I demand that they put out. I remember the way I felt when I was a player about certain men on the ball club who weren't putting out all they might have." Fitzgerald revealed that the ever-ambitious Greenberg viewed his position with Cleveland "as a stepping-stone," hoping someday to purchase a big league team.[5]

The Indians, who had finished third and fourth, respectively, during the two previous seasons, hired Al Lopez as their manager in 1951. The Indians proved competitive during the next few years under Greenberg's guidance, finishing second behind the New York Yankees from 1951 to 1953. The Indians were led by star pitchers Bob Feller, Early Wynn, and Mike Garcia and slugging third baseman Al Rosen, major league baseball's latest Jewish star, who was twice the league homer run titlist and the 1953 American League MVP. Rosen long considered Greenberg one of his heroes and had closely followed his attempt to break Babe Ruth's home run mark in 1938. Rosen later recalled, "I can remember that there was very strong anti-Semitic feeling in America about not letting a Jew break the revered Babe Ruth's record." By the time Rosen entered the majors in 1947, he believed that "more acceptance" of Jewish ballplayers existed. Rosen then stated, "Remember, Greenberg was to Jewish ballplayers what Jackie Robinson was to blacks. I'm not trying to draw an analogy between the problem the blacks have and the Jews, but there were problems nevertheless. Whenever people don't come to grips with that there can be a real problem. And Greenberg went through a great deal and he paved the way for people like me." Greenberg was unique, in his estimation. As Rosen reflected, "There were some Jewish ballplayers but no one of his kind—don't forget, when you talk about Greenberg you're talking about a man of great stature in the minds of people who never knew anything about baseball. He was a cultured, intelligent, bright, good-looking, massive sort of a man." Greenberg was also "polished and he was all the things people would aspire to." As Rosen acknowledged, "You feel you're in a vast sea of mediocrity out there and then someone rises above the crowd. Now here comes a Jew who is rising above and going for Babe Ruth's revered record and it's very obvious that more people are going to take shots at him. He was the first big name. The rest of the Jews who came along after that had some problems, but he made it easier." Knowingly or not Rosen patterned himself after Greenberg. "I always felt that I had to conduct myself . . . in a courtly manner, and I wanted people to think of me in a certain frame of mind, in a certain way. Dignity is the word I am searching for."[6]

Greenberg was drawn into a conflict involving players and baseball management during the winter of 1953. The owners were threatening to terminate the players' rather paltry pension plan. Commissioner Ford Frick agreed to meet with Pirate slugger Ralph Kiner and Yankee pitching ace Allie Reynolds, who had been selected to represent the National League and American League, respectively, but refused to let them bring along their unpaid lawyer, J. Norman Lewis. When asked why Lewis could not participate, as the owners always had legal representation at the meetings, Frick simply stated, "That's different." Kiner and Reynolds responded, "J. Norman Lewis attends the meeting, or there's no meeting," and left. Told by his friends Kiner and Detroit manager Fred Hutchinson that a strike now loomed, Greenberg relayed that information to baseball magnates. They in turn named him and Pittsburgh Pirates owner John Galbreath to a committee that would meet with the player representatives. Galbreath said to Greenberg, "I'll go along with whatever you want to do." Greenberg then met with Kiner and Reynolds and allowed Lewis to join in the session, staving off the threatened strike.[7]

The Indians broke through in 1954 by winning a record 111 regular-season games to take the American League pennant, defeating the Yankees by 8 games. The heavily favored Indians were then swept by the New York Giants in the World Series. The Indians fell back to their customary runner-up position behind the Yankees in both 1955 and 1956. A highlight of the 1956 season was the induction of the Indians general manager into baseball's Valhalla; he entered the Hall of Fame as a member of the Detroit Tigers, one year after his former rival, Joe DiMaggio, did so representing the New York Yankees. On July 23, 1956, Hank Greenberg joined Joe Cronin, a longtime star with the Washington Senators and Boston Red Sox and a two-time pennant-winning manager, as the newest inductees. Cronin expressed pleasure at being inducted alongside Greenberg, "the greatest right-handed hitter I ever saw." Greenberg became the first Jewish player to be so honored; as of 2012, only Sandy Koufax had duplicated that feat. Hank declared on being enshrined at Cooperstown, "In all my years of being on the playing field, I never dreamed that this would be the final result. I can't possibly express how I feel. It's just too wonderful for words. I'm deeply grateful and humble for this great honor."[8]

In his column in the *New York Times*, Arthur Daley suggested that the selection of Greenberg and Cronin might prove more inspirational than the earlier entry into the Hall of Fame by Ty Cobb, Babe Ruth, Honus Wagner, and Walter Johnson. Those four men were "true immortals, demi-gods of such enormous skills" possessing "almost legendary grandeur." By contrast, Greenberg and Cronin succeeded through "the hardest kind of work." Daley admitted that he now had to wait until Ted Williams, Bob Feller, Stan Musial, and Jackie Robinson became eligible for the Hall of Fame. The election of Greenberg and Cronin brought him "a sense of personal satisfaction . . . because both are old and valued friends." He had voted for them not because of friendship but rather due to what they had accomplished, Daley assured his readers. As for Greenberg, Daley indicated that the local boy brought up in New York City had to learn everything. Daley suggested, "If ever a man hauled himself up by his bootstraps, that man was Hank. He hired peanut vendors and park attendants to help him practice every morning, polishing his fielding and his hitting. No one worked harder to cure his weaknesses than the big fellow from the Bronx." Along with his contemporary Jimmie Foxx, Greenberg went on to hit more homers in a single season than any other player besides Babe Ruth. Greenberg became one of the first major leaguers to head off to war but returned to guide Detroit to a pennant after four-and-a-half years in the service. His late season homer clinched the American League title for the Tigers, and he then starred in the World Series. "But it was tough work," Daley reported.[9]

The 1957 season proved the least successful of Greenberg's tenure with the Indians. A career-altering injury to star pitcher Herb Score resulting from a line drive by Gil McDougald that tore into the young southpaw's eye helped to bring about the downslide that resulted in a 76–77 season mark. That was good for only sixth place in the American League. In October 1957 Cleveland dumped Greenberg—who had become a 20 percent owner of the ball club—as its general manager. Franklin Lewis of the *Cleveland Press* explained the reasons for Greenberg's ouster. Greenberg's dealings with reporters were sometimes contentious. Greenberg's firing of the much-idolized player-manager Lou Boudreau at the end of the 1950 season had been unpopular. So too was his campaign to drive fading slugger Al Rosen into retirement at the close of the 1956 campaign. The replacement of Al Lopez by Kerby Farrell as Indian skipper after that season had proven to be a bust. Some of Greenberg's other player moves were questionable, such as his signing of fading home run king and close friend Kiner. Still, the Indians had performed well under Greenberg's tutelage, placing second five times and winning the 1954 AL pennant.[10]

Cleveland president Myron H. Wilson indicated that fan displeasure led to Greenberg's ouster. He acknowledged, "No one will tell us what they think is the matter with him." Greenberg was clearly troubled by the decision. He admitted being "keenly disappointed that the board of directors chose to terminate my contract" and expressed pride in the team's performance during his tenure. "I have gained many honors in baseball, but feel that my work in Cleveland is one of my greatest achievements."[11]

Daley blamed Cleveland sportswriters for Greenberg's dismissal from the Indians. Those writers "all profess vast admiration for Hennery as a person" while condemning his performance as Cleveland general manager, Daley stated. Greenberg's greatest problem was that he experienced "wonderful press relations everywhere in baseball" except for Cleveland. "He's a warm and delightful companion whose friendship has long been treasured in this corner. Some of his ideas have been singularly keen and perceptive, geared for the greater good of the sport." Greenberg had long urged the introduction of interleague play that would have allowed fans in American League cities, including New York, which both the Dodgers and Giants had now fled, to enjoy National League stars like Willie Mays, Stan Musial, Hank Aaron, and Duke Snider. Greenberg also called for teams that finished in the second division to conduct transactions without trade deadlines. He presented "good suggestions" regarding an expansion of the player draft. "In short, he's brought a young, refreshing and ingenious mind to the upper echelons of the game," Daley continued. Only in the last season had his team performed poorly, although its annual attendance had plummeted from a record 2,620,627 fans in 1948 to 724,000 during the past season. Daley acknowledged that Greenberg had made mistakes, including his trading away of outfielder Minnie Miñoso, that got the Indians little in return. The columnist still considered Greenberg's firing unfortunate.[12]

Greenberg and other minority stockholders of the Cleveland Indians sold their stock to chairman William Daley in November 1958 and accepted the general manager position for the Chicago White Sox, now managed by Al Lopez, whose team captured the 1959 American League pennant, their first title since the Black Sox scandal forty years earlier. The White Sox finished in third place in 1960 and slipped to fourth place the following season, after which Ed Short replaced Greenberg, who remained on the White Sox payroll for a time, serving as a team vice president and adviser to Arthur C. Allyn, president of the ballclub. Allyn indicated, "I greatly respect Hank's knowledge of baseball. He was a great player in his day, knows baseball talent, has good business judgment and is invaluable to a club in an advisory capacity."[13] Greenberg indicated that he planned to head back to New York City, where he intended to reside and take it easy. Instead within months he had formed a stock-investment partnership with David Marx, a toy manufacturer. Fortunately for the new partners, a bull market soon followed. Greenberg also purchased a five-story town house on 70th Street in Manhattan and became involved with B-movie star Mary Jo Tarola, whose screen name was Linda Douglas.

His marriage to Caral had fallen apart as she spent her time on show horses and cultural affairs while Hank focused on baseball. Caral had been attracted to his "gentleness" and "wonderful sense of humor" and hoped to draw him into her world, which included regular attendance at the symphony, participation in the arts, and horseback riding.[14] Hank instead remained engrossed in baseball, even spending weekends at the ballpark. Caral returned to New York, and Hank, following a bitter, drawn-out battle, got joint custody of their three children, Glenn, Stephen, and Alva. Glenn attended Andover before graduating from Yale, where he played varsity football, and later Columbia University, where he studied business administration. Stephen played baseball and soccer at Yale before signing a minor league contract with the Washington Senators. Uncertain that he would ever make the majors, Stephen went to law school at UCLA and became an agent for big league players (and eventually a top sports official). Alva attended Kenyon College and later purchased majority ownership of a newspaper in Connecticut. On November 18, 1966, Hank married Mary Jo, and the two later moved to California, eventually buying a house in Beverly Hills. He continued investing in the stock market and began playing tennis frequently at the Beverly Hills Tennis Club.

When interviewed for Lawrence Ritter's book *The Glory of Their Times*, a revealing collection of interviews with former major leaguers, Greenberg spoke of his career and the tribulations he had encountered as a Jewish player. He admitted, "It's a strange thing. When I was playing, I used to resent being singled out as a Jewish ballplayer. I wanted to be known as a great ballplayer, period." Then he stated, "I'm not sure why or when I changed, because I'm still not a particularly religious person. Lately, though, I find myself wanting to be remembered not only as a great ballplayer, but even more as a great *Jewish* ballplayer."[15] Neither Greenberg nor Caral sought to expose their children to Judaism. Nevertheless, Glenn, Stephen, and Alva came to believe that their father possessed a strong sense of his own Jewish identity, which became more pronounced as he aged. He remained opposed to organized religion, never taking his children to temple for services, but he became more attuned to political matters involving the state of Israel.

Major league baseball owners began searching for a new commissioner to replace William Eckert during the latter stages of the 1960s. Bill Veeck suggested Greenberg as a possible replacement. "The most qualified man in the country is Hank Greenberg," Veeck declared. "In the first place he doesn't need the job and secondly he's known so well nationally as a Hall of Fame baseball player, as an operator and as an owner. He knows every facet of the business." Veeck admitted, "He once was associated with me and that probably has put the curse on him with the owners."[16] Early the next year, Greenberg's name was one of those suggested by Arthur Allyn and Atlanta Braves president Bill Bartholomay, among others. Greenberg expressed only mixed interest in the position, declaring, "Bill is a good friend of mine and I'm highly flattered. But I'm not available for the job. I have a very successful investment business and I'm running my own mutual fund." Greenberg admitted, reflecting about the possibility of a draft, "That's a different ball game. But I haven't talked to anyone at all about it and I don't know if they are even considering it."[17]

Greenberg expressed displeasure with how baseball magnates had mishandled the advent of free agency. "I feel very disgusted that the people who run baseball have permitted the game to fall into what might be called complete chaos," he complained in mid-October 1977. He considered it all too predictable "that something like this was bound to happen eventually . . . baseball was operating contrary to the laws of the land." Greenberg recalled that he and Bill Veeck had testified during the Curt Flood case, eight years earlier. They recognized that changes needed to be made regarding organized baseball's reserve clause, which effectively bound a player to the team that signed him until he was released, traded to another team, or retired. Those in management, however, foolishly "fought it as they do anything new. Instead of taking a realistic look at the situation, they tried to preserve the status quo, as they always do. Now they are paying for it." Greenberg was most disturbed about how free agency would change baseball's competitive balance, fearing that a few teams would be able to stockpile "most of the talent." He concluded, "It's the system that's wrong, and we could have had a better one if management had sat down with the players 10 years ago and tried to work something out."[18]

In May 1980 with a baseball strike looming, Greenberg believed the kind of get together he had participated in nearly three decades earlier could prevent that from taking place. "It just might work," he said. Sportswriter Dick Young offered that owners and players might consider bringing in Greenberg once again. "There is no man around who has experienced the player-owner relationship from both sides as has he." Greenberg warned, "The issue seems so reconcilable compared to what they all have to lose."[19]

On June 13, 1983, the Detroit Tigers retired Charlie Gehringer's No. 2 and Greenberg's No. 5, the second and third players in team history so honored. Al Kaline's No. 6 had been retired three years earlier. Another ex-Tiger and Hall of Famer, George Kell, spoke of playing with Hank. "I remember one of the first things he told me once when I came up to bat with a runner on second. He said, 'You get him over to third and I'll bring him home.'" Kell noted, "That's the kind of player he was. He loved to drive in runs."[20] That same year, American League president Bobby Brown selected Greenberg to serve as honorary captain of his circuit's All-Star team.

Following a thirteen-month battle with cancer, Hank Greenberg died at his Beverly Hills home on December 4, 1986, at the age of seventy-five. Ralph Kiner, now working for the New York Mets, told broadcast partner Tim McCarver, "This is the worst day of my life. My dearest friend, and the man who was like a father to me, Hank Greenberg, has died."[21] Detroit president and chief executive officer Jim Campbell stated, "Hank Greenberg was a tribute to baseball on and off the field. He was one of the most feared home run hitters of all time. Later he proved to be equally productive as a baseball executive. More than anything, though, he was a gentleman. The Tigers and all of baseball will miss him."[22] Bob Broeg of the *St. Louis Post-Dispatch* referred to Greenberg as "one of the most devastating sluggers in baseball history" who "also was one of the most determined, self-made players."[23] Maury Allen of the *New York Post* bemoaned Greenberg's passing: "It's a loss for all who keep score of how many decent men are around."[24] Some three hundred people attended the memorial service, held at the Wadsworth Theater in Los Angeles. Kiner declared, "Hank was the type of person that would give his time freely, who would help anybody." After revealing that Greenberg had helped him "live the right way," Kiner stated, "There has never been anyone with his class and there never will be anyone with his class in baseball." The actor Walter Matthau, who had met Hank at the Beverly Hills Tennis Club, spoke of growing up on Manhattan's Lower East Side idolizing Greenberg. Matthau continued, "Greenberg for me put a stop to the perpetuation of the myth at the time that all Jews wound up as cutters or pants pressers. Or, if they were lucky, salesmen in the garment center." Desirous of becoming an athlete himself, Matthau saw "Greenberg amongst all those ferocious, skilled, tough, tobacco-chewing, cursing, and spitting ballplayers who were the best in the world." Matthau admitted, "When you're running around in the jungle of the ghetto on the Lower East Side you couldn't help but be exhilarated by the sight of one of our guys looking like a Colossus. He eliminated for me all those jokes which start out: Did you hear the one about the little Jewish gentleman?"[25]

In his autobiography, *Hank Greenberg: The Story of My Life*, coauthored with sportswriter Ira Berkow and released posthumously in 1989, Hank discussed how anti-Semitism had affected him. After indicating that people presumed that "it was a terrible burden," Greenberg stated, "I found it to be a big help." Throughout the course of the long baseball season, players admittedly dogged it on occasion, Greenberg revealed. Back when he was having a tough time in Detroit and a fan hollered, "Come on, you big Jew, can't you do better than that?" Hank felt as if he had been belted with "a cold shower." When angered he resolved to perform better. He recognized that during his playing career, he had been the only prominent Jewish competitor, and began to reflect on what that meant.[26]

The January 13, 2000, edition of the *New York Daily News* contained an editorial by Vic Ziegel examining the recently released documentary on Greenberg, *The Life and Times of Hank Greenberg*. Ziegel compared him with Jackie Robinson. Ziegel called Greenberg "a Jew, and superstar" who entered the public consciousness a dozen years prior to Robinson's breaking of organized baseball's color barrier. The two men had, "to this country's great disgrace, too much in common," Ziegel wrote. "Robinson's crime was the color of his skin. Greenberg's mistake was being Jewish." Still as Harvard Law School professor Alan Dershowitz noted in the film, Greenberg represented "what 'they' said we could never be." Jews could play pinochle or chess and could work in sporting goods stores, but they did not lead the American League in homers four times.[27] In his review of the documentary, *New York Times* columnist Richard Sandomir noted that "worshipful fans" lovingly referred to Greenberg as Hankus Pankus. They saw him as "a 'messiah,' 'a Jewish god,' a Moses-like savior" who challenged negative stereotypes about Jews. In the film, Rabbi Reeve Brenner admitted, "I had this Captain Marvel, Hank Greenberg, on my shoulder. He was my big brother, my *mishpocheh* [family]." Author Peter Levine offered, "Hank Greenberg was a tough Jew when tough Jews were important. . . . He was a role model for my parents' generation."[28]

Later that year, Senator Joe Lieberman became the first Jew to run on the national ticket of a leading American political party, serving as the running mate of Democratic nominee Al Gore. Lieberman was at the time one of ten Jews serving in the U.S. Senate, while thirty Jews were in the House of Representatives. That Rosh Hashanah, Rabbi Marc Gellman of Dix Hills, New York, praised Lieberman's placement on the Democratic Party ticket. He declared that no Jew since Los Angeles star pitcher Sandy Koufax, who like Greenberg had refused to play on Yom Kippur, had so "entered the national consciousness of America in so deep and complex a way."[29]

13

The Greatest Brooklyn Dodger

In 1948 Jackie Robinson returned for his second big league season, having signed a new contract for $12,500, a figure that disappointed both Rachel and him. He was twenty-five pounds overweight and somewhat out of shape, to the chagrin of manger Leo Durocher, returned from his year-long suspension. Robinson also encountered a particularly trying moment during spring training, when the Dodgers stopped at a roadside restaurant in Florida, following a game against the Yankees. Road secretary Harold Parrott recalled that all the white players enjoyed steaks in the restaurant while Robinson and Roy Campanella stayed on the team bus. Parrott carried trays out to the two black players, with Robinson "seething" and Campanella typically conciliatory. Roy said, "Let's not have no trouble, Jackie. This is the [only] thing we can do right now, 'lessen we want to go back to them crummy Negro leagues." Undoubtedly thinking about how he had helped propel the Dodgers into the World Series, Jackie refused to eat, while Campanella "tore into the meal."[1]

The failure of their teammates to defend Robinson and Campanella remains startling, albeit less so in the case of "Campy," who had just joined the Dodgers for the 1948 season. Robinson's resentment was perfectly understandable, as he became the catalyst who helped to turn a good team into the mythical Boys of Summer. Before Robinson's arrival, the Dodgers had been unable to repeat their 1941 pennant. Brooklyn's 1946 squad actually had a better record than the following year's team, but the latter captured the Dodgers' fourth league title, initiating a period of sustained excellence that lasted throughout Robinson's tenure. Although no one could have foreseen, it was clear that Jackie made a difference, that his intelligence, drive, brilliance on the base paths, and skills at the plate and in the field transformed the Dodgers, just as he helped alter the game altogether. Robinson had become a genuine star during the 1947 campaign, receiving recognition as the major league Rookie of the Year (in 1949 each league began selecting its own top rookie) for helping to carry the Dodgers back to the World Series when post-season checks were sometimes larger than regular season ones. Many of the Dodger players proved to be men of great merit, and not only on the playing field, and their inability to move beyond the easy racial norms of the era is noteworthy.

As the 1948 season opened, Wendell Smith reflected back on the previous year, which he considered "the greatest of all time" for black athletes. "Without any question," he wrote, "Jackie Robinson's graduation to the Brooklyn Dodgers was the most momentous event of all." His brilliant performance on the playing field "only added more luster" to Rickey's plan to integrate baseball, which gave lie to the argument that Southern players would not allow a black into the majors. Instead "they not only played with and against Jackie, but many rallied to his defense at crucial moments." All the while Robinson accomplished more than any athlete "in the face of so many obstacles."[2] Smith delivered a revealing observation later that year, even as organized baseball slowly began to incorporate additional black players. He reflected on the large number of black ballplayers back in the 1920 and early 1930s who were of major league-caliber and suggested that there were fewer presently. Smith recalled outfielders Pete Hill, Oscar Charleston, Cristóbal "Carlos" Torriente, Ted Page, and Cool Papa Bell. He remembered infielders Ray Dandridge, John Henry Lloyd, Martín Dihigo, Buck Leonard, Willie Wells, and José Méndez. He pointed to catchers Biz Mackey, Josh Gibson, and Bruce Petway. He mentioned pitchers Dave Brown, Willie Foster, Smokey Joe Williams, Dick Redding, Bullet Joe Rogan, and Slim Jones.[3]

In early April the Brooklyn Dodgers played a series of games against the Atlanta Crackers at the minor league team's home ballpark. A record crowd showed up at Ponce de Leon Park, announced at 25,221, with over half of those in attendance black patrons. Robinson was now stationed at second base, Eddie Stanky having been traded to the Boston Braves. After struggling early in the season, Robinson began batting over .300, but to his astonishment the Dodgers placed him on waivers in June, and sportswriters indicated that his performance lacked the "dashing, daring" quality on the base paths characteristic of his first year in the big leagues.[4] As the season approached its midpoint, Robinson had yet to steal a base, and his batting average had fallen to .270. At the end of June, he began pulling out of his slump, even smacking his first grand slam. He soon stole a base for the first time all season and delivered an inside-the-park homer against the New York Giants. He also witnessed Leo Durocher's departure, after the Dodgers struggled to a 41–38 start, replaced by the Dodgers manager from the previous campaign, Burt Shotton. In August 1948 Robinson got ejected from a major league game for the first time and informed a radio audience that his new ability to let off steam enabled him to relax more. Having quickly rounded into form, Robinson nevertheless struggled until the middle of the season. At that point he took off and ended up batting .296 for the year, scoring 108 runs, and driving in 85 while again hitting 12 homers along with 38 doubles and 8 triples. He stole 22 bases during the disappointing 1948 season when the Dodgers fell to third place in the National League, six-and-a-half games behind the St. Louis Cardinals and another game in back of the pennant-winning Boston Braves.

About the midpoint of the 1948 season, Jackie, Rachel, and Jackie Jr. relocated to a duplex in Brooklyn's Flatbush section. In a recent decision, *Shelley v. Kraemer*, the U.S. Supreme Court had unanimously ruled that the Fourteenth Amendment prevented states from sustaining racially restrictive covenants pertaining to the purchase or occupancy of housing. Residents in the largely Jewish neighborhood of Flatbush were little pleased about the presence of the Robinsons and their black landlady, but as Jackie recounted in his autobiography, his young son helped change people's attitudes.

Slipping into the backyards of his neighbors, Jackie Jr. invariably asked for a snack while charming those who encountered him. A small number of neighbors became very close to the Robinsons.

The informal pact that Robinson—who now signed for $17,500—had made with Rickey to rein himself in for three years ended following the 1948 season. Consequently Jackie felt free to respond when a young team-mate, pitcher Chris van Cuyk, began harassing him during spring training. Robinson threatened to fight after Van Cuyk threw at his head. Writing in the *New York World-Telegram*, sportswriter Bill Roeder warned that "in the future, those who step on him, or on his feelings, are likely to hear about it just as young Chris van Cuyk did yesterday." The new season took on a different note as exemplified by Robinson's response to a sportswriter who quoted him as warning, "They'd better be rough on me this year because I'm sure going to be rough on them." Displeased by Robinson's apparent threat, baseball commissioner Happy Chandler called him in to discuss that statement. Robinson informed Chandler that he had no desire to cause trouble but simply would no longer tolerate insults, an explanation that apparently satisfied the game's top official.[5]

Nevertheless sportswriter Wendell Smith, long Robinson's champion, chastised him in a column that appeared in the *Pittsburgh Courier* on March 19, 1949. Smith reminded Robinson that the press had "been especially fair to him." Without journalistic coverage, Robinson would have remained "just another athlete insofar as the public is concerned." In fact he would likely still be "t[r]amping around the country with Negro teams, living under what he has called 'intolerable conditions.'" However, presently, "Mr. Robinson's memory, it seems, is getting shorter and shorter. That is especially true in the case of the many newspapermen who have befriended him throughout his career."[6]

Branch Rickey for his part continued to sing Robinson's praises to the press. Dismissing the battle with Van Cuyk as "a tempest in a teapot," Rickey urged that it "be forgotten." More important was the fact that "Jackie's the same high-class boy he was the first year we brought him up. He's entitled to all the rights of any other American citizen. He's a great competitor and resents any violation of those rights. . . . We couldn't have picked a finer boy than Robinson for our experiment of introducing a Negro into organized baseball."[7]

Midway through the 1949 season, Robinson spoke before the House Un-American Activities Committee, which had targeted the great African American singer and actor Paul Robeson, among others on the left who were seen as sympathetic to the Soviet Union. Speaking in Paris at the recent World Congress of the Partisans of Peace, a pro-communist gathering, Robeson had explained the unwillingness of "American Negroes to go to war on behalf of those who have oppressed us . . . against a country [the Soviet Union] which in one generation has raised our people to the full dignity of mankind." During his House testimony, some of which he later regretted having delivered, Robinson said, "I am a religious man. Therefore I cherish America where I am free to worship as I please, a privilege which some countries do not give. And I suspect that nine hundred and ninety-nine out of almost any thousand colored Americans you meet will tell you the same thing." Robinson nevertheless warned, "White people must realize that the more a Negro hates communism because it opposes democracy, the more he is going to hate the other influences that kill off democracy in this country—and that goes for racial discrimination in the Army, and segregation on trains and buses, and job discrimination because of religious beliefs or color or place of birth."[8] Robinson continued, "And other things the American public ought to understand, if we are to make progress in this matter: the fact that it is a Communist who denounces injustice in the courts, police brutality, and lynching when it happens doesn't change the truth of his charges." Indeed, "Negroes were stirred up long before there was a Communist Party, and they'll stay stirred up long after the Party has disappeared—unless Jim Crow has disappeared by then as well." Regarding Robeson's declaration about the disinclination of American blacks to fight against the Soviets, Robinson dismissed it as "very silly" while indicating that Robeson "has a right to his personal views."[9]

The Dodgers captured their second pennant in three years, nipping the Cardinals by a single game. Robinson and Stan Musial battled for individual honors, with the St. Louis first baseman leading the league in hits, doubles, triples, total bases, and on-base percentage; coming in second in runs scored, homers, batting average, and slugging percentage; and finishing third in RBIs. Making the All-Star team for the first time, Jackie led the league in batting average with a .342 mark and stolen bases with 37; finished second in hits with 203, RBIs with 124, and on-base percentage; coming in third with 38 doubles, 12 triples, and a .528 slugging average; and ending up fifth in total bases. Robinson, who also hit 16 homers, was eventually named National League MVP. The Dodgers went against the Yankees once again in the World Series but fell in five games, with Robinson batting only .188, although he notched the lone run in Brooklyn's second game victory.

After the 1949 baseball season, Robinson also signed a contract for the upcoming year for $35,000, one of the top salaries in major league baseball. He began hosting a pair of sports programs on television as well as a radio show for ABC. His daughter, Sharon Robinson, was born on January 13, 1950, and the Robinsons purchased a comfortable home in Queens. The house was located in St. Albans, where Roy Campanella, Count Basie, and Herbert Mills of the Mills Brothers all lived. Robinson also became more concerned about issues pertaining to social justice, including anti-Semitism. At the same time, Jackie wanted to help ensure that his family was as financially secure as possible, and he readily appeared in a number of advertisements, ranging from Wheaties to Chesterfield cigarettes.

He also signed a deal for a movie about his life for which he was paid $50,000 and a percentage of the profits. Before the new season began, Alfred E. Green directed that film, with the ballplayer in the lead role. Also appearing in *The Jackie Robinson Story* was actress Ruby Dee, who played the part of Rachel Robinson. Referring to Jackie's magnetism, Dee recalled, "He had the most gorgeous smile you ever saw. It just lit up a room." Bosley Crowther of the *New York Times* underscored "the sincerity of the dramatization and the integrity of Mr. Robinson playing himself." Robinson "displays a calm assurance and composure that might be envied by many a Hollywood star," Crowther wrote. The film critic particularly praised the scenes in which Robinson met Branch Rickey to discuss breaking organized baseball's color barrier and when Robinson was razzed by fans at a Montreal Royals game who proceeded to hurl a black cat onto the playing field. Crowther called the scene of Jackie's first at bat in the majors "tingling." Throughout the film, "the magnificent athlete conducts himself with dignity," and his story was told "with honest pride . . . a story of which all Americans with respect and gratitude, may be proud, too."[10] Robinson garnered still more publicity when *Life* magazine placed him on the cover of its May 8, 1950, issue, which contained a feature article on him. The following month, in a pair of rulings—*Sweatt v. Painter* and *McLaurin v. Oklahoma State Regents*—the U.S. Supreme Court unanimously declared unconstitutional legislative attempts to provide segregated education at the professional or graduate level.

At the midpoint of the 1950 season, sportswriter Dan Burley discussed Robinson's more aggressive performance on the playing field and the subsequent response of umpires. During his season with the Montreal Royals and his first years with the Dodgers, Robinson "took it like a man," suffering abuse from "all sides, insults as to color and race, insults to his ability, to his manhood." This was ironic for the "high-spirited young man with not an ounce of Uncle Tom in him [who] suddenly found himself situated into the role of champion Uncle Tom." He was compelled to keep "his blazing tempers under wraps" to set the stage for "future Campanellas, Newcombes, Bankheads, Irvins, Dobys, and Thompsons." During the past spring training, Robinson had indicated he planned to play "a rough, aggressive game, tit for tat." Consequently Robinson was now "emerging as a full-blown personality, big if not bigger than any contemporary in the game, including Joe DiMaggio and Ted Williams." Like other ballplayers, Robinson acted as bench jockey, questioned close calls at second base that went against the Dodgers, and continued to run and play hard.[11]

The Dodgers battled to the final game of the 1950 season, when they fell to the Philadelphia Phillies, 4–1 in the tenth inning. Robinson had another superb year, coming in second to Musial this time around with a .328 batting average, scoring 99 runs, belting 39 doubles, swatting 14 homers, driving in 81 runs, and compiling a .423 on-base percentage. Along with failing to repeat as pennant winner, the Dodgers witnessed the departure of Branch Rickey from their organization, undoubtedly owing to a dispute with owner Walter O'Malley, who had a highly contentious relationship with Robinson. Jackie thanked Rickey "for all you have meant not only to me and my family but to the entire country and particularly to the members of our race." Robinson praised Rickey's "constant guidance" and stated that "being associated with you has been the finest experience that I have had." Rickey answered, "My acquaintanceship with you has ripened into a very real friendship."[12]

The next year again proved to be heartbreaking for the Brooklyn Dodgers, who led the New York Giants by 13½ games in August but fell into a tie with their archrivals at season's end. The Giants won the decisive contest in a best of three game playoff series, coming all the way back from a 4–1 deficit in the bottom of the ninth inning when Bobby Thompson walloped the most famous home run in major league history. In yet another stellar season, Robinson, now paid $39,750, scored 106 runs, drove in 88, managed 185 hits, knocked out 33 doubles, rapped 19 homers, and batted .338 while stealing 25 bases. This time Robinson finished third in batting average, behind the Phillies' Richie Ashburn and title-winner Stan Musial; third in stolen bases, with former Negro leaguer Sam Jethroe setting the pace for the National League; and third in on-base percentage, following the Pirates' Ralph Kiner and Musial. In the field Robinson committed only seven errors, setting a league record for second basemen.

In a full-length article in the October 1951 issue of *Sport*, which featured a cover shot of Robinson, Milton Gross discussed "The Emancipation of Jackie Robinson," during which the baseball pioneer had discarded "an armor of humility." Deliberating restraining himself early in his professional baseball career "chafed continually" and at times "dug ruthlessly into both his flesh and his spirit." The humility hardly came easily "to the gifted Negro," Gross suggested. "No meek and humble man could possibly play baseball with the fire and dash Robinson exhibits." After five years on the Dodgers, Robinson had become "his own man," battling in recent times with umpires, former manager Leo Durocher, and pitchers who threw at his head or at those of his Dodger teammates. Robinson anticipated nasty letters, generally rough treatment, segregation, and hostility from some opponents and even from some of the Brooklyn players. Gross presciently asked, "What happens to a man within whom emotion rages, yet who is not allowed to let the searing feelings escape him?"[13]

Continuing to carve out necessary niches away from baseball during the off-season, Robinson became involved in a significant real estate project, the Jackie Robinson Houses, intended to provide housing for low-income blacks. Jackie also sought to make money off his partnership with developer Arnold H. Kagan, who promised to pay him 16 percent of the profits.

Sportswriter Roger Kahn followed the Brooklyn Dodgers as the 1952 season unfolded, viewing Robinson differently than many others did. To Kahn "Robinson was a gentle, thoughtful, loving man, disguised as a fire-brand" who confronted "bigots on the field, in the grandstands, in the press box." He responded by displaying "a bristling personality, needling and jockeying in sharp and sometimes nasty ways." Robinson admitted, "It's like I've got an antennae. I can tell who's an *anti* before they even speak." No longer were sportswriters willing to argue that blacks could not compete in big league baseball, but they readily referred to Jackie as "uppity." Kahn considered this absurd. Those same sportswriters admired the qualities that Robinson displayed when exhibited by white players: fierceness and "hard-nosed" competitiveness.[14] Pitcher Joe Black, another Negro league veteran who joined the Dodgers during the 1952 season, pointed to Robinson as the key to Brooklyn's great team. In Black's estimation, Robinson fostered competitiveness. "If you went out there and didn't give one hundred per-cent, Jackie would let you know." Dodger pitching ace Carl Erskine under-scored the fact that "the personality of this team centered around Jackie."[15]

As Jackie and Rachel welcomed their third child, David, born on May 14, 1952, the Dodgers marched to another pennant, besting the Giants by 4½ games. Robinson had another fine year, batting .308 with 19 homers, 75 RBIs, 104 runs scored, and a league-leading, career-best on-base per-centage of .440. He also stole 24 bases and made the All-Star team for the fourth straight time. Robinson had another rocky time in the World Series, batting only .174, with a home run, 2 RBIs, and 4 runs scored as the Dodgers again fell to the Yankees, this time in seven games.

After the baseball season ended, Robinson opened up the Jackie Robinson Store, located at 111 West 125th Street in Harlem and featuring quality goods. Robinson owned the store for six years, enjoying the time spent there interacting with customers. His real estate dealings with Arnold Kagan expanded as they acquired a multiacre lot in the Bronx for the proposed Jackie Robinson Apartments, intended for low-income tenants. Robinson remained in the news during the off-season in other ways, such as when he chastised the Yankees management for failing to integrate major league baseball's greatest team. The following spring, Jackie became editor of *Our Sports*, a magazine targeting a black audience.

Having signed his latest contract, which paid him $42,000, Robinson readied for the 1953 season but soon was forced to shuffle between second base and left field. Nevertheless he excelled at the plate, batting .329, scoring 109 runs, belting 34 doubles, 7 triples, and 12 homers while driving in 95 and still managing to steal 17 bases. During the season, the *New York Post*'s Jimmy Cannon praised Robinson, stating he could do more to beat the competition than any other contemporary ballplayer. The Dodgers raced to their second straight pennant, winning 105 contests and finishing 13 games ahead of the runner-up Milwaukee Braves. In a six-game World Series, Brooklyn once more came up short against the New York Yankees, this time despite Robinson's fine performance, which resulted in a .320 batting average.

On November 23, 1953, Robinson attended a dinner honoring the Anti-Defamation League of B'nai B'rith at which President Dwight Eisenhower served as guest of honor. After Eisenhower delivered his address, implicitly critical of the antics of Senator Joseph McCarthy, the president deliberately went over to Robinson's table to shake his hand. An excited Robinson told a reporter, "To think the President of the United States would come halfway across a room just to shake my hand!"[16]

On a less happy note, Robinson's relations with Dodger management continued to decline. Robinson conducted something of a war of wills with new manager Walt Alston, at least indirectly challenging his authority. Jackie also had to contend with the sometimes-petty antics of O'Malley, such as when the Dodgers owner criticized him roundly with Rachel present, referring to her husband as a prima donna. Little helpful too was the fact that the black players on the Dodgers remained segregated from their teammates when it came to spring training accommodations.

Early in the 1954 season, the U.S. Supreme Court, led by Chief Justice Earl Warren, cast another blow against segregation. In the case of *Brown v. Board of Education of Topeka*, the court ruled unanimously that "separate educational facilities are inherently unequal." Warren asserted that Jim Crow practices in public schools violated the Equal Protection Clause of the Fourteenth Amendment. Many white Southerners were enraged by the decision and efforts to implement the subsequent ruling that desegregation proceed "with all deliberate speed." African Americans took heart, envisioning a second Reconstruction. As resistance mounted, particularly in former Confederate states, a black civil rights movement burgeoned in which the young black Baptist minister Martin Luther King Jr. became a leading spokesperson.

Still the most integrated team in baseball, the Dodgers finished behind their National League rivals, the New York Giants, during the 1954 race, despite winning 92 games. That left them 5 back of the Giants, who would sweep to the World Series title in a stunning upset of the record-setting Cleveland Indians. Alternating between the outfield and third base, Robinson appeared in a then career-low 124 games, with only 386 official trips to the plate. He managed 22 doubles and 15 homers, in addition to a .311 batting average, but scored only 62 runs and contributed but 59 RBIs. He also stole a mere 7 bases. After an incident in Milwaukee on June 2 in which he tossed a bat that inadvertently fell into the stands, crowds heckled Robinson throughout the remainder of the season. As *Sport* magazine reported, he became baseball's most despised player.

In a column that appeared in the *New York Herald Tribune* in late August 1954, Roger Kahn discussed Robinson, who was now clearly in the latter stages of his playing career. Kahn called Robinson "an angry man" who was "proud and dedicated, loyal and tempestuous." Angry men like Robinson were needed, Kahn pointed out, to battle against "stupidity and bigotry and conformity." Some in baseball circles criticized Robinson for his passionate nature, condemning the way he needled players on other teams or disputed umpires' calls. For Kahn it made no sense to compare Robinson with the hot-headed Eddie Stanky or Leo Durocher. "The ordinary standards don't apply to Robinson. He is larger than life," Kahn recognized. Robinson's rage came from his competitive nature, which drove him to strive to keep the Dodgers out of second place. It also existed because of the conditions he faced during his first year in organized baseball, the very real prejudices he continued to encounter when his team trained in the South, and the fact that he had been so frequently thrown at while batting during his eight-year major league career. More tellingly Kahn appreciated the fact that "this fury of Robinson's . . . enabled him to do the great and immensely difficult thing he did only nine years ago. Without the anger he wouldn't be Jackie Robinson." And "without Jackie Robinson the world of baseball would be an infinitely poorer place."[17]

During the off-season, the Robinsons moved to Stamford, Connecticut, where they built a large suburban house that cost over $90,000. Jackie delivered a series of public speeches on behalf of the National Conference of Christians and Jews and served as cochair of the New York Men's Committee of the United Negro College Fund. When the 1955 season opened, the Dodgers sprinted to a torrid start, taking all but three of their first twenty-five games. While Robinson limped along to his worst major league campaign, hitting only 6 doubles and 8 homers, driving in only 36 runs, and batting .256, Brooklyn captured another National League pennant, winning 98 games to finish 13½ games ahead of Milwaukee. The New York Yankees swept the first two games of the World Series at Yankee Stadium, despite Robinson's disputed theft of home in the opener. The Dodgers rebounded to win three straight at Ebbets Field, then the Yankees evened the Series with a 5–1 win in Game 6. In Game 7, the young Dodger southpaw Johnny Podres outdueled Tommy Byrne to win 2–0, clinching Brooklyn's first and only World Series championship. Robinson's contribution on the playing field was mixed at best, as he batted only .182, but he scored five runs and was credited with serving as the Dodgers' inspirational leader.

A decade after he broke organized baseball's color barrier, Robinson was again the subject of a major essay by Roger Kahn that appeared in *Sport* magazine. Kahn wanted to title the piece, "The Ordeal of Jackie Robinson," but his editor, Ed Fitzgerald, said, "I don't think so. But his ordeal will jump off the pages that you write. We don't need to telegraph our punches in the title."[18] At that stage of Robinson's playing career, he "could converse with Eleanor Roosevelt and curse at Sal Maglie with equal intensity and skill," Kahn observed. Because Robinson early endured "outrage and vituperation with an almost magic mixture of humility and pride," some considered him a saint. Because Robinson now fought back, sometimes instigating the "mudslinging," some deemed him a troublemaker. Because he shattered baseball's system of apartheid, some viewed him as a hero. And because he had failed to lighten in color during his major league career, some called him a villain. Thus Robinson remained baseball's "most controversial" figure. Earlier the game's "most exciting player," Robinson was applauded by former managers Leo Durocher and Chuck Dressen, with the former stating, "He comes to win. He beats you," and the latter declaring, "There never was an easier guy for me to manage and there never was nothing I asked that he didn't do. Hit-and-run. Bunt. Anything. He was the greatest player I ever managed." Walter O'Malley, however, charged he was "always conscious of publicity and is always seeking publicity." Teammate Duke Snider offered, "I'll say this for Jack. When he believes something is right, he'll fight for it as hard as anybody I ever saw." By contrast, a well-known columnist acknowledged, "I'm just about fed up with Robinson fights and Robinson incidents and Robinson explanations. He's boring. I'm going to heave a great sigh of relief when he gets out of baseball. Then I won't have to bother with him any more." Despite such an analysis, Kahn subsequently contended that Rickey "chose Robinson with wisdom that borders upon clairvoyance, to right a single wrong. Robinson had the playing ability to become a superstar, plus the intelligence to understand the significance of his role. He had the fighting temperament to wring the most from his ability, and he had the self-control to keep his temper in check. His ten years in major-league baseball will never be forgotten."[19]

The 1956 season, which proved to be Robinson's last, saw the Dodgers, with their ninety-three wins, squeak by the Milwaukee Braves and the Cincinnati Reds by one game and two games, respectively. Robinson rebounded somewhat, hitting fifteen doubles and ten homers and lifting his batting average to .275. This time the Dodgers took the first two contests of the Subway Series, but the Yankees came back to win in seven games. Robinson did his best to help the Dodgers retain their World Series crown, batting .250, scoring five runs, and smacking a home run. Following the loss to the Yankees, the Dodgers undertook an extensive playing tour of Japan.

Back home he again spoke frequently on behalf of the National Conference of Christians and Jews while becoming more involved with the operations of the National Association for the Advancement of Colored People. In fact the NAACP had recently given Robinson its Spingarn Medal, awarded each year to the black American viewed as having most honored "the race." Previous recipients included the social critic and long-time editor of the NAACP's *Crisis* magazine, W. E. B. DuBois; singer Marian Anderson; author Richard Wright; actor-activist Paul Robeson; labor leader and editor of *The Messenger* magazine A. Philip Randolph; and diplomat Ralph Bunche. The citation from the NAACP referred to Robinson as "a brilliant and versatile athlete" who had served as "an inspiration to the youth of the nation and especially to Negro youth for whom denial of opportunity has been a source of frustration." Moreover "the entire nation is indebted to him for his pioneer role in breaking the color barrier in organized baseball."[20] In receiving his award at a banquet held in Manhattan on December 8, 1956, Robinson asserted, "I am now quite convinced that the way I have played and the way I have tried to conduct myself was the right way." Yes, many had attempted to convince him "not to speak up every time I thought there was an injustice." Indeed, "I was often advised to look after the Robinson family and not to worry about other people." Admittedly the "biting criticism" he endured sometimes left him wondering if he had responded as he should have.[21]

Shortly after Robinson received the Spingarn Medal, William H. Black, who operated Chock full o'Nuts, a chain of coffee shops, offered Jackie a position as vice president and director of personnel. The job paid $30,000, provided a company car, and offered stock options. The initial contract ran for two years, but Black promised that this was "a lifetime job" if Robinson desired. Jackie also agreed to discuss his retirement in the pages of *Look* magazine, receiving $50,000 for a three-part series. Before the series ran, Robinson received a call from Buzzie Bavasi of the Dodgers front office, informing him that he had been traded to the New York Giants. When the Dodgers announced the trade of Robinson to the Giants for $30,000 and pitcher Dick Littlefield, Arthur Daley of the *Times* indicated that although Jackie's legs would not hold up for 154 games, he could still be "a matchless performer, the best money player in the business."[22] Jimmy Cannon wrote, "You are Jackie Robinson, who is consumed by rage and pride. You're a complicated man, persecuted by slanderous myths, using anger as a confederate. No athlete of any time has been assaulted by such an aching loneliness which created your personality and shaped your genuine greatness." Referring to the trade to the Giants, Cannon continued, "It's a challenge and you won't back down."[23] However, Robinson soon announced his retirement from the game, in the pages of *Look* magazine, rather than accept the trade. Bavasi then blasted Robinson, charging that the ballplayer was seeking to draw more money from his new team. Robinson fired back, declaring that he was retiring because of Bavasi's unfair attacks on his integrity. The Giants purportedly continued to attempt to convince Robinson to join them, offering as much as $65,000 for the upcoming season. He decided instead to conclude his major league career and become an executive with Chock full o'Nuts.

Daley argued for Robinson's admission to baseball's Hall of Fame, calling him "the goad" that drove Brooklyn to six pennants during his decade with the team. Daley contended that Robinson deserved this distinction because of merit but also due to the fact that "he was the trail-blazer for his race." Branch Rickey, Daley wrote, selected "the perfect pioneer before he triggered his revolution. He wanted a college graduate possessing intelligence, character, integrity, dignity, high athletic skill and courage that would be both moral and physical." As Daley saw it, "Robbie has all those qualities and then some." He became "a superior ballplayer" despite entering the majors at the relatively late age of twenty-eight. "Otherwise he might have been one of the greatest." Still "he was great enough."[24]

During his 10 years in the big leagues, Robinson delivered 1,518 hits, including 273 doubles, 54 triples, and 137 homers. He scored 947 runs, 6 times going over the 100-run mark, and drove in 734, with a single-season high of 124. He stole 197 bases, twice leading the league. He hit .311 for his career, with one batting championship. His on-base percentage was a brilliant .410, as he walked 740 times and struck out only 291 times. Robinson was named to six All-Star teams and was the 1949 National League Most Valuable Player. But his contributions to the game far exceeded statistics, however impressive. Robinson was a baseball, and consequently a racial, pioneer, who shattered the color barrier that had afflicted that national pastime for over a half century. That breakthrough required tremendous fortitude in addition to considerable baseball skill, no small accomplishment even for an athlete as gifted as Robinson. Baseball, after all, was hardly his best sport and was not one he had played regularly for very long. Nevertheless the seemingly boundless pride and determination that drove Jackie Robinson enabled him both to succeed and star in the most difficult sport of all. And he did so in the face of continuous ridicule, taunts, vicious diatribes, and sheer hatred emanating from the stands, opposing players, and sometimes even his own teammates.

Battling against fierce odds, he became the National League's best-known player, as well as the majors' most controversial one. His accomplishments at the plate, in the field, on the bases, and in the clubhouse were hugely significant, enabling other great athletes such as Willie Mays, Hank Aaron, Ernie Banks, and Frank Robinson to enter the major leagues. Because of Robinson and his small band of black brothers—Roy Campanella, Don Newcombe, and Larry Doby, among them—other players whose skin color or racial heritage would have previously prevented them playing in the major leagues were able to do so. They thus avoided the fate of the legendary black stars of the first half of the twentieth century, including Rube Foster, John Henry Lloyd, Oscar Charleston, Josh Gibson, and many other Negro leaguers who shone so brilliantly on a baseball diamond tainted by segregation and racial prejudice.

The collapse of the color barrier in organized baseball was ultimately liberating for black Americans in general, whether they were athletes or not. Not only did other major sports begin to open their doors to African American performers, but gradually, albeit far too slowly and often at great cost for many individual blacks, the American landscape itself began to shift. As professional football and basketball discarded their own racial lines, American jurisprudence underwent dramatic alterations that ultimately underscored the right of all citizens to fundamental protections afforded by the U.S. Constitution. The federal court system, led by the U.S. Supreme Court, began to issue a series of rulings that tossed aside racial restraints in housing, employment, and education. This achieved considerable momentum during the very period when Jackie Robinson was starring for the Brooklyn Dodgers, whose interracial makeup made the Boys of Summer America's team in many ways. Particularly following Earl Warren's appointment in 1953 as chief justice, the Supreme Court provided judicial weight to demands for racial justice. However, even rulings such as *Brown v. Board of Education of Topeka* hardly sufficed to batter Jim Crow altogether. Instead it required steadfast courage by individuals who followed Robinson's lead to contest practices and policies involving segregation and the debasement of American citizens. Moreover, a figure like Martin Luther King Jr., who employed nonviolent direct action tactics to challenge segregation, discrimination, and racially induced prejudice, literally drew on Robinson's examples, as King himself often acknowledged. All of this made Robinson not merely one of the great baseball players of his generation but among the most important Americans of the twentieth century.

14

Jackie Robinson's Final Years

For many athletes, their careers following their playing days amount to little more than an afterthought. In some ways that was true for Jackie Robinson, possibly the second greatest all-around athlete in America in the first several decades of the twentieth century. Indeed a poll taken at mid-century placed him just behind Jim Thorpe, the Native American track-and-field Olympic gold medalist, football legend, and major leaguer. Nevertheless Robinson remained committed to making his mark, while providing comfortably for his family. He did so with characteristic determination, seeking to become a success in business, the media, and public service. He loved his new house in Connecticut and raised his children in a pristine small community there. Jackie played golf regularly, spent a great deal of time with his family, and, along with Rachel, nurtured a number of close friendships in both Stamford and New York City. Leaving baseball behind, he traveled widely for the NAACP, supporting its Fight for Freedom Fund, designed to legally confront segregation. He chaired the fund in 1957 and served on the NAACP's board of directors for a full decade. He greatly enjoyed his work for Chock full o'Nuts and possessed the luxury of a wholly supportive employer who refused to contest his ability to express himself freely. He also considered it essential that blacks acquire the economic means to achieve genuine autonomy.

Robinson's political views tilted in the direction of the Republican Party as he became a strong backer of both President Eisenhower and Vice President

Richard M. Nixon, whom he considered sympathetic to the cause of civil rights. He appeared on programs like *Meet the Press*, where he fielded questions concerning discrimination in housing but denied rumors that he might enter the political arena. He pressed the NAACP to adopt a more assertive attitude regarding civil rights and served as marshal for the Youth March for Integrated Schools, which took place on October 25, 1958, when three thousand participants marched to the Lincoln Memorial. The following January he began hosting *The Jackie Robinson Show*, a thirty-minute radio program heard on WRCA in New York City. Robinson interviewed guests from the American political world, including New York mayor Robert Wagner and Eleanor Roosevelt, still the first lady of the Democratic Party. He soon joined in a second Youth March for Integrated Schools. In April 1959 his column "Jackie Robinson" began appearing in the *New York Post*; he promised to write about both national and international events. He particularly displayed a continuing interest in civil rights but took a leave of absence from the newspaper in September 1960 to serve on Nixon's presidential campaign team. Robinson proved disappointed when Nixon refused to call Martin Luther King Jr. after the civil rights leader was arrested in Georgia. Following a meeting in which he urged Nixon to contact King, a bitterly frustrated Robinson determined that the Republican candidate did not deserve the presidency. Rather he drew close to New York governor Nelson Rockefeller, a liberal Republican.

As students became more involved with the civil rights campaign, participating in sit-ins and freedoms rides, Robinson backed their efforts. In 1960 he helped establish the Student Emergency Fund to provide support for the early sit-in protesters while at the same time working on behalf of the NAACP's voter-registration efforts. He became more sympathetic to John Kennedy, appreciating the new president's moral leadership but questioning his legislative skills. Robinson also became more appreciative of Robert F. Kennedy, who served as his brother's attorney general and became intimately involved with civil rights developments.

On January 23, 1962, Robinson received word that he, along with former major-leaguer Bob Feller, had been named to Baseball's Hall of Fame.

The *New York Daily News*'s Dick Young, who had frequently criticized Robinson, had predicted his selection. He recalled how Robinson during his first years in the major leagues "endured, with a tight-lipped mouth, all the physical and mental abuse that it is possible for men to inflict on other men." Young remembered Robinson's "ability to beat you with his bat, with his globe, with his waddling speech." In the columnist's estimation, "Jackie Robinson made baseball history and that's what the Hall of Fame is, baseball history."[1] Robinson responded graciously to the announcement that his plaque would be placed in Cooperstown, New York, the site of the Hall of Fame: "I am so grateful. I have had a lot of wonderful things happen to me in my life. . . . But to make the Hall of Fame on the first go-around, where do you put that on the list?"[2] Robinson stated during his induction speech, "Today everything is complete. I could not be here without the advice and guidance of three of the most wonderful people I know—my advisor, a wonderful friend and a man who has treated me as a father, Branch Rickey; my mother; and my wife. I never thought I'd make it in my lifetime."[3]

That same month, Robinson began delivering a column, "Jackie Robinson Says," for the *New York Amsterdam News*. In his column Robinson praised Attorney General Robert Kennedy while criticizing President Kennedy's position on civil rights. Later that year, after hearing that black churches had been burned down, Robinson accepted King's suggestion that he head a rebuilding drive. Now sporting a cane and gray hair, Robinson also became cochair of a fund-raising effort to refurbish the operations of the YMCA's Harlem branch. Black nationalists nevertheless increasingly viewed Robinson with disdain. Ignoring their criticisms, Robinson traveled to Birmingham, Alabama, in the spring of 1963, during King's campaign there. In August Jackie and Rachel, along with their younger children Sharon and David, participated in the March on Washington. With 200,000 others, they delighted in the address by King during which he invoked his "I have a dream" refrain. The following month's murder of four young girls stemming from the bombing of Birmingham's Sixteenth Street Baptist Church enraged Robinson. The assassination of President Kennedy in November 1963 led him to admit that while he had often criticized the president, Kennedy had nevertheless accomplished more in the area of civil rights than any of his predecessors.

In early 1964 Robinson left Chock full o'Nuts to take a position as a deputy national director of Nelson Rockefeller's presidential campaign. He continued to be involved with several business ventures and served on various boards of directors while becoming more engaged in the political arena. He was displeased with both Muhammad Ali and Malcolm X, condemning what he considered their extreme views, as he closely followed the civil rights movement. After the murder of three young civil rights workers—two Jews and one black—during the Mississippi Freedom Summer drive in 1964, he chaired a fund-raising effort to construct a community center in Meridian. As riots rippled across the nation, including in Harlem in July of that year, Robinson worried about the brutality of police tactics. In an effort to keep hope alive, Robinson served as cochair of a committee that sought to establish a bank in Harlem, which opened its doors in January 1965. He also began appearing on ABC broadcasts of major league baseball games, which paid $500 per contest, and cowrote *Breakthrough to the Big League* and wrote *Baseball Has Done It*.

He followed with pride, and, sometimes admitted bewilderment, his wife Rachel's career. She had received a graduate degree in nursing from New York University and became head of psychiatric nursing at the Albert Einstein College of Medicine in the Bronx. Then in 1965 Rachel headed the nursing division at the state mental health center in New Haven, where she also joined the faculty of the Yale University School of Nursing. Jackie and Rachel had to contend with their troubled son, Jackie Jr., a high school dropout who had entered the U.S. military, undergoing basic training at Fort Riley, Kansas, where his father had temporarily been stationed during the war. The two other Robinson children, Sharon and David, thrived in school as their brother headed for Vietnam, where he was wounded in an ambush. Jackie suffered a grievous loss in December 1965 when eighty-four-year-old Branch Rickey died. The two men had remained close since their first encounter two decades earlier. Indeed their relationship had deepened following Robinson's departure from baseball. By contrast Jackie's dealings with Jackie Jr. proved troubled, worsening when the young man returned from Southeast Asia.

Robinson continued to follow the civil rights movement, growing concerned with the tendency of many young activists to adopt a militant posture far removed from King's nonviolent ideals. In 1966 Robinson's column again appeared in the *Amsterdam News*, where he supported Rockefeller's reelection bid for the New York governorship. In February Rockefeller named Robinson his special assistant for community affairs. When the House of Representatives expelled Adam Clayton Powell Jr. for financial improprieties, talk was heard that Robinson might run to replace him as Harlem's representative. Helping to pique such rumors was the purchase of two apartments on 93rd Street by Jackie and Rachel Robinson. Jackie possessed no desire for political office and actually defended Powell from furious assaults. His support for the Johnson administration's waging of war in Vietnam also probably lessened the likelihood of Robinson's joining the political fray. Despite that stance, Robinson now considered Muhammad Ali heroic for his principled opposition to the war, and yet he was unhappy when King began openly criticizing the war in 1967. Still, Robinson continued to refer to King as his leader, and he remained personally devoted, affirming, "This is a personal commitment and a public pledge." Some black activists dismissively called Robinson an Uncle Tom.

Early in 1968 Robinson became associated with Sea Host Incorporated, which hired him to help promote the sale of fast food franchises. He remained active in the public arena, serving as national chairman of the National Conference of Christians and Jews' Brotherhood Week. Then he learned on March 4 that Jackie Jr. had been arrested and charged with possessing marijuana, heroin, and a .22 caliber pistol. Notwithstanding this personal setback, Robinson remained heavily involved in presidential politics, hoping that Governor Rockefeller would win the Republican nomination. King's assassination on April 4 upset Robinson greatly, and he referred to the slain minister as the greatest figure of the twentieth century. Another blow came Robinson's way in May when his mother, Mallie

Robinson, died. Then on June 6, Senator Robert F. Kennedy, in the midst of his bid for the Democratic Party presidential nomination, was gunned down. In his column in the *Amsterdam News*, Robinson expressed sorrow for the loss of a man whose dedication to social justice had become so great. Talk was soon heard that Rockefeller might select Robinson to fill Kennedy's spot in the U.S. Senate. Late in June, however, Robinson suffered a mild heart attack. In August Jackie Jr. was arrested yet again, this time while in the company of a young woman who was apparently a prostitute. Despite having pointed a gun at a policeman, Jackie Jr. received a suspended sentence. Refusing to support the presidential run of Richard Nixon, whom Robinson thought was pandering to Southern racists, Jackie instead backed Democratic nominee Hubert Humphrey, which diminished his standing within the Rockefeller administration.

During the late 1960s, Robinson's health continued to deteriorate. In August 1970 his doctor gave him a battery of tests, which revealed that his diabetes was in an advanced state and that he had experienced a stroke. He soon suffered another stroke and was hemorrhaging in his eyes, threatening blindness. In October, experiencing shortness of breath, he entered the Mayo Clinic in Minneapolis but was soon released. Still he followed with satisfaction the progress of his children. David had entered Stanford University. Sharon was remarried, after a troubled first marriage, and was enrolled in a nursing program at Howard University. Jackie Jr. completed a rehabilitation program for addicts. On February 10, 1971, Jackie and Rachel celebrated their twenty-fifth wedding anniversary. Days later new tests revealed that Jackie had advanced heart disease and chronic lung disease. Despite his physical ailments, Robinson reached out to the Rev. Jesse Jackson, who was running Operation Breadbasket and had established PUSH (People United to Save Humanity). In June 1971 Jackie received word that Jackie Jr. had died following a car crash. The death of her eldest son devastated Rachel, and the marriage of Jackie and Rachel Robinson temporarily reached its rockiest point.

At the beginning of the 1970s, discussion occurred about the possibility of a separate wing at the Baseball Hall of Fame to honor Negro league greats like Satchel Paige and Josh Gibson. Buzzie Bavasi, the longtime Dodgers executive who was now working for the San Diego Padres, wrote to Robinson about that idea. Bavasi expressed his opposition to the black greats being segregated from Ruth, Gehrig, and other white legends. Robinson shared Bavasi's concerns and asserted forthrightly, "1971 is no time to go backwards and frankly I personally would refuse this dubious honor."[4]

In 1971 Roger Kahn's brilliant examination of the Brooklyn Dodgers, *The Boys of Summer*, contained a moving tribute to the player he respected more than any other, in a chapter titled "The Lion at Dusk." Robinson's playing career far transcended the statistics he compiled during his ten years in the major leagues, Kahn explained. "Troops of people . . . believe that in his prime Jackie Robinson was a better player than any of the others." Kahn quoted from Leo Durocher, who said, "Ya want a guy that comes to play. This guy didn't just come to play. He come to beat ya. He come to stuff the goddamn bat right up your ass." As Kahn prepared to speak with Robinson, he spotted Jackie, looking "astonishingly handsome," with his coal-black skin and shockingly white hair. Robinson had lost some weight, under doctor's orders, having endured "diabetes, high blood pressure, and . . . a heart attack" despite abstaining from both cigarettes and alcohol.[5]

In 1971, *Sport* magazine named Robinson its "Man of the last 25 years." At the luncheon on December 6 honoring Robinson, *Sport*'s editor Al Silverman referred to the breaking of organized baseball's color barrier: "What Jackie has done can never be told. He endured, somehow, he endured it all." Robinson himself questioned how far blacks had actually come, contending instead, "We are still somewhere back in the nineteenth century" with no African American managers and many roads yet to travel "as men, as athletes."[6]

In his autobiography, *I Never Had It Made*, released in 1972, Robinson related the story of his struggles as an African American confronting racial barriers, including those pertaining to major league baseball. He reiterated a longstanding concern of his: blacks were still denied leadership opportunities in organized baseball, with not a single African American yet hired as a big league manager. Robinson attributed that phenomenon to the discrimination and prejudice by the same kinds of individuals who had opposed Branch Rickey's determined effort to integrate the game. Jackie reported that he would have leapt at the chance to manage and knew he would have done a good job. In the epilogue to *I Never Had It Made*, Robinson admitted that he nevertheless considered himself "very fortunate." Still he recognized that "everything I got I fought hard for," and yet he remained unable "to say truthfully that I have it made." He expressed pride in having become the first vice president of Jesse Jackson's PUSH. Robinson acknowledged hope that some day racial and religious divides in America would be transcended.[7]

In concluding his autobiography, Robinson recalled "standing alone at first base—the only black on the field." He had to grapple with "loneliness" and "abuse," along with the recognition that any mistakes on his part would be exaggerated. In the beginning he was compelled to "deny my true fighting spirit" to enable Rickey's "noble experiment" to take root, Robinson reminded readers. Throughout his playing career, he most cared about winning respect, not being accepted. He followed the same principle in both his business and political affairs. A loving family sustained him. "I have always fought for what I believed in," Robinson wrote. And yet "I was a black man in a white world. *I never had it made.*"[8]

On June 4, 1972, the Dodgers held Old Timers' Day at Dodger Stadium in Los Angeles. The team retired three numbers: Sandy Koufax's, Roy Campanella's, and Jackie Robinson's. Robinson revealed to the crowd, "This is truly one of the greatest moments of my life." During that same period, he sat as Rachel read aloud from the galleys of his forthcoming book, *I Never Had It Made*, written with Alfred Duckett. All the while, his health continued to worsen, with his physician certain that Robinson's legs would soon have to be amputated. He managed to throw out the first ball at the second game of the 1972 World Series between the Oakland Athletics and the Reds, which took place in Cincinnati on October 15. Encountering friends like Roger Kahn and Jim Murray, the great sportswriters, Robinson acknowledged not being able to see.

On October 24, 1972, at 7:10 in the morning, fifty-three-year-old Jackie Robinson died at Stamford Hospital. Red Smith wrote a moving essay for the *New York Times* following Robinson's death. He recalled how Robinson kept the Brooklyn Dodgers in the pennant race by making a spectacular catch in the 12th inning and then smashing a homer two frames later on the last regular day of the 1951 campaign, which of course ended with Bobby Thomson's "shot heard 'round the world." Nevertheless for Smith, Robinson's performance suggested "the unconquerable doing the impossible." Robinson "would not be defeated. Not by the other team and not by life." Smith also recalled how Robinson transformed baseball, as he "could bring a game to a stop just by getting on base." Then he "established the black man's right to play second base" as he "fought for the black man's right to a place in the white community" after leaving the sport that made him famous throughout the world.[9]

At a funeral ceremony for Robinson, attended by 2,500 at the Riverside Church on the Upper West Side in Manhattan, Reverend Jackson remembered, "When Jackie took the field, something reminded us of our birthright to be free." Other luminaries in attendance included New York governor Nelson Rockefeller, New York City mayor John Lindsay, former cabinet official Robert Finch, ex-Peace Corps chairman Sargent Shriver, NAACP executive director Roy Wilkins, and civil rights activist A. Philip Randolph, the man who planned the 1963 March on Washington.[10] Also present were baseball commissioner Bowie Kuhn; former Dodgers teammates such as Jim Gilliam, Don Newcombe, Ralph Branca, Pee Wee Reese, Joe Black, Roy Campanella, Carl Erskine, Gene Hermanski, and Billy Loes; baseball executive Bill Veeck; basketball great Bill Russell; and baseball legends Willie Mays, Ernie Banks, Warren Spahn, and Hank Greenberg.

On the fiftieth anniversary of Jackie Robinson's entrance into the major leagues, analysts reflected on his role as an American pioneer. An editorial in the *Los Angeles Times* acknowledged that "there may have been better ballplayers" but asked, "Who among them could have blazed the path Robinson did?" While leading the Dodgers to six pennants and one World Series championship in ten years, Robinson "knocked the cover off racism in baseball." The *Chicago Tribune* discussed Robinson's importance as a trailblazer, stating he "carried the fortunes of a whole people on his broad shoulders" while "pushing against a stone wall of prejudice." The paper wondered: If Robinson had not existed, would Hank Aaron, Bob Gibson, and Frank Thomas have made it in professional baseball? Would Jim Brown and Walter Payton have thrived on the gridiron for the National Football League? Would Bill Russell and Michael Jordan have succeeded on the National Basketball Association courts? Would Lee Elder and Tiger Woods have competed in Professional Golf Association tournaments? *Boston Globe* sports columnist Bob Ryan affirmed that Robinson "was one of the most distinguished and significant Americans of the 20th century." He "was a true pioneer and a true hero" who "simply could not fail." Robinson "had to be great on the field and even greater off the field. The entire nation was watching him." Sports columnist Thomas Boswell of the *Washington Post* affirmed that Robinson was "the most important player" in baseball history. Frank Deford, a sports columnist for *Newsweek*, referred to Robinson's role in triggering "the utter African American domination of so many of our most popular sports." The *Philadelphia Inquirer* praised Robinson's "dignity, courage, intelligence and ferocious competitiveness that can be summed up only by one word: *greatness.*"[11] On April 15, 1997, major league baseball announced that Jackie Robinson's number 42 would be retired by all teams. No other player had been so honored.

15

Two Pioneers

From the time he became a regular with the Detroit Tigers in 1933, Hank Greenberg served as a model for his fellow American Jews who were desperately in need of such a figure. At home anti-Semitism had hardly disappeared, although the United States had long been viewed as a special place where Jews avoided the kinds of legal restraints that afflicted them elsewhere. Yet European anti-Semitism remained prevalent and became far fiercer the same year Greenberg joined the Tigers everyday lineup, with the ascendancy of Adolf Hitler to the chancellorship of Germany. A new, more virulent brand of anti-Semitism soon swept across central Europe. Hitler's Nazi Party, during its first years in power, fueled the gospel that Jews were a parasitical force to be shunned, ostracized, and disfranchised, at a minimum. Throughout that same period the movie-star handsome Greenberg belied the absurd stereotypes spun about Jews: that they were ugly, weak, cowardly, lacking in spirit, and devoid of morality. Far more physically powerful than most baseball players of his generation, Greenberg also displayed genuine courage in overcoming the slurs, innuendoes, and racial aspersions that Tigers foes and fans hurled at him. In the face of it all and as stories of anti-Semitic horrors poured out of Germany, Greenberg became one of the greatest sluggers in major league baseball, on a par with Lou Gehrig, Jimmie Foxx, Joe DiMaggio, and Ted Williams. That enabled him to become an icon for American Jews who needed a different kind of hero, one outside the realms of vaudeville, cinema, business, or even politics. What better venue than the national pastime, whose most famous players possessed allure and stature equal to that of any entertainer or politician other than President Franklin D. Roosevelt.

In the midst of FDR's historic lengthy tenure, Jackie Robinson, with cinematic good looks of his own, became another icon, one who drew from Greenberg's inspiration and served as a model for his fellow African Americans in the 1930s, when blacks Americans continued to face discriminatory treatment. This was true far beyond the Deep South, where a solid Jim Crow edifice remained in place. In Robinson's adopted state of California, African Americans endured segregation edicts and easy characterizations that they were inferior, lazy, mentally deficient, and lacking in physical courage. Racism, pure and simple, remained a potent force in the United States and was resorted to in both conscious and unconscious manners designed to keep blacks in their place. That was something Robinson, like Greenberg, was never willing to accept easily, if at all. First as a high school star and then as a collegian, Robinson began to make his mark on a variety of playing fields, competing at the top level against white and black athletes. Word emerged that he was an all-around athlete, perhaps the nation's finest since Jim Thorpe, as he excelled on the gridiron, the hardtop, the baseball diamond, and track circuits. Dropping out of college before graduation, Robinson foundered, notwithstanding a stellar showing in the College All-Star Game against the National Foootball League champion Chicago Bears.

World War II, which resulted in unprecedented disasters for European Jews as well as opportunities for their American brethren and for African Americans, proved transformative for Greenberg and Robinson while adding to their legends. Greenberg was the first major league star to enter the U.S. Armed Forces and lost more playing time because of military service during WWII than any of his contemporaries. Entering the army as the reigning American League MVP, Greenberg was applauded for his readiness to sacrifice. Robinson enlisted in the U.S. military while it was still segregated. Despite having earned a commission, he encountered the very Jim

Crow practices that he had sometimes been able to avoid and that sometimes slammed him in the face. Although a brilliant athlete, he had been
unable to enter the NFL or organized baseball. Contesting segregation practices while wearing his lieutenant bars, Robinson soon faced a court-martial in which he was acquitted. Their military service kept Greenberg and
Robinson in the public limelight, assuring that when they left the army,
fans would readily follow their next endeavors.

Greenberg returned to the Detroit Tigers in 1945, a genuine American
hero boasting battlefield stars and time spent in the Asian theater of the
war. Robinson joined the Kansas City Monarchs of the Negro National
League that same year, undoubtedly better known because of the controversy surrounding his court-martial. Slamming a homer in his first game
back in the majors, Greenberg went on to smash a pennant-winning grand
slam for the Tigers before leading them to the World Series championship.
This delighted American Jews who had recently received word that six million European Jews had been murdered by the Nazis and their allies.
Robinson starred with the Monarchs, then signed a contract with the
Brooklyn Dodgers of the National League that enabled him to become the
first black to play in organized baseball in the twentieth century. African
Americans cheered reports of Robinson's signing, which promised to break
one of the most entrenched Jim Crow barriers. As Greenberg returned to
his prewar position as the American League's home run and RBI champ,
Robinson starred for the Montreal Royals of the International League,
encountering both racial abuse and tremendous fan support. The same
would be true the following year, 1947, when Greenberg played his last
major league season with the Pittsburgh Pirates and Robinson joined the
Brooklyn Dodgers. The two men met on the playing field, where they
shared words of praise and support. Robinson went on to become the
National League Rookie of the Year while helping the Dodgers advance to
the World Series.

Greenberg retired to the sidelines to enter big league management, where
he still endured anti-Semitism on occasion. Robinson continued blazing
his way to glory as one of the best-known members of the famed Boys of

Summer. Greenberg thrived as an executive with the Cleveland Indians. Robinson, the "black Ty Cobb," helped transform major league baseball, bringing back speed and a thinking man's approach to the game. As the Indians won a pair of pennants and one World Series championship, the Dodgers won six National League titles and their own World Series crown, all in competition against the hated New York Yankees. A small number of Jews starred in major league baseball during this period, including Indian slugger Al Rosen and All Star infielder-outfielder Sid Gordon. Far more African Americans, following Robinson's lead, made their mark in big league baseball, including his teammates Roy Campanella and Don Newcombe, the New York Giants' Willie Mays, the Milwaukee Braves' Hank Aaron, the Chicago Cubs' Ernie Banks, and the Cincinnati Reds' Frank Robinson. Ironically and appropriately, 1956 was Robinson's last major league campaign and the year that Hank Greenberg became the first Jew inducted into baseball's Hall of Fame. Six years later, Robinson, a different kind of American hero, joined Greenberg there as he became the first African American and former Negro leaguer admitted into Cooperstown.

During their post-baseball careers, Greenberg and Robinson remained in the public realm, sought out for comments about contemporary events involving the game that made them such storied figures and other matters as well. Robinson particularly spoke about civil rights, remaining controversial as some wanted him to adopt a more militant posture and others believed that he was not appreciative enough of the opportunities afforded him. Until their deaths in 1972 and 1986, respectively, Jackie Robinson and Hank Greenberg continued to serve as models and mentors for African Americans, Jews, and anyone interested in fair-minded treatment of their fellow citizens. Each was an American hero. Each represented the best that their country stood for: equality of opportunity and fair treatment for all. Each worked diligently for everything he accomplished, with Robinson possessing more natural athletic ability but having to confront, as Greenberg did, seemingly inordinate obstacles on the path to athletic stardom. Each possessed a driving athletic ambition, but rare gifts too, resulting in a majestic baseball career and considerable success thereafter. Each paid a heavy price along the way. The stress each man endured was enormous, leading to considerable discomfort for Greenberg and the far too early breaking down of Robinson's once magnificent physique. Hank Greenberg and Jackie Robinson nevertheless opened the doors for countless others, both in the sporting world and beyond, and for non-Jews and non–African Americans who also did not easily fit into long accepted religious and racial norms.

NOTES

Introduction

1   Jackie Robinson, *Jackie Robinson: My Own Story* (New York: Greenberg, 1948), 146–47; Hank Greenberg, *Hank Greenberg: The Story of My Life*, ed. Ira Berkow (New York: Times Books, 1989), 191.

2   Bob Considine, "The Will to Overcome," *Boston Herald*, October 27, 1972.

Chapter 1. Discrimination and the National Pastime

1   "The Brooklyn Eagle," *American Chronicle of Sports and Pastimes*, 1868, File RE, National Baseball Hall of Fame Library, Cooperstown, New York.

2   Robert Peterson, *Only the Ball Was White: A History of Legendary Black Players and All-Black Professional Teams* (New York: Oxford University Press, 1992), 16–17.

3   Robert C. Cottrell, *Blackball, the Black Sox, and the Babe: Baseball's Crucial 1920 Season* (Jefferson, North Carolina: McFarland & Company, Inc., 2002), 5.

4   "Do They Need Protection?," *Sporting Life*, April 13, 1887.

5   "No Color for Him, Please," *Sporting Life*, October 10, 1888.

6   *The Sporting News*, March 23, 1889.

7   Peterson, *Only the Ball Was White*, 41.

8   Sol White, *Sol White's History of Colored Base Ball, with Other Documents on the Early Black Game, 1886–1936* (Lincoln: University of Nebraska Press, 1995), 111; Rube Foster, "Success of the Negro as a Ball Player," *Indianapolis Freeman*, April 16, 1910.

9   "The Colored Clubs," *Baseball Magazine* 22 (December 1918): 117–18.

10 David Spaner, "From Greenberg to Green: Jewish Ballplayers," in *Total Baseball V*, ed. John Thorn et al. (New York: Viking, 1997): 172.

11 Steven A. Riess, "From Pike to Green with Greenberg in Between," in *The American Game: Baseball and Ethnicity*, eds. Lawrence Baldassaro and Richard A. Johnson (Carbondale: Southern Illinois University Press, 2002), 123.

12 "We Are in Receipt," *Baseball Magazine* 27 (June 1921): 290, 296.

13 W. J. Cameron, "Jewish Gamblers Corrupt American Baseball," *Dearborn Independent*, September 3, 1921.

14 W. J. Cameron, "Jewish Degradation of American Baseball," *Dearborn Independent*, September 10, 1921.

15 Orval W. Baylor to August Herrmann, May 31, 1924, 1–2, RE, National Baseball Hall of Fame Library; Herrmann to Baylor, June 4, 1924, RE, National Baseball Hall of Fame Library.

16 Henry Montor letter, May 29, 1925, JW, National Baseball Hall of Fame Library; Harry Conzell, "An Open Letter to the Baseball Magnates," June 5, 1925, JW, National Baseball Hall of Fame Library.

17 Conzell, "An Open Letter"; Spaner, "From Greenberg to Green," 172.

18 F. Scott Fitzgerald, *The Great Gatsby* (New York: Charles Scribner's Sons, 1925), 73–74.

19 F. C. Lane, "Why Not More Jewish Ball Players?," *Baseball Magazine* 36 (January 1926): 341, 372.

20 Oliver S. Arata, "The Colored Athlete in Professional Baseball," *Baseball Magazine* 42 (May 1929): 555–56; Robert Charles Cottrell, *The Best Pitcher in Baseball: Rube Foster, Negro League Giant* (New York: New York University Press, 2002), passim.

21 Arata, "Colored Athlete," 556.

22 *New York Daily News*, February 1, 1933; Richard O'Connor, *Heywood Broun: A Biography* (New York: Putnam, 1975).

23 Jimmy Powers, "Colored B.B. Players—O.K.," *New York Daily News*, February 8, 1933.

24 "Comiskey Says 'Color' on Diamond Is Sox Problem," *Chicago Defender*, March 4, 1933.

25 Ibid.

26 Ibid.

27 Ben Field, "The Brooklyn Dodgers Win a Game," *Daily Worker*, August 29, 1933.

28 "Sultan of Swat Talks," *Pittsburgh Courier*, August 11, 1933.

29 "East-West Poll Is Sweeping Nation," *Pittsburgh Courier*, August 19, 1933; Chester Washington, "Sez 'Ches,'"*Pittsburgh Courier*, August 26, 1933.

30 Al Monroe, "Speaking of Sports," *Chicago Defender*, February 3, 1934.

31 Lester Rodney, "Fans Oppose Jim Crow in Big League Baseball," *Sunday Worker*, August 16, 1936.

32 Fred Farrell, "Fanning with Farrell," *Sunday Worker*, August 23, 1936.

33 Ted Benson, "'League Open to Negroes'—Frick," *Sunday Worker*, August 23, 1936.

34 Mike Kantor, "Dodgers 'Ready' to Sign Negro Star," *Sunday Worker*, January 17, 1937.

35 "DiMaggio Calls Negro Greatest Pitcher," *Daily Worker*, September 13, 1937.

36 Chester L. Washington, "Pirates' Owner Would Favor Sepia Players in Organized Baseball; Lauds Gibson, Satchell [*sic*]," *Pittsburgh Courier*, February 12, 1938.

37 Fay Young, "Dandridge as Good as Ott at His Best," *Chicago Defender*, March 24, 1938.

38 Neil Lanctot, *Negro League Baseball: The Rise and Ruin of a Black Institution* (Philadelphia: University of Pennsylvania Press, 2004), 221.

39 Al Monroe, "It's News to Me," *Chicago Defender*, September 17, 1938.

40 Wendell Smith, "Cincinnati Reds' Manager, Players Laud Negro Stars," *Pittsburgh Courier*, July 15, 1939.

41 "'Negroes Will Never Crash Majors,' Says Bill Terry; Carl Hubbell Lauds Colored Players," *Pittsburgh Courier*, July 22, 1939.

42 Wendell Smith, "'I Would Use Negro Ball Players on My Team If Permitted,' Says 'Doc' Protho, Manager of the Philadelphia Phillies," *Pittsburgh Courier*, July 29, 1939.

43 Wendell Smith, "Brooklyn Dodgers Admit Negro Players Rate Place," *Pittsburgh Courier*, August 5, 1939.

44 Wendell Smith, "Would Be a Mad Scramble for Negro Players if Okayed," *Pittsburgh Courier*, August 12, 1939.

45 Wendell Smith, "'Owners Must Solve Color Problem in Majors,'" *Pittsburgh Courier*, August 26, 1939.

46 Ibid.

47 Fay Young, "Through the Years: Past Present Future," *Chicago Defender*, July 22, 1939.

48 *Daily Worker*, September 19, 1939; *Sunday Worker*, October 15, 1939; *Daily Worker*, September 17, 1940; John C. Chalberg, *Rickey & Robinson: The Preacher, the Player, and America's Game* (Wheeling, Illinois: Harlan Davidson, 2000), 95; Kelly E. Rusinack, "Baseball on the Radical Agenda: *The Daily Worker* and the *Sunday Worker* Journalistic Campaign to Desegregate Major League Baseball, 1933–1947," 75–85, in *Jackie Robinson: Race, Sports, and the American Dream* (Armonk, NY: M. E. Sharpe, 1998), eds. Joseph Dorinson and Joram Warmund.

49 William Hageman, "Chicago's 55-Year-Old Secret: Jackie Robinson's Tryout with the White Sox," *Chicago Tribune*, March 26, 1997, Tempo sec.

Chapter 2. Anti-Semitism and a Detroit Tiger

1 Sidney M. Bolkosky, *Harmony & Dissonance: Voices of Jewish Identity in Detroit, 1914–1967* (Detroit: Wayne State University Press, 1991), 80.

2 "Henry Ford's Anti-Semitic Crusade," *Current Opinion* 69 (August 1920): 222.

3 Max Wallace, *The American Axis: Henry Ford, Charles Lindbergh, and the Rise of the Third Reich* (New York: St. Martin's, 2003), 12.

4 Henry Ford, *My Life and Work* (Garden City, NY: Doubleday, 1922), 250–52.

5 Lewis S. Gannett, "Is America Anti-Semitic?," *The Nation* 116 (March 21, 1923): 330–32.

6 Hank Greenberg, *Hank Greenberg: The Story of My Life*, ed. and with an introduction by Ira Berkow (Chicago: Triumph Books, 2001), 4–5.

7 Ibid., 1; Spaner, "From Greenberg to Green," 171.

8 Greenberg, *Hank Greenberg*, 1–3.

9 Ed Fitzgerald, "Hank Greenberg: A Study in Success," *Sport* (March 1951): 29.

10 Ibid., 28; Greenberg, *Hank Greenberg*, 9.

11 "Hank Greenberg" in Lawrence Ritter, *The Glory of Their Times: The Story of the Early Days of Baseball Told by the Men Who Played It* (New York: Quill, 1985), 308–9.

12 Charles P. Ward, "Hammering Hank," *Baseball Monthly* 66 (March 3, 1941): 437.

13 Johan J. Smertenko, "The Jew: A Problem for America," *Outlook and Independent* 152 (August 7, 1929): 574–77.

14 Fitzgerald, "Hank Greenberg," 29.

15 Morris Weiner, "Hank Greenberg the 'Local' Hero," *Detroit Jewish Chronicle*, April 12, 1935.

16 Greenberg, *Hank Greenberg*, 16.

17 Ibid.; "Hank Greenberg," *Glory of Their Times*, 310.

18 Greenberg, *Hank Greenberg*, 17.

19 Ibid.

20 Ward, "Hammering Hank," 437.

21 Greenberg, *Hank Greenberg*, 17; Hank Greenberg, interview by Eli Wohlgelernter, July 25, 1980, American Jewish Committee Oral History Collection, Dorot Jewish Division, New York Public Library, New York, NY

22 Greenberg, *Hank Greenberg*, 24; Greenberg, interview.

23 Ward, "Hammering Hank," 437–38.

Chapter 3. A Major League Star

1   Alan Brinkley, *Voices of Protest: Huey Long, Father Coughlin & the Great Depression* (New York: Vintage Books, 1983), 93.

2   Wallace, *The American Axis*, 9.

3   Annetta Halliday Antona, "Five Minutes with Men in Public: Adolf Hitler, the Man without a Country," *Detroit News*, December 31, 1931.

4   Bolkosky, *Harmony & Dissonance*, 172.

5   Charles E. Coughlin, *By the Sweat of Thy Brow* (Detroit: Radio League of the Little Flower, 1931), 75, 108.

6   J. Woodford Howard Jr., *Mr. Justice Murphy: A Political Biography* (Princeton, New Jersey: Princeton University Press, 1968), 28.

7   Peter Levine, *Ellis Island to Ebbets Field: Sport and the American Jewish Experience* (New York: Oxford University Press, 1992), 141.

8   Greenberg, *Hank Greenberg*, 50–51.

9   Aviva Kempner, "The Game Came Second," *Washington Post*, September 18, 1994.

10 Ritter, *Glory of Their Times*, 328.

11 Greenberg, *Hank Greenberg*, 53.

12 "Rosh Hashanah," *Detroit Free Press*, September 9, 1934.

13 Charles P. Ward, "Greenberg's Two Home Runs Give Tigers 2 to 1 Victory," *Detroit Free Press*, September 11, 1934.

14 Kempner, "The Game Came Second."

15 Jack Carvath, "Henry Prayed and Swung His Way to Baseball Glory," *Detroit Free Press*, September 11, 1934.

16 "A Happy New Year for Everybody," *Detroit Free Press*, September 11, 1934.

17 Ward, "Greenberg's Two Home Runs."

18 William M. Simons, "Hank Greenberg: The Jewish American Sports Hero," in *Sports and the American Jew*, ed. Steven A. Riess (Syracuse, NY: Syracuse University Press, 1998), 194–95.

19 "A Happy New Year for Everybody."

20 Iffy the Dopester, "Hank's Homers Strictly Kosher," *Detroit Free Press*, September 11, 1934.

21 Greenberg, *Hank Greenberg*, 56–57.

22 Bolkovsky, *Harmony & Dissonance*, 142.

23 Bud Shaver, *Detroit News*, September 21, 1934.

24 H. G. Salsinger, *Detroit News*, September 21, 1934.

25 Morris Weiner, "Hank Greenberg the 'Local' Hero," *Detroit Jewish Chronicle and the Legal Chronicle*, April 12, 1935.

26 Ibid.

27 Greenberg, *Hank Greenberg*, 75.

28 "Number One G-Man Shows Mickey's G-Men How It's Done," *Detroit Free Press*.

29 Frederick G. Lieb, "Oi, Oi, Oh, Boy! Hail That Long-Sought Hebrew Star," *The Sporting News*, September 12, 1935.

30 Ibid.

31 "Iffy . . . the Dopester rises to remark . . . ," *Detroit Free Press*, September 19, 1935.

32 F. C. Lane, "Baseball's New Sensation, 'Hank' Greenberg," *Baseball Magazine* 55 (October 1935): 483.

33 Ibid., 483–484; Harold U. Ribalow, *The Jew in American Sports* (New York: Bloch, 1966), 37.

34 Jules Tygiel, *Baseball's Great Experiment: Jackie Robinson and His Legacy* (New York: Oxford University Press, 1983), 182.

35 George Morris, *Black Legion Rides* (New York: Workers Library, 1936), 12–20.

36 Ritter, *Glory of Their Times*, 317.

37 Greenberg, *Hank Greenberg*, 109.

38 Ibid., 110.

39 Roger Kahn, "The Homer Heard Round the World," from "Sport," in *Beyond the Boys of Summer: The Very Best of Roger Kahn*, ed. Rob Miraldi (New York: McGraw-Hill, 2005), 88.

40 "Editorial Comment," *Baseball Magazine* 61 (November 1938): 530, 576.

41 Louis Effrat, "Hank Greenberg Roots for Mark in Homers by Maris or Mantle," *New York Times*, September 14, 1961.

42 Charles Coughlin, "Persecution: Jewish and Christian," *Social Justice* (November 28, 1938): 9–10.

43 "The Week in the Nation," *Social Justice* (December 12, 1938): 9.

44 Charles Coughlin, "Shrine Dinner Chats," *Social Justice* (June 5, 1939): 2.

45 Bolkosky, *Harmony & Dissonance*, 235–36.

Chapter 4. Baseball in a Time of War

1 Speech by Lou Gehrig, Yankee Stadium, July 4, 1939.

2 Greenberg, *Hank Greenberg*, 157.

3 Ibid., 111.

4   Charles P. Ward, "Tiger Claws," *Baseball Magazine* 64 (December 1939): 319–20.

5   Bolkosky, *Harmony & Dissonance*, 236–37.

6   Ward, "Hammering Hank," 438.

7   Ritter, *Glory of Their Times*, 322.

8   "September's Brightest Star: Henry (Hank) Greenberg," October 3, 1940, Hank Greenberg file, National Baseball of Fame Library.

9   Charles P. Ward, "Ward to the Wise," *Detroit Free Press*, September 26, 1940.

10 Daniel M. Daniel, "Greenberg Chosen Player of Year," *Baseball Magazine* 66 (December 1940): 291.

11 Robert W. Creamer, *Baseball in '41* (New York: Penguin, 1992), 123–32.

12 Ibid., 132–35

13 Ibid., 136–37.

14 Bill Gilbert, *They Also Served: Baseball and the Home Front, 1941–1945* (New York: Crown, 1992), 12.

15 Shirley Povich, "Greenberg: One of Cooperstown's Finest," *Washington Post*, September 9, 1986.

16 *Total Baseball* V, ed. John Thorn, et al., 174.

17 Charles A. Lindbergh, "Who Are the War Agitators?" (speech, Des Moines, Iowa, September 11, 1941), http://www.charleslindbergh.com/americanfirst/speech.asp.

18 John N. Sabo, "Hank Declares He's Ready for Baseball Now," *Detroit Free Press*, December 6, 1941.

19 "Greenberg, Released from Army, Is Eager to Return to Baseball," *New York Times*, December 6, 1941.

20 "Greenberg to Re-Enlist," *Detroit Free Press*, December 10, 1941.

21 "Greenberg Will Return," *New York Times*, December 10, 1941.

22 J. G. Taylor Spink, "Hank Greenberg, Back to Colors, Becomes the Hank Gowdy of '41," *The Sporting News*, December 18, 1941.

23 "Rejoining Army, Greenberg Says," *New York Times*, January 3, 1942.

24 James M. Gould, "War and Baseball," *Baseball Magazine* (February 1942): 389.

25 Ibid., 390, 427.

26 Kenesaw M. Landis, letter to President Franklin D. Roosevelt, January 14, 1942, National Baseball of Fame Library.

27 Franklin D. Roosevelt, letter to Kenesaw M. Landis, January 15, 1942, National Baseball Hall of Fame Library.

28 James M. Gould, "The President Says 'Play Ball,'" *Baseball Magazine* (March 1942), 435–36, 475.

29 James MacDonald, "Himmler Program Kills Polish Jews," *New York Times*, November 25, 1942; "Wise Gets Confirmations," *New York Times*, November 25, 1942.

30 John Underwood, "War Bond," *The 1992 Information Please Sports Almanac* (Boston: Houghton Mifflin, 1991), 55; Arthur Daley, "Sports of the Times," *New York Times*, February 14, 1945.

31 "Detroit is Dynamite," *Life*, September 7, 1942.

32 Bolkosky, *Harmony & Dissonance*, 265.

33 Henry L. Feingold, *A Time for Searching: Entering the Mainstream 1920–1945* (Baltimore: The Johns Hopkins University Press, 1992), 255.

Chapter 5. Racism and the Making of a Sports Star

1 Madison Grant, *The Passing of the Great Race* (New York: Argo, 1970), 167.

2 "Negro Leaders to Present War Aims to Negroes," *The Messenger* 2 (July 1918): 8; "Pro-Germanism Among Negroes," *The Messenger* 2 (July 1918): 13.

3 Arnold Rampersad, *Jackie Robinson: A Biography* (New York: Ballatine Books, 1998), 16.

4 "The Negro at Bay," *The Nation* 108 (June 14, 1919): 931.

5 "Reaping the Whirlwind," *Chicago Defender*, August 2, 1919.

6 "President Harding Discourses on the Color Line," *Current Opinion* 71 (December 1921): 704–6.

7 Ibid., 707.

8 David E. Lilienthal, "A Trial of Two Races," *The Outlook* 141 (December 23, 1925): 629.

9 Ibid., 629–30.

10 Jackie Robinson, *I Never Had It Made: Jackie Robinson; An Autobiography* (New York: Ecco, 1995), 5–6.

11 Rampersad, *Jackie Robinson*, 34.

12 Robinson, *I Never Had It Made*, 7–8.

13 Rampersad, *Jackie Robinson*, 55.

14 David Falkner, *Great Time Coming: The Life of Jackie Robinson from Baseball to Birmingham* (New York: Touchstone, 1996), 43.

15 Woody Strode and Sam Young, "The Goal Dust Gang," in *The Jackie Robinson Reader: Perspectives on an American Hero*, ed. Jules Tygiel (New York: Dutton, 1997), 27.

16 Rampersad, *Jackie Robinson*, 65.

17   Glenn Stout and Dick Johnson, *Jackie Robinson: Between the Baselines* (San Francisco: Woodford, 1997), 24.

18   Falkner, *Great Time Coming*, 55.

19   Strode and Young, "The Goal Dust Gang," 27.

20   Ibid., 56.

21   Robinson, *I Never Had It Made*, 11.

22   Stout and Johnson, *Jackie Robinson*, 27.

23   Vic Kelley, "Jackie Robinson's Athletic Career at UCLA," Jackie Robinson Papers, National Baseball Hall of Fame Library.

24   Robinson, *I Never Had It Made*, 12.

Chapter 6. Out of School and Into the Army

1   Wilfrid Smith, "Robinson Leads All-Star Drive," *Chicago Tribune*, August 16, 1941.

2   Wilfrid Smith, "Play 7-7 Tie in All-Star Drill," *Chicago Tribune*, August 20, 1941.

3   "'Pass Defense-Where Was It?' All-Stars Ask," *Chicago Tribune*, August 29, 1941.

4   Edward Prell, "Weary Bears Admit It Was a Tough Game," *Chicago Tribune*, August 29, 1941.

5   Falkner, *Great Time Coming*, 67.

6   "'Get after Landis, We'd Welcome You,' Sox Manager Tells Young Negro Stars," *Daily Worker*, March 23, 1942.

7   Herman Hill, "Chi White Sox Reject Race Players," *Pittsburgh Courier*, March 21, 1942.

8   Phil Dixon with Patrick J. Hannigan, *The Negro Baseball Leagues: A Photographic History* (Mattituck, NY: Amereon House, 1992), 245.

9   Lester Rodney, *Daily Worker*, May 6, 1942.

10   Peterson, *Only the Ball Was White*, 178.

11   David Pietrusza, *Judge and Jury: The Life and Times of Judge Kenesaw Mountain Landis* (South Bend, IN: Diamond Communications, 1998), 418.

12   Fay Young, "Through the Years: Past Present Future," *Chicago Defender*, August 1, 1942.

13   Conrad Komorowski, "'No Comment,' Says Landis," *Daily Worker*, June 24, 1942.

14   Lanctot, *Negro League Baseball*, 234.

15   Nat Low, "An Open Letter to Joe McCarthy," *Daily Worker*, May 4, 1942.

16   Lester Rodney, "Can You Read, Judge Landis?," *Daily Worker*, May 26, 1942.

17   "CIO Convention Wires Landis, 'Lift the Ban,'" *Daily Worker*, May 27, 1942.

18 "Has Your Union Wired Landis?," *Daily Worker*, May 29, 1942.

19 Lester Rodney, "On the Score Board," *Daily Worker*, May 31, 1942.

20 "Chicago Catholic Bishop Joins Campaign to Lift Ban against Negro Ball Players," *Daily Worker*, June 6, 1942.

21 Nat Low, "The Low Down," *Daily Worker*, May 7, 1942.

22 Nat Low, "City C.I.O. Demands 'End Jim Crow,'" *Daily Worker*, June 8, 1942.

23 "Jim-Crow Ban Sure to Go, Says Diamond Fan Cacchione," *Daily Worker*, June 19, 1942.

24 Komorowski, "'No Comment,' Says Landis."

25 "Negroes and Baseball," *Newsweek* 20 (August 10, 1942): 58.

26 Fay Young, "Through the Years," *Chicago Defender*, July 25, 1942.

27 Fay Young, "Through the Years," *Chicago Defender*, August 1, 1942.

28 J. G. Taylor Spink, "No Good from Race Issue," *The Sporting News*, August 6, 1942.

29 Carl T. Rowan and Jackie Robinson, *Wait Till Next Year: The Life Story of Jackie Robinson* (New York: Rowan House, 1960), 74.

30 Rampersad, *Jackie Robinson*, 95.

31 Robinson, *I Never Had It Made*, 14.

32 Ibid., 17.

33 "Transfer Card," December 27, 1943, Jackie Robinson Papers, Manuscript Division, Library of Congress.

34 Proceedings of Disposition Board, January 28, 1944, Jackie Robinson Papers, Manuscript Division, Library of Congress.

35 Falkner, *Great Time Coming*, 72–73, 75.

36 Robinson, *I Never Had It Made*, 18.

37 Military Records, Jackie Robinson Papers, Manuscript Division, Library of Congress.

38 Robinson, *I Never Had It Made*, 19.

39 Statement of Mr. Milton N. Renegar, July 7, 1944, Jackie Robinson Papers, Manuscript Division, Library of Congress.

40 Statement of Mr. Bevlia B. Younger, July 7, 1944, Jackie Robinson Papers, Manuscript Division, Library of Congress.

41 H. L. Jaworski and Sloan G. Stewart, "Proceedings of Disposition Board," June 26, 1944, Jackie Robinson Papers, Manuscript Division, Library of Congress; Statement of Capt. Puelor L. Wiggington, Jackie Robinson Papers, Manuscript Division, Library of Congress.

42 Statement of Jack R. Robinson, July 7, 1944, Jackie Robinson Papers, Manuscript Division, Library of Congress.

43 Robinson, *I Never Had It Made*, 20–21.

44 Statement of Gerald M. Bear, n.d., Jackie Robinson Papers, Manuscript Division, Library of Congress.

45 Falkner, *Great Time Coming*, 80.

46 Edward R. Dudley to Jack Robinson, August 3, 1944, Jackie Robinson Papers, Manuscript Division, Library of Congress.

47 J. A. Ulio to Commanding General, Camp Hood, August 15, 1944, Jackie Robinson Papers, Manuscript Division, Library of Congress.

48 Walter D. Buie to Colonel Kimball, July 17, 1944, Jackie Robinson Papers, Manuscript Division, Library of Congress.

49 Transcript of a meeting of the Army Retiring Board with Jackie Robinson, July 21, 1944, Jackie Robinson Papers, Manuscript Division, Library of Congress.

50 Record of Court-Martial Trial, August 2, 1944, Jackie Robinson Papers, Manuscript Division, Library of Congress.

51 Arden Freer and R. K. Farnham to the Adjutant General, Officers Branch, August 3, 1944, Jackie Robinson Papers, Manuscript Division, Library of Congress.

52 Robinson, *I Never Had It Made*, 23.

53 Herbert M. Jones, "Official Statement of the Military Service of Jack R. Robinson," Jackie Robinson Papers, Manuscript Division, Library of Congress.

54 Robinson, *I Never Had It Made*, 23–24.

Chapter 7. The Color Barrier Remains

1 Lanctot, *Negro League Baseball*, 244–45.

2 Wendell Smith, "Publishers Place Case of Negro Players before Big League Owners," *Pittsburgh Courier*, December 11, 1943; Wendell Smith, "Frick Says Owners Were Impressed by Publishers," Pittsburgh Courier, December 11, 1943;

3 "Ira F. Lewis's Factual Speech to Judge Landis and Major League Owners," *Pittsburgh Courier*, December 11, 1943.

4 Eric Enders, "A Legacy Remembered," *Austin American-Statesman*, April 15, 1997.

5 "Will Our Military Policy Change?," *Pittsburgh Courier*, January 6, 1945.

6 Wendell Smith, "'Smitty's' Sport Spurts," *Pittsburgh Courier*, January 27, 1945.

7 Wendell Smith, "'Smitty's' Sports Spurts," *Pittsburgh Courier*, March 10, 1945.

8 *Chicago Defender*, March 10, 1945; Dick Clark and Larry Lester, eds., *The Negro Leagues Book* (Cleveland, OH: The Society for American Baseball Research, 1994), 29.

9 James Bankes, *The Pittsburgh Crawfords: The Lives & Times of Baseball's Most Exciting Team!* (Dubuque, IA: Wm. C. Brown, 1991), 135.

10 Wendell Smith, "'Smitty's' Sports Spurts," *Pittsburgh Courier*, March 24, 1945.

11 Wendell Smith, "Boston Councilman Joins in Crusade," *Pittsburgh Courier*, April 14, 1945.

12 "Birmingham, Monarchs Split Two Sunday Tilts," *Pittsburgh Courier*, April 14, 1945.

13 Jimmy Smith, "McDuffie, Thomas First Negroes in Big League Uniforms," *Pittsburgh Courier*, April 14, 1945.

14 Wendell Smith, "Red Sox Consider Negroes," *Pittsburgh Courier*, April 21, 1945.

15 "Players Get Try-Outs," *Pittsburgh Courier*, April 21, 1945.

16 Glenn Stout, "Tryout and Fallout: Race, Jackie Robinson, and the Red Sox," *Massachusetts Historical Review* 6 (2004): 29.

17 "Roosevelt: The Man!," *Pittsburgh Courier*, April 21, 1945.

18 Wendell Smith, "'Smitty's' Sports Spurts," *Pittsburgh Courier*, April 21, 1945.

19 "The Baseball Situation," *Pittsburgh Courier*, April 28, 1945.

20 Wendell Smith, "Three Players Who Received Try-Out with Boston Red Sox," *Pittsburgh Courier*, April 28, 1945.

21 Wendell Smith, "'Smitty's' Sports Spurts," *Pittsburgh Courier*, April 28, 1945.

22 Robinson, *I Never Had It Made*, 29.

23 Wendell Smith, "The Sports Beat," *Pittsburgh Courier*, January 4, 1947.

24 "Chandler's Chance," *Pittsburgh Courier*, May 5, 1945.

25 "Rickey Claims That 15 Clubs Voted to Bar Negroes from the Majors," Jackie Robinson File, National Baseball Hall of Fame Library.

26 Ric Roberts, "New Czar Must Face Bias Issue," *Pittsburgh Courier*, May 5, 1945.

27 Cum Posey, "Many Problems League Must Solve," *Pittsburgh Courier*, May 5, 1945.

28 Wendell Smith, "The Sports Beat," *Pittsburgh Courier*, May 12, 1945.

29 "'Our Boys' Fought in All Major Battles," *Pittsburgh Courier*, May 12, 1945.

30 "Chandler Plays Parley on Issue of Negroes in Majors," *Pittsburgh Courier*, May 12, 1945.

31 James Edmund Royack, "Committee Proposed to Study Problem," *Pittsburgh Courier*, May 12, 1945.

32 Wendell Smith, "The Sports Beat," *Pittsburgh Courier*, May 19, 1945.

33 Robinson, *I Never Had It Made*, 24–25.

34 John Holway, *Voices from the Great Black Baseball Leagues* (New York: Da Capo, 1992), 344.

35 Joe Posnanski, *The Soul of Baseball: A Road Trip through Buck O'Neil's America* (New York: Harper, 2008).

36 Robinson, *I Never Had It Made*, 25.

37 Wendell Smith, "The Sports Beat," *Pittsburgh Courier*, May 26, 1945.

38 J. Cordell White to Mr. Clark Griffith, *Pittsburgh Courier*, June 2, 1945.

39 Wendell Smith, "The Sports Beat," *Pittsburgh Courier*, June 9, 1945.

40 Wendell Smith, "The Sports Beat," *Pittsburgh Courier*, July 14, 1945.

41 Wendell Smith, "The Sports Beat," *Pittsburgh Courier*, July 28, 1945.

Chapter 8. Greenberg Returns

1 Arthur Daley, "Sports of the Times," *New York Times*, February 14, 1945.

2 "Hank's Back; Ability to Hit Fast Ball His Only Worry," *Detroit Free Press*, September 21, 1945.

3 Red Smith, "It Doesn't Sound Like Greenberg," *New York Herald Tribune*, August 27, 1946.

4 Greenberg, *Hank Greenberg*, 145–46.

5 Lyall Smith, "As of Today," *Detroit Free Press*, June 22, 1945.

6 Lyall Smith, "Hank Displays Old Eye, Power in First Workout," *Detroit Free Press*, June 22, 1945.

7 Frank Williams, "Hank Can Provide an Answer," *Detroit Free Press*, June 24, 1945.

8 Lyall Smith, "Greenberg Starts Comeback against A's Sunday," *Detroit Free Press*, June 26, 1945.

9 "Welcome Back, Hank Greenberg," *Detroit Free Press*, June 30, 1945.

10 Herbert Simons, "The First Things They Did," *Baseball Magazine* 76 (January 1946): 262.

11 Andrew Kopkind, "Bess Bets," *The Village Voice*, November 12, 1979, 19–20. Greenberg's ancestors were Romanian.

12 "Greenberg Hailed by Joyous Tigers," *New York Times*, October 1, 1945.

13 Greenberg, *Hank Greenberg*, 148.

14 Lyall Smith, "Hank's Bat Wins Flag," *Detroit Free Press*, October 1, 1945.

15 Iffy the Dopester, "Iffy Sees in Homer Hank a Never-Say-Die Detroit," *Detroit Free Press*, October 2, 1945.

16 Lee Greene, "Hammerin' Hank Greenberg," *Sport* (June 1960): 79.

Chapter 9. The Signing of Jackie Robinson

1 Dave Anderson, "The Days That Brought the Barrier Down," *New York Times*, March 30, 1997.

2 "Rickey Claims Base Ball Is Moral Guide," *Sporting Life*, December 4, 1915.

3 Phil Pepe, "Through the Press Gate," July 20, 1972, Jackie Robinson Papers, 1970–1979, National Baseball Hall of Fame Library.

4 "Memorandum of Conversation between Mr. Rickey and Mr. Sukeforth," Monday, January 16, 1950, Arthur Mann Papers, Library of Congress.

5 Robinson, *Jackie Robinson*, 30–31; "Memorandum of Conversation Between Mr. Rickey and Mr. Sukeforth"; Dan W. Dodson, "The Integration of Negroes in Baseball," *Journal of Educational Sociology* 28 (October 1954): 78.

6 Robinson, *Jackie Robinson*, 31–34.

7 Wendell Smith, "The Sports Beat," *Pittsburgh Courier*, September 1, 1945.

8 Wendell Smith, "The Sports Beat," *Pittsburgh Courier*, September 8, 1945.

9 Wendell Smith, "Sepia Shortstop and Dodgers' Boss Meet in Brooklyn," *Pittsburgh Courier*, September 8, 1945.

10 Janet Bruce, *The Kansas City Monarchs: Champions of Black Baseball* (Lawrence: University Press of Kansas, 1985), 111.

11 Wendell Smith, "The Sports Beat," *Pittsburgh Courier*, September 29, 1945.

12 Herman Hill, "Robinson Sparkling on the Coast," *Pittsburgh Courier*, October 13, 1945.

13 Herman Hill, "Sepia Stars Blank Big Leaguers, 1-0," *Pittsburgh Courier*, October 13, 1945.

14 Branch Rickey to Arthur Mann, October 7, 1945, Arthur Mann Papers, Library of Congress.

15 Wendell Smith, "Branch Rickey Tells Couriers Why He Signed Jackie Robinson to Play with Montreal Club," *Pittsburgh Courier*, November 3, 1945.

16 Tommy Holmes, "Rickey Signs Negro Amid Complications," *Brooklyn Eagle*, October 24, 1945.

17 Harold C. Burr, "Robinson's Road All Cleared; Monarchs Refuse to Block It," *Brooklyn Eagle*, October 26, 1945.

18 "Closer Relations Between Big Leagues, Negroes Seen As Robinson Sequel," *Brooklyn Eagle*, October 25, 1945.

19 Tommy Holmes, "Public Will Decide On Jackie Robinson," *Brooklyn Eagle*, October 31, 1945.

20   Jackie Robinson, "Glad of Opportunity and Will Try to Make Good," *Pittsburgh Courier*, November 3, 1945.

21   Peterson, *Only the Ball Was White*, 192.

22   Phil Gordon, "Won't Fight Robinson Singing, Says Baird, Negro Team Owner," *Daily Worker*, October 26, 1945.

23   Wendell Smith, "The Sports Beat," *Pittsburgh Courier*, November 3, 1945.

24   "Martin Congratulates Rickey on Signing," *Pittsburgh Courier*, November 3, 1945.

25   "Fans Say Brooklyn Should Pay Monarchs for Robinson," *Michigan Chronicle*, November 3, 1945.

26   "The Courier Supports Organized Negro Baseball?," *Pittsburgh Courier*, November 3, 1945.

27   Russ J. Cowans, "Sports Chatter," *Michigan Chronicle*, November 3, 1945,

28   Bill L. Weaver, "The Black Press and the Assault on Professional Baseball's 'Color Line,' October, 1945–April, 1947," Phylon 40 (4th Qtr., 1979): 305–6.

29   Dan Burley, "Jackie Robinson Greater on College Grid Than on Diamond, Record Reveals," *New York Amsterdam News*, November 3, 1945.

30   Dan Burley, "What's Ahead for Robinson?," *The Crisis* LII (December 1945): 364.

31   John B. Holway, *Josh and Satch: The Life and Times of Josh Gibson and Satchel Paige* (New York: Carroll & Graf, 1991), 179–80.

32   Holway, *Great Black Baseball Leagues*, 267–68.

33   Peterson, *Only the Ball Was White*, 193.

34   Holway, *Great Black Baseball Leagues*, 345.

35   "What 'Name' Writers Wrote about Signing of Jackie Robinson," *Pittsburgh Courier*, November 3, 1945.

36   Wendell Smith, "The Sports Beat," *Pittsburgh Courier*, November 10, 1945; Peterson, *Only the Ball Was White*, 193.

37   Harold C. Burr, "B.R. to Have More than One Negro Player," *The Sporting News*, November 8, 1945.

38   Wendell Smith to Branch Rickey, December 19, 1945, Wendell Smith Papers, 1945–1949, National Baseball Hall of Fame Library.

39   "Feller Says Jackie Can't Hit Inside Pitches," *Pittsburgh Courier*, November 3, 1945.

40   Smith, "The Sports Beat," November 10, 1945.

41   Wendell Smith, "The Sports Beat," *Pittsburgh Courier*, December 29, 1945.

42   "Hooded Hate Group Opens All-Out Attack on Minorities in the South," *Pittsburgh Courier*, December 15, 1945.

Chapter 10. A Year of Transition and Hope

1   Hank Greenberg, *Hank Greenberg*, 152.

2   David Charnay and Neal Patterson, "Hank Greenberg, Caral Gimbel Wed in Georgia Judge's Home," February 10, 1946, Hank Greenberg File, National Baseball Hall of Fame Library.

3   Greenberg, *Hank Greenberg*, 156.

4   Ibid., 160–61.

5   Red Smith, "Views of Sport: It Doesn't Sound Like Greenberg," *New York Herald Tribune*, August 27, 1946.

6   Greenberg, *Hank Greenberg*, 162.

7   Ibid., 160.

8   Ibid., 163.

9   "Chandler and the Negro Baseball Problem," *The Sporting News*, January 31, 1946.

10   Sgt. Bob Stone, "Jackie Robinson, Pathfinder," *Baseball Digest* 5 (February 1946): 19.

11   Wendell Smith, "The Sports Beat," *Pittsburgh Courier*, February 23, 1946.

12   Nora Holt, "Jackie Robinson's Main Manager Ain't Mr. Rickey," *New York Amsterdam News*, April 27, 1946.

13   Robinson, *I Never Had It Made*, 39–40.

14   Rachel Robinson, *Jackie Robinson: An Intimate Portrait* (New York: Harry N. Abrams, 1996), 48.

15   Ibid., 52.

16   Arthur Mann, "Say Jack Robinson," *Collier's* (March 2, 1946): 67–68.

17   Faulkner, *Great Time Coming*, 130, 132.

18   Robinson to Ralph P. Norton, March 12, 1946, Jackie Robinson Papers, Manuscript Division, Library of Congress.

19   Rampersad, *Jackie Robinson*, 145.

20   Wendell Smith, "The Sports Beat," *Pittsburgh Courier*, March 30, 1946.

21   Tommy Holmes, "Robinson Collects First Hit, Gets Boost From the Mahatma," *The Sporting News*, April 11, 1946.

22   Bud Poliquin, "Rachel Robinson Says It's True: There Was a Black Cat," *Syracuse Herald American*, June 15, 1997.

23   Lloyd McGowan, "Robinson Rivets Royal Keystone Job on Hitting, Fielding and Base-Stealing," *The Sporting News*, June 5, 1946.

24   Tom Meany, "What Chance Has Jackie Robinson?," *Sport* (January 1947): 13.

25 Ralph P. Norton to Jackie Robinson, May 16, 1946, Jackie Robinson Papers, Manuscript Division, Library of Congress.

26 Ed English to Jackie Robinson, July 1946, Jackie Robinson Papers, Manuscript Division, Library of Congress.

27 Tygiel, *Baseball's Great Experiment*, 122.

28 Meany, "What Chance Has Jackie Robinson?," 13.

29 Jackie Robinson to Branch Rickey, July 13, 1946, Branch Rickey Papers, Manuscript Division, Library of Congress.

30 Wilbur Jones to Jackie Robinson, August 13, 1946, Jackie Robinson Papers, Manuscript Division, Library of Congress.

31 Red Smith, "Views of Sport," *New York Herald Tribune*, August 4, 1946.

32 McGowan, "Robinson, Topping Int Hitters, Rated Ready for Dodgers in '47," *The Sporting News*, August 21, 1946.

33 J. G. Taylor Spink, "Looping the Loops," *The Sporting News*, September 11, 1946.

34 "Jackie Makes Good," *Time* 48 (August 26, 1946): 63–64.

35 "Baseball-Royal Robinson," *Newsweek* 28 (August 26, 1946): 71–72.

36 "Report of Major League Steering Committee for Submission to the National and American Leagues at Their Meetings in Chicago," August 27, 1946, Baseball Hall of Fame Library, 18.

37 Ibid., 18–20.

38 Ibid., 20.

39 Arthur Mann, *The Jackie Robinson Story* (New York: Grosset & Dunlap, 1951), 162–63.

40 "Report of Major League Steering Committee," 20; J. G. T. Spinks, "Looping the Loops," *The Sporting News*, September 11, 1946.

41 Sam Maltin, "Fans 'Mob' Jackie in Great Tribute to Star," *Pittsburgh Courier*, October 12, 1946.

42 Rampersad, *Jackie Robinson*, 157.

43 Wendell Smith, "The Sports Beat," *Pittsburgh Courier*, November 16, 1946.

Chapter 11. Greenberg's Final Season and Baseball's Great Experiment

1   Ed Fitzgerald, "Hank Greenberg: A Study in Success," *Sport* (March 1951): 87.

2   Daniel M. Daniel, "Hank Greenberg's Shift to Pirates Presents Case without Any Precedent," *Baseball Magazine* 78 (May 1947): 415.

3   Ritter, *Glory of Their Times*, 325.

4   Dan Daniel, "Daniel's Dope," *New York World Telegram*, January 20, 1947.

5   Ribalow, *Jew in American Sports*, 42–43.

6   Ritter, *Glory of Their Times*, 325–26.

7   Greenberg, *Hank Greenberg*, 175.

8   Red Smith, "A Day for Hank Greenberg," *New York Herald Tribune*, August 24, 1947.

9   Greenberg, *Hank Greenberg*, 185–86.

10 Ibid., 187.

11 Wendell Smith, "The Sports Beat," *Pittsburgh Courier*, January 4, 1947.

12 Tom Meany, "What Chance Has Jackie Robinson?," *Sport* 7 (January 1947): 13.

13 Meany, "What Chance Has Jackie Robinson?," 12–13.

14 Robinson, *Jackie Robinson*, 56; Harold C. Burr, "Robinson May Be Dodgers' 1st Sacker After Royal Series," *Brooklyn Eagle*, March 17, 1947.

15 Faulkner, *Great Time Coming*, 154.

16 Leo Durocher, "Durocher Says: Robby Can Influence Any Dodger With Hits," *Brooklyn Eagle*, March 21, 1947.

17 Wendell Smith, "The Sports Beat," *Pittsburgh Courier*, March 15, 1947.

18 Robinson to Ralph P. Norton, March 24, 1947, Jackie Robinson Papers, Manuscript Division, Library of Congress.

19 William Nack, "The Breakthrough," *Sports Illustrated*, May 5, 1997, 65.

20 Tommy Holmes, "Jackie Robinson Natural Player," *Brooklyn Eagle*, March 31, 1947.

21 Tommy Holmes, "Rickey and Jackie Are Both on Spot," *Brooklyn Eagle*, April 9, 1947.

22 Wendell Smith, "The Sports Beat," *Pittsburgh Courier*, April 12, 1947.

23 Tom Meany, "Robbie Will Find It Rough in NL," *PM*, April 11, 1947.

24 Harold C. Burr, "Robby Makes Debut With Dodgers Today," *Brooklyn Eagle*, April 11, 1947.

25 Wendell Smith, "The Sports Beat," *Pittsburgh Courier*, April 19, 1947.

26 Bill Veeck, *Veeck as in Wreck: The Autobiography of Bill Veeck* (1962; repr., Chicago: University of Chicago Press, 2001), 175.

27 Richard Sandomir, "A Hard-Hitting Profile on Robinson by ESPN," *New York Times*, February 28, 1997.

28 "Robinson's Debut Not Startling, But Gets Friendly Reception," *Brooklyn Eagle*, April 12, 1947.

29 Tommy Holmes, "Negro Track Star With Grid Dodgers?," *Brooklyn Eagle*, April 17, 1947.

30 Harold C. Burr, "Giants Turn Back Dodgers 4–3," *Brooklyn Eagle*, April 20, 1947.

31 "Triumph of Whole Race Seen in Jackie's Debut in Major-League Ball," *Boston Chronicle*, April 19, 1945.

32 "Jackie Robinson," *Atlanta Daily World*, April 16, 1947.

33 *New York Amsterdam News*, April 19, 1947; Bill L. Weaver, "The Black Press and the Assault on Professional Baseball's 'Color Line,' October, 1945–April, 1947," *Phylon* 40 (4th qtr., 1979): 303–17.

34 "Jackie Makes Auspicious Debut with Brooklyn," *Michigan Chronicle*, April 19, 1947; "Who Said We Can't Get To First Base?," *Michigan Chronicle*, April 19, 1947; "Another Hero," *Michigan Chronicle*, April 19, 1947; "Newest Dodger's Batting Form," *Michigan Chronicle*, April 19, 1947; "Press Is Unanimous in Robinson Approval," *Michigan Chronicle*, April 19, 1947; "Jackie's Phenomenal Rise to Majors An Unusual Story," *Michigan Chronicle*, April 19, 1947; Russ J. Cowans "Sport Chatter," *Michigan Chronicle*, April 19, 1947; Bill Matney, "Jumpin' the Gun," *Michigan Chronicle*, April 19, 1947.

35 Peter Golenbock, *Bums: An Oral History of the Brooklyn Dodgers* (New York: Contemporary Books, 2000), 151.

36 See Jonathan Eig's account in *Opening Day: The Story of Jackie Robinson's First Season* (New York: Simon & Schuster, 2007), 105.

37 Jackie Robinson, "Jackie Robinson Says," *Pittsburgh Courier*, May 3, 1947.

38 Ibid., 153.

39 Harold Parrott, *The Lords of Baseball: A Wry Look at a Side of the Game the Fan Seldom Sees—The Front Office* (Atlanta: Longstreet, 2002), 242.

40 Jules Tygiel, *Baseball's Great Experiment: Jackie Robinson and His Legacy* (New York: Oxford University Press, 1983), 185–86.

41 Telegram from the NAACP to Ford Frick, May 15, 1947, Jackie Robinson Papers, Manuscript Division, Library of Congress.

42 Eig, *Opening Day*, 94–96.

43 Jimmy Cannon, *New York Post*, May 10, 1947.

44 Robinson, *Jackie Robinson*, 63–64.

45 Rodney Fisher to Jackie Robinson, May 19, 1947, Jackie Robinson Papers, Manuscript Division, Library of Congress.

46 G. Gilbert Smith to Jackie Robinson, June 1, 1947, Jackie Robinson Papers, Manuscript Division, Library of Congress.

47 Mrs. Bernice Franklin to Jackie Robinson, August 20, 1947, Jackie Robinson Papers, Manuscript Division, Library of Congress.

48 Greenberg, *Hank Greenberg*, 181–82.

49   Wendell Smith, "The Sports Beat," *Pittsburgh Courier*, May 24, 1947.

50   Robinson, *Jackie Robinson*, 146–47.

51   Wendell Smith, "The Sports Beat," *Pittsburgh Courier*, May 24, 1947.

52   Ibid.

53   Levine, *Ellis Island to Ebbets Field*, 139; Wendell Smith, "The Sports Beat," *Pittsburgh Courier*, June 28, 1947.

54   "Editorial Comment," *Baseball Magazine* 79 (June 1947): 217.

55   Tommy Holmes, "Jackie Robinson Is No Longer Unique," *Brooklyn Eagle*, July 22, 1947.

56   Golenbock, *Bums*, 156–57.

57   "Rookie of the Year," *Time* 50 (September 22, 1947): 70–76.

58   Robinson, *I Never Had It Made*, 67.

59   *PM*, September 14, 1947, Sunday supplement.

60   "Rookie of the Year," *Time*, 70–76.

61   J. G. Taylor Spink, "Rookie of the Year . . . Jackie Robinson," *The Sporting News*, September 17, 1947.

62   Robinson, *I Never Had It Made*, 68.

63   David Halberstam, "History's Man," in *Jackie Robinson: Between the Baselines*, eds. Glenn Stout and Dick Johnson (San Francisco: Woodford Press, 1997), 64.

Chapter 12. A Tiger's Horizons Expand

1   Dan Coughlin, "Steve Greenberg Talks about Dad," *Cleveland Plain Dealer*, September 13, 1979.

2   Greenberg, *Hank Greenberg*, 200.

3   Wendell Smith, "Wendell Smith's Sports Beat," *Pittsburgh Courier*, December 3, 1949.

4   Ed Rumill, "Henry B. Greenberg, Executive," *Baseball Magazine* 84 (March 1950): 335.

5   Fitzgerald, "Hank Greenberg," 88.

6   Greenberg, *Hank Greenberg*, 211–13.

7   Dick Young, "Greenberg: Personal Touch Might Avert Strike," *New York Daily News*, May 22, 1980, Greenberg File, National Baseball Hall of Fame Library.

8   "Greenberg Eulogized," *Boston Globe*, September 5, 1986.

9   Arthur Daley, "Sports of the Times: The Swinging Door," *New York Times*, January 30, 1956.

10 Franklin Lewis, "Hank Showed Class Right to Bitter End," *Cleveland Press*, October 30, 1957, Greenberg File, National Baseball Hall of Fame Library.

11 "Club Fell to 6th and Lost Money," October 17, 1957, Greenberg File, National Baseball Hall of Fame Library.

12 Arthur Daley, "Sports of the Times: Scalped Indian," *New York Times*, October 22, 1957.

13 Jerry Holtzman, "Comisky Raps 3-Grand Chisox Pay for Greenberg," November 1, 1961, Greenberg File, National Baseball Hall of Fame Library.

14 Greenberg, *Hank Greenberg*, 219.

15 Ritter, *The Glory of Their Times*, 330.

16 Arthur Daley, "Veeck, the Outcast, Lists Ideas for Troubled Baseball," *Utica Observer-Dispatch*, December 15, 1968.

17 "Greenberg, Lombardi Crop Up in Commissioner Race," *The Sporting News*, February 1, 1969.

18 Wayne Lockwood, "Greenberg: Baseball 'Stuck Head in Sand,'" *San Diego Union*, October 16, 1977, Greenberg File, National Baseball Hall of Fame Library.

19 Young, "Greenberg."

20 "Tigers Hand Up Nos. 2 and 5," *New York Times Union*, June 14, 1983, Greenberg File, National Baseball Hall of Fame Library.

21 Greenberg, *Hank Greenberg*, 268.

22 "Baseball's Hank Greenberg, Hall of Fame Slugger, Dies," *Washington Times*, September 5, 1986.

23 Bob Broeg, "Self-Made Slugger Greenberg Hankered to Play," *St. Louis Post-Dispatch*, September 7, 1986.

24 Maury Allen, "Greenberg, a Great, Is Remembered," *New York Post*, September 5, 1986.

25 Greenberg, *Hank Greenberg*, 270–71.

26 Ibid., 255–56.

27 Ziegel, "In Greenberg."

28 Richard Sandomir, "He Batted for the Tigers, Himself and American Jews," *New York Times*, January 9, 2000.

29 Marc Gellman, "Joe Lieberman as Rorschach Test," *First Things* 108 (December 2000): 9–11.

Chapter 13. The Greatest Brooklyn Dodger

1 Golenbock, *Bums*, 190–91.

2 Wendell Smith, "Sports Beat," *Pittsburgh Courier*, January 3, 1948.

3 Wendell Smith, "Wendell Smith's Sports Beat," *Pittsburgh Courier*, October 2, 1948.

4   Rampersad, *Jackie Robinson*, 201.

5   Robinson, *I Never Had It Made*, 79.

6   Wendell Smith, "The Sports Beat," *Pittsburgh Courier*, March 19, 1949.

7   Rampersad, *Jackie Robinson*, 207.

8   Golenbock, *Bums*, 228.

9   Hearings Regarding Communist Infiltration of Minority Groups, Hearings Before the Committee on Un-American Activities, House of Representatives, Eighty-First Congress, July 18, 1949, 479–83.

10   Bosley Crowther, "The Jackie Robinson Story," *New York Times*, May 17, 1950.

11   Dan Burley, "Dan Burley on Sports," *New York Age,* July 15, 1950.

12   Jackie Robinson to Branch Rickey, n.d., Branch Rickey Papers, Manuscript Division, Library of Congress.

13   Milton Gross, "The Emancipation of Jackie Robinson," *Sport* 11 (October 1951): 13–14.

14   Roger Kahn, *Memories of Summer: When Baseball Was an Art, and Writing about It a Game* (New York: Hyperion, 1997), 67.

15   Falkner, *Great Time Coming*, 223–24.

16   Rampersad, *Jackie Robinson*, 261.

17   Roger Kahn, "Another Viewpoint," *New York Herald Tribune*, August 29, 1954

18   Roger Kahn, "The Ten Years of Jackie Robinson," *Sport* 20 (October 1955): 12, 76–77.

19   Ibid.; Roger Kahn, *Beyond the Boys of Summer* (New York: McGraw-Hill, 2005), 270.

20   Citation for Jackie Robinson, 41st Spingarn Medalist, December 8, 1956, NAACP Records, Manuscript Division, Library of Congress.

21   "Acceptance Address by Jackie Robinson at Special Luncheon Honoring Him on Presentation of 41st Spingarn Medal," December 8, 1956, Jackie Robinson Papers, Manuscript Division, Library of Congress.

22   Arthur Daley, "Sports of the Times," *New York Times*, December 17, 1956.

23   Rampersad, *Jackie Robinson*, 306.

24   Daley, "Sports of the Times." Daley did not realize that Robinson never graduated from UCLA.

Chapter 14. Jackie Robinson's Final Years

1   Arthur Mann, *The Jackie Robinson Story* (New York: Grosset & Dunlap, 1963), 253.

2   Rampersad, *Jackie Robinson*, 361.

3   Jackie Robinson's Hall of Fame Induction Speech, July 23, 1962, Cooperstown, New York.

4   E. J. Bavasi to Jackie Robinson, February 11, 1971, Jackie Robinson Papers, Library of Congress; Robinson to Buzzie, n.d., Jackie Robinson Papers, Library of Congress.

5   Roger Kahn, *The Boys of Summer* (1972; repr., New York: Harper & Row, 1987), 386–411.

6   Eric Lincoln, "Robinson Sees Little Progress After 25 Years," *New York Mirror*, December 8, 1971, Jackie Robinson File, National Baseball Hall of Fame Library.

7   Robinson, *I Never Had It Made*, 268.

8   Ibid., 278–79.

9   Red Smith, "Death of an Unconquerable Man," *New York Times*, October 25, 1972.

10   "Jackie Goes Home to Brooklyn," *New York Times*, October 28, 1972.

11   "Jackie Robinson: Heroic Pioneer," *USA Today*, April 18, 1997.

INDEX